ROCK CONCERT

Also by Marc Myers

Anatomy of a Song

Why Jazz Happened

ROCK CONCERT

AN ORAL HISTORY AS TOLD BY
THE ARTISTS, BACKSTAGE INSIDERS,
AND FANS WHO WERE THERE

MARC MYERS

Grove Press

New York

FIRST EDITION

Published simultaneously in Canada
Printed in the United States of America

This book was designed by Norman E. Tuttle at Alpha Design & Composition.

This book was set in 11-pt. Goudy Oldstyle by Alpha Design & Composition of Pittsfield, NH.

First Grove Atlantic hardcover edition: November 2021

Library of Congress Cataloging-in-Publication data is available for this title.

ISBN 978-0-8021-5791-1
eISBN 978-0-8021-5793-5

Grove Press
an imprint of Grove Atlantic
154 West 14th Street
New York, NY 10011

Distributed by Publishers Group West

groveatlantic.com

21 22 23 24   10 9 8 7 6 5 4 3 2 1

To Alyse, Olivia, and Dylan,
my rock stars

CONTENTS

Part 4: The 1980s

INTRODUCTION

Live music has a long past. The Hurrian songs—one of the world's oldest examples of written music, composed 3,400 years ago—were meant to be performed in front of an audience. Scratched onto clay tablets, the ancient songbook was unearthed by archeologists in the 1950s at the entrance to a royal palace in Syria. The tablets even included tuning instructions for a Babylonian lyre, an early stringed relative of the guitar. Though many of the songs survived only in fragments, the one complete tablet was a hymn to Nikkal, the Hurrian goddess of orchards and wife of the moon god. Love songs and concerts weren't far behind.

From the beginning, live music's purpose was to transform a gathering into a community by unifying an audience's mood. Live music could accomplish what oratory often failed to achieve—collective agreement and a sense of belonging. Through the centuries, live performances that had once been held only at palaces, churches, and the homes of the wealthy expanded to public spaces. The arrival of printed sheet music in America in the mid-1800s and wax phonograph cylinders in 1889 gave rise to popular music and at-home entertainment, but they didn't replace live music. In fact, the proliferation of parlor pianos and recorded music boosted the public's interest in performance. At the start of the twentieth century, live music not only was a diversion but also helped assimilate millions of newly arrived immigrants by making them feel American.

The first rock concerts went one step further. For the first time, a genre of popular music was recorded and performed specifically for adolescent listeners. In addition to uniting this market, the music empowered the

1

youth culture to air its grievances and stand up for its rights. Throughout the first half of the twentieth century, traditional popular music certainly attracted teens, but they were listening to their parents' music. What changed in the mid-1950s was access and allowance money.

Starting in the early 1950s, sales of portable phonographs for teens and preteens began to climb. Parents were happy to shell out for lightweight record players, since the turntables and 45s kept children at home in their rooms and allowed parents to watch their new TV sets undisturbed. Smaller night-table radios also wound up in children's rooms, giving them an opportunity to find new music anywhere on the dial. But as parents soon discovered, the music teens found was provocative and liberating.

From the start, rock 'n' roll artists, records, and concerts sided with teens in their battle for independence from parents. Over time, the music would support a wide range of teen grievances. Between 1950 and 1985, rock echoed the American youth culture's concerns with segregation, lousy teachers, the threat of nuclear war, middle-class conformity, the draft, the Vietnam War, civil rights, women's rights, pollution, gay rights, world hunger, imperiled family farms, and more. Through rock, the youth culture had a voice.

Rock's roots date back to 1944 and the emergence of hundreds of independent record labels. A good number of these labels recorded Black artists pioneering a new form of saxophone-driven dance music known broadly as jump blues. This extension of boogie-woogie led directly to R&B in 1949, which relied on smaller ensembles, vocals, and a distinct backbeat. By then, the use of tape in studios reduced the cost of recording and enabled a greater number of small labels to record R&B artists. Unlike pop and jazz, R&B exhibited a new level of earthiness and blunt sexuality, and R&B concerts added visual excitement.

In the mid-1950s, the music shifted and a new, gentler form of R&B was marketed to teens. Instead of dwelling on sex, drinking, cheating, and other adult themes that dominated R&B records, rock 'n' roll concerned itself with teen anxieties and social issues such as cars, school life, dances, dating, breaking up, and falling in love. Uplifted by animated disk jockeys who played rock 'n' roll records and championed the youth culture on the radio, teens embraced the music and concerts as a way to bond socially and rebel against the restrictions imposed by authority figures. They also began to question and challenge adult values.

Before the arrival of rock 'n' roll, popular music made little effort to win over young listeners. One of the first significant pop concerts was Paul Whiteman's An Experiment in Modern Music at New York's Aeolian Hall in February 1924. The concert was notable for the debut of George Gershwin's "Rhapsody in Blue," a classical-jazz suite commissioned exclusively for the event. Whiteman's intent was to show that American jazz in the hands of a Broadway songwriter could impress a highbrow audience weaned on European classical music. The paying audience was composed mostly of adults.

Louis Armstrong's lyrical and bold trumpet playing during performances with the Fletcher Henderson Orchestra in the 1920s and in his own Hot Five and Hot Seven ensembles helped jazz's raucousness and dance steps connect with young adult audiences. Armstrong also helped establish the electrifying improvised solo. Bix Beiderbecke's horn did the same with college-age audiences in the 1920s. Throughout the decade, jazz was so potent that the syncopated music left its mark not only on young adults but also on everything from fashion and design to architecture and the English language. There's a reason the 1920s was known as the Jazz Age.

With the onset of the Depression in the early 1930s, radio became the country's most popular source of live music. You paid once for a radio and all of its programming was free, thanks to the sponsorship of advertisers. Once the sound quality of radio vastly improved with the advent of the ribbon microphone in 1931, live on-air music and announcers' voices were clearer and more lifelike. Radio sales climbed and programming became more diversified. By the mid-1930s, radio house bands and orchestras performed popular and classical music live in the radio studio throughout the day. To protect those jobs, the musicians' union prohibited the airplay of records.

The first inkling that live dance music might gain traction with young audiences nationwide came during Benny Goodman's appearance at Los Angeles's Palomar Ballroom in August 1935. Since the early 1930s,

3

Black bands led by Jimmie Lunceford, Fletcher Henderson, Chick Webb, and others had already been playing a new, looser form of dance music at ballrooms in Black communities. White radio listeners were largely unaware of these bands or their performances in the early 1930s, since "race records," as they were known then, were sold mostly in Black neighborhoods.

In the summer of 1935, Goodman's final cross-country tour performance was to be held at the Palomar Ballroom, with the NBC radio network set to air the show. When the Goodman band launched into up-tempo arrangements of "Sugar Foot Stomp," "King Porter Stomp," and other instrumentals, a thunderous cheer went up from the mostly white teens attending, who had followed the band on the radio during its travels. Goodman's three-week Palomar engagement launched what became known as the swing era—when Black big band dance music crossed over to young white audiences listening to national radio networks.

The impact of the swing era's groove on the youth culture can be seen in a YouTube documentary clip of the Carnival of Swing concert held at New York's Randall's Island Stadium in May 1938. The benefit concert—known now as one of the first outdoor jazz festivals—ran about six hours and attracted an estimated 23,000 young white and Black fans, who danced freely in place and in the aisles as Count Basie and other leading swing bands performed.

But swing's rise and hold over the youth market was cut short in 1941, when America entered World War II. During the war, millions of young men enlisted or were drafted—limiting the size of paying audiences and making it difficult for bands to hold on to musicians, since many wound up in the service. War worries and the declining number of eligible young men on the home front gave rise to a new teen pop phenomenon—Frank Sinatra.

Thin, seemingly vulnerable, and brashly charismatic, with a new, conversational approach to singing romantic standards, Sinatra became pop's first teen idol and superstar. Between late 1942, when he became a solo act, and 1944, when a near riot broke out in Manhattan due to crowds too large for the number of seats available at one of his Paramount

Theatre concerts, Sinatra's sensitive persona and caressing vocals were entrancing, particularly for young women.

After the war, a new tax on dance establishments gave rise to clubs that hired smaller jazz and lounge groups. Many of these ensembles played a new form of jazz in which improvisation, speed, and poly-rhythms dominated. While artistically spectacular, this form of modern jazz wasn't exactly conducive to dancing. Many in the Black community who still favored dance music shifted to jump blues and then R&B, which grew in popularity in the late 1940s.

By the start of the 1950s, with the musicians' union now permitting radio stations to play records on the air, DJs found they could earn extra income by spinning R&B records at neighborhood dance parties. They also began holding concerts where teens could see the artists who had hit records. The youth market for R&B grew, and more radio stations began playing the music to meet the demand and to attract sponsors. The R&B concert trend began in Los Angeles and quickly spread to Cleveland in the early '50s and then—as rock 'n' roll—jumped to Chicago, Memphis, and New York in the mid-'50s. Local rock 'n' roll TV shows modeled after Philadelphia's *American Bandstand* also captured the imaginations of school-age teens.

In the early 1960s, pop-rock performances in theaters and on TV along with the Beatles' arrival in America and the subsequent British invasion turned rock 'n' roll into a cultural phenomenon. Bob Dylan's 1965 electric performance at the Newport Folk Festival led to a more introspective and personal form known simply as rock. Reliant on poetry and social commentary, Dylan's music inspired a growing number of artists to write and record original songs while jazz artists such as John Coltrane encouraged them to take extended solos. The emerging rock album soon found a home on FM radio, where stations needed content to fill airtime. Broadcasting in stereo, FM helped launch a new era in live rock performed at ballrooms, theaters, and free outdoor festivals. In the 1970s, rock splintered into subcategories and major bands began filling sporting arenas and stadiums. Meanwhile, outdoor concert attendance records were set at events such as Summer Jam at Watkins Glen in New York, and California Jam in Ontario, California.

By 1980, the rock concert had become a theatric extravaganza as progressive-rock bands such as Pink Floyd staged opera-size performances. The launch of MTV in 1981 brought visual rock performances into homes and placed new demands on performing bands to look and sound more like their stylized videos. Easy access to credit cards and computerized ticketing in the early 1980s not only provided convenience but also led to higher ticket prices, angering audiences that had grown accustomed to free or inexpensive shows. Live Aid in 1985 was perhaps the last spectacular rock concert before ticket prices climbed significantly and concert revenue, not albums, became the leading moneymaker for rock artists.

Rock Concert is a five-decade story of how enterprising songwriters, producers, disc jockeys, managers, promoters, and artists sided with the youth culture as it struggled to be heard and changed society at large. Once the music became more accessible on the radio and grew in popularity, the trial-and-error approach to staging a concert resulted in standardized production strategies, better sound, improved security, sophisticated concert technology, shrewder ticketing, and, ultimately, a multibillion-dollar industry and a successful model for all large-scale music concerts. To endure between 1950 and 1985, rock wisely remained in sync with the youth market rather than chase after a single generation as it aged. But the rock concert hardly remained static. Over time, artists adapted to larger spaces, the latest speaker systems and lighting, new instruments and enhancements, longer tours, special effects, more sophisticated media coverage, and branding.

This book isn't meant to be an all-inclusive, day-by-day history of the rock concert. Nor does it weigh in on rock's glamorization of drugs and alcohol or the sexual abuse of underage and adult fans by some performers and those who worked for or accompanied them. The book also isn't intended to touch on every major event and artist within the thirty-five-year period covered. I'm sure readers will click off plenty of concerts and artists who they feel should have been included in these pages, which is only natural. Instead, *Rock Concert* is a vivid narrative in the words of those who performed at, promoted, witnessed, or participated in events that contributed to the rock concert's development.

I hope that by reading this book, readers will come away with a sense of how the rock concert flowered and influenced American culture over the decades and how it went from small and dynamic in the 1950s to massive and meaningful by the early 1980s. To help fill in any historical blanks, I've included lists of my fifty favorite live albums, fifty favorite concert videos, and fifty favorite rock documentaries.

For many readers, the book will stir memories of the early rock concerts they attended and how they became turning points along the road to adulthood. Sitting in the dark, we saw and heard musicians we knew only from album covers and bedroom turntables. Yet the music was deeply personal. Experienced live, the rock concert allowed us to see and hear our idols onstage for the first time. It was our introduction to celebrity and to artists who embodied their audience's spirit.

My first rock concert was Santana, with Booker T. and Priscilla as the opening act, at New York's Felt Forum on October 16, 1971. I had just turned fifteen and went with my best friend, Glenn. As you read this book, I'm sure you'll think about your first and the others that followed, and I hope you'll learn a few things along the way.

PART 1
THE 1950s

The rock concert can be traced to Los Angeles in the late 1940s, when R&B revues were held at Johnny Otis's Barrelhouse in the city's Watts section. At the time, L.A. was filled with young jazz and blues musicians, newly formed independent record labels, and clubs featuring nearly every type of popular music. The city and its surrounding suburbs also were flush with independent radio stations newly granted licenses by the FCC in hopes of keeping radio alive as TV proliferated. In 1950, in the South Central section of the city, where most Black residents lived, a few disc jockeys at low-signal stations began playing R&B records by local artists. By 1951, Black, white, Mexican-American, and Asian teens who lived in the area began to pick up R&B on their radios. One of those disc jockeys, Hunter Hancock, was hosting live R&B concerts and promoting them on his radio show. Teens soon showed up at the concerts in droves. Captivated by the music onstage, they ignored L.A.'s segregation laws and mingled freely with each other. Rebellion against adult norms had begun.

Word of L.A.'s growing R&B market soon reached *Billboard* and other music trade publications. In Cleveland, disc jockey Alan Freed started playing R&B records. When he first tried to hold a concert there in 1952, too many people showed up and the concert was canceled. More Freed concerts followed at regional theaters.

By mid-decade, an electric blues guitarist in Chicago named Chuck Berry began performing at clubs and recording what would become rock 'n' roll. In Memphis, Elvis Presley combined country and R&B and performed live on the radio and at county fairs, clubs, and sports arenas. Known as rock 'n' roll, the music reached New York in 1955, when Freed, who had taken a DJ job there, began holding concerts at a large Brooklyn movie theater, launching the multiday rock 'n' roll revue for integrated teenage audiences.

By the late 1950s, rock 'n' roll held sway over teens nationwide. The music and artists were also featured regularly on TV jukebox shows and in movies for the teenage market. The music's surging popularity was helped in great measure by payola—hefty cash payments and gifts of value provided by middlemen to radio DJs to ensure the repeated airplay of specific records. Payola also took the form of ad dollars that record companies spent at specific radio stations in exchange for airplay. Interestingly, such gifts weren't illegal at the time if broad legal loopholes were exploited. The value of payola was immeasurable and immediate. The frequent play of a record increased its sales potential and improved the odds of it becoming a national hit.

Chapter 1

LOS ANGELES AUDITORIUMS

Since 1916, Los Angeles had been a prime destination for millions of Black people migrating from the South for better-paying factory jobs and freedom from the threat of racial terrorism. They brought with them a passion for the blues and dance music. Before long, Black musicians in the city combined the blues and dance beats, and the music landed on jukeboxes at bars and clubs in Black neighborhoods. In addition, many early R&B songs had adult themes camouflaged by lyrics laced with innuendo, and most of the artists who recorded them were young adults. Those who were too young to drink in bars could hear R&B live in theaters and ballrooms or listen to it on small local radio stations. Rising sales of affordable nightstand radios let white teens in the L.A. suburbs pick up the signals. The question was: Where could they see the artists perform?

Ernie Andrews
    (Los Angeles jazz, blues, and pop singer)
    Los Angeles was wide open in the mid-1940s. All the major big bands and acts stopped in the city to perform and kick back, especially in the winter, when touring the country was harder. Top bands made short films in Hollywood or appeared in feature films. The city really became a music center after America's entry into World War II in December '41, when L.A. was a major military port. Soldiers and sailors stationed on bases near the city as well as crowds of defense workers sought out

entertainment. So did the many Blacks who had already migrated to the city from all over the country to work in the region's war plants.

After school and over the weekends, I worked as an usher at the 2,000-seat Lincoln Theatre, one of Central Avenue's major concert halls. When I was seventeen, I was promoted at the Lincoln to head usher. Amateur nights, on Wednesdays, were packed. Everyone who was trying to break into show business would appear. I sang on those nights in my uniform. After each performance, you'd wait for Pigmeat Markham or Bardu Ali or Sybil Lewis to come out and hold a hand over your head. If the audience didn't like you, they'd let you know it, and you'd have to get off. But they loved me, and I'd be onstage so long that Pigmeat and Dusty Fletcher would have to cut me off to let others get on.

There were plenty of places to hear music and dance in L.A. in the 1940s, like the 5-4 Ballroom on the corner of Fifty-Fourth and Monet, and the Elks Hall on Central Avenue. They'd have dancing and singing and a mixture of jazz and R&B. The Downbeat on South Central Avenue was always hot. You'd have to be twenty-one to get into many of them, but I was tall for my age. In 1945, I was discovered by songwriter Joe Greene during one of those Lincoln Theatre amateur shows. Overnight, he wrote "Soothe Me" for me. I recorded the ballad with the Clara Lewis Trio on Greene's Gem label. We sold 300,000 copies. Then Joe wrote another one for me, "Don't Let the Sun Catch You Cryin'." It was even bigger.

I performed on Central Avenue with everybody you could name. I was trying to gain momentum. I performed at the Downbeat, the Last Word, the Dunbar Hotel, and Club Alabam. Many of the people who came up from the South loved the blues. They grew up with it and lived it. Unlike other vocalists, R&B singers didn't just stand there and sing. They moved with the music. That's true of the blues shouters and the vocal groups, too. Many of these artists were earthier than jazz singers but not as schooled or as polished. Blues with a dance beat became hugely popular. Young people caught the music in L.A. on radio shows on small stations, hosted by guys like Hunter Hancock and Dick "Huggy Boy" Hugg. Though these DJs were white, they sounded Black and created opportunities for everyone in the Black community.

In the late 1940s, I remember seeing R&B tenor saxophonist Big Jay McNeely at the Last Word, across from Club Alabam on Central Avenue. He'd leave the stage playing his horn and lead everyone out into the street, honking and stomping. Bardu Ali had a full band that featured Johnny Otis on drums. They were partners in a club called the Barrelhouse. Johnny Otis was a giant. He was a great drummer and he got the beat. He brought a lot of Black R&B artists along. Even though he was white, he was dark and sounded Black.

Mike Stoller
(songwriter and record producer with Jerry Leiber)

In 1940, when I was seven, I began spending summers at an interracial summer camp called Wo-Chi-Ca, which stood for Workers' Children's Camp. It was near Hackettstown, New Jersey, about an hour outside of New York. Such camps were unusual then. One day, I heard someone playing boogie-woogie on a piano in the camp's barn. I slipped inside and saw a Black teenager sitting at a beat-up upright. I was mesmerized. When he left, I approached the piano and tried to do what I heard him doing. After the summer, when I went home to the Sunnyside section of Queens, New York, I kept trying.

I was crazy about boogie-woogie. For the next few years, I couldn't hear enough of it. My interest was so obsessive that when I was ten, I traveled by subway to take six or seven lessons from the famous pianist and composer James P. Johnson. He lived in Jamaica, Queens. This was in 1943 and '44. My life would have been very different if I hadn't taken those lessons. While I may have picked up some of the blues listening to the radio, getting it firsthand from James P. was much more powerful.

Still, like many kids after World War II, my imagination was awakened by the radio. Before television, that's all we had on each day. The radio was my doorway to the adult world, especially adult music. Black artists were foreign to most other white kids then. I listened to stations that played R&B and jazz, with disc jockeys like "Symphony Sid" Torin. I heard musicians such as Lionel Hampton, Dinah Washington, and Louis Jordan and vocal groups like the Ravens and the Orioles. In my early teens, I spent a lot of time with a friend, Al Levitt, taking the subway

13

into Manhattan to Fifty-Second Street, where all the jazz clubs were and the bebop musicians played. On Saturdays, we went to a social club on 124th Street in Harlem. The music was remarkable and exciting.

In 1949, when I was sixteen, my family moved to Los Angeles. L.A. then was a city of transplants: there were whites from the Southwest, Blacks from the South, Mexicans, and Asians. They were largely isolated in their own neighborhoods with distinct borders, but I socialized with kids from all these groups in my senior year at Belmont High. That was a lot more exciting than my all-white high school back in Forest Hills, Queens. In May 1950, when I was a freshman at Los Angeles City College and living at home, someone called me on our phone. It was a guy named Jerry Leiber. He'd heard about me from a drummer he knew and asked if I wanted to write songs with him. Jerry said he had moved with his mother to L.A. in 1945 from Baltimore and that he wrote lyrics. I politely told him I wasn't interested in pop music. Jazz was my thing.

Less than an hour later, Jerry was at my front door. He handed me pages of lyrics. When I saw that his lyrics were in the form of twelve-bar blues, I agreed to write with him. I turned Jerry on to some of the jazz artists I loved and he got me into R&B and the blues. Of course, I'd always been into boogie-woogie, which is really what brought us together. Many boogie-woogie records at the time had a blues song on the flip side. Jerry and I were like two sides of the same record.

Jerry and I hung out at record shops, theaters, and clubs on South Central Avenue. After I met Jerry, we'd go see producer Gene Norman's annual Blues Jubilee concerts at the Shrine Auditorium near the University of Southern California. Gene was a big disc jockey then, more on the jazz side than R&B. One day we met Gene, and he told us where a lot of the R&B musicians performed. So Jerry and I went to the theaters and clubs in search of artists who might record our songs.

At one of these places—Club Alabam, next to the Dunbar Hotel—we met Wynonie Harris, Percy Mayfield, and others. We also met Jimmy Witherspoon and gave him our song "Real Ugly Woman." He wound up recording it live at a concert at the Shrine in 1950. Through sheer luck, the concert was taped, and the tape of our song was released on a record. Jerry and I went everywhere and met everyone we could on

South Central Avenue. It was a thriving main street in the city's Black community. Jerry and I felt like we belonged.

In 1950 and '51, Gene Norman and Hunter Hancock were the big R&B concert promoters in L.A. At some concert, I remember writing a big band arrangement for the Robins after they had a hit with our song "Loop De Loop Mambo" in 1954. I wrote out the trumpets the same way my right hand would play the notes on the keyboard. I was thrilled with the result. There also were concerts in larger clubs, like the 5-4 Ballroom with Big Jay McNeely. A lot of white and Mexican-American kids came to hear him, Chuck Higgins, Gil Bernal, and other performers. Even in cases where radio stations were aimed primarily at a Black audience, DJs would announce where concerts were held. White kids who otherwise never would have heard of these events found their way there.

At the time, there were five or six independent R&B record companies in the city, labels like the Mesner brothers' Aladdin, Art Rupe's Specialty, Otis and Leon René's Excelsior and Exclusive, and the Bihari brothers' Modern. Lester Sill, who did sales and promotion for Modern, first met Jerry at Norty's Music, a record store on Fairfax where Jerry worked after school. Lester introduced us to a few people, including Ralph Bass of Federal Records. Ralph in turn introduced us to Johnny Otis. All Jerry and I wanted was to write good R&B and blues songs for the Black artists we revered. Our heroes were Charles Brown and Jimmy Witherspoon. When Johnny Otis introduced us to artists like Little Esther and Big Mama Thornton, they needed songs to perform and record. You didn't have to ask us twice. We wrote "Hound Dog" for Big Mama in about fifteen minutes. Those fifteen minutes changed our lives.

Bob Willoughby
(Los Angeles photographer)

In 1947, when I was twenty, I lived at my mother's house on Marvin Avenue in Los Angeles. I loved listening to jazz and R&B on the radio. The music's energy, soul, and beat were mesmerizing. I also admired the cool confidence of these musicians on- and offstage. I was passionate about photography then and had been from the age of twelve, when my parents first bought me a camera. By 1948, I sat in on photography

15

classes at the University of Southern California's School of Cinematic Arts. I couldn't afford college, so auditing classes was the next best way to learn. Before long, I began working as an assistant for several photographers I had been studying with. During my downtime, I photographed dancers and jazz musicians. I set up a darkroom in the garage, where it was pitch-black at night. In the garage, I always had my radio tuned to jazz and R&B stations.

One night in late '51, I was listening to KFOX, an R&B station. The DJ, Hunter Hancock, began promoting a midnight concert he was hosting at the Olympic Auditorium. He was urging listeners to come down to see the show. The Olympic was an arena on South Grand Avenue built in 1924 and often used for boxing matches. The idea of starting a concert at midnight was so intriguing I had to take my cameras and see what it was all about. I walked into the Olympic sometime after midnight, when the concert was already underway. The hall felt as if it was rocking on its foundation. I could see the audience on their feet, screaming. You could taste the energy. I had never seen or heard anything to match it. It was my introduction to the amazing tenor saxophonist Big Jay McNeely. Big Jay stood where the fight ring was normally set up, in the center. He was playing his heart out, and the crowd was exploding around him. He had created some sort of resonance with the audience. In some weird way, he seemed to be playing them.

What I saw was so mind-boggling that I found myself scrambling for the cameras around my neck as I ran down the aisle toward the fireworks. I was afraid I was going to miss it all. But I didn't really have to worry. Big Jay was a marathon player. I was so caught up in the excitement, I climbed up on the stage without thinking. Big Jay was strutting back and forth onstage, playing run after run on his sax and honking his way through forty-five minutes of pulsating, explosive rhythm. While playing, he kneeled down, he sat, he lay flat on his back. He played into the faces of orgasmic girls. He was on some spaceflight. He perspired until his clothes were soaking. And then he took off his wet jacket without missing a beat.

The crowd was nearly hysterical. Big Jay literally was a pied piper. I was told that at another concert in San Diego, he had swept the entire audience out of the theater and led them on a tour around the block while honking on his saxophone. All of this was much to the dismay of the local police. In L.A., the police weren't too sure what might happen at this gig either. You could see them in the crowd, probably looking for drugs. But with Big Jay in orbit onstage, the crowd was already euphoric.

Big Jay McNeely
(R&B tenor saxophonist)

I decided to play the saxophone when I was sixteen, around 1943. My brother played the instrument and was an excellent musician. When he was drafted during World War II, he left his saxophone home. I was working at the Firestone Tire and Rubber Company at the time. I decided music would be a better bet for me. I rode my bike each day to Alma Hightower's house and took lessons for twenty-five cents. Then I took lessons with a gentleman who played first saxophone chair with the RKO Studio Orchestra. When my brother, Robert, came home from World War II, we both studied voice with a guy who would teach the Hi-Lo's and the McGuire Sisters. My brother and I figured eventually we'd have to sing and that studying singing would help us with our blowing.

In 1947, I played at the Barrelhouse Club, owned by drummer Johnny Otis. It was right down the street from my home in Watts. There was a lot of blues energy there. At the end of 1948, Ralph Bass, an A&R guy who was at Savoy Records at the time, asked me if I wanted to do a record. I said yeah. He told me to put a tune together. A kid I knew in Watts had a record shop. He gave me a record by Glenn Miller that opened with a drummer playing the sock cymbal. I can't remember the name of the song. But I built a blues off of it called "Deacon's Hop," which became a #1 hit on *Billboard*'s jukebox "race records" chart in early '49. Hunter Hancock broke in the record by playing it a lot. He's the one who started playing race music, our music, in L.A.

One night on tour in 1950, we played Clarksville, Tennessee. When we played for the first time, the audience didn't respond. They just sat there. I couldn't understand that. The music usually got people going. So on the next set I did something different. I got down on my knees to play. Then I laid down on the stage and played from there. People went crazy. After the concert, I said to myself, "I'm going to try this again." So I did it in Texas. And again, everyone went crazy. Back in L.A., I did it, too. The kids went nuts. They loved that I was on my back blowing like that. My energy fired up theirs.

Pete Foxx
(Los Angeles singer-guitarist and original member of the Flairs)

My friends in junior high school and I first heard the Swallows, Sonny Til and the Orioles, the Clovers, and Billy Ward and His Dominoes on Hunter Hancock's show. These were the vocal groups we tried to imitate. The Swallows were from Baltimore. We listened carefully to their records—like "Will You Be Mine" and "Eternally." Then we copied what they were doing, humming harmony notes as our lead vocalist sang. I sang baritone. Eventually, four of us in school started singing songs these groups recorded.

We first started singing in junior high school in 1949. The first group we formed in high school in early 1952 was the Debonairs. We went through several different incarnations with guys coming and going. By the time we were in Jefferson High School that fall, a couple of the guys in the group were from Fremont High and Manual Arts. As the Debonairs, we sang in a talent show at the Lincoln Theatre on South Central Avenue. Whoever got the most audience applause won. We won, because we had the most friends there. The guys in our group were from different schools, so our friends came from all over.

In December '52, we wrote some songs and felt we were ready to record. Somehow, we hooked up with John Dolphin, whose record store, Dolphin's of Hollywood, was near Jefferson High. We recorded two sides: "I Had a Love" and "Tell Me You Love Me." He renamed us the Hollywood Blue Jays on the record, probably because his label was called Recorded in Hollywood and bird groups were popular then. But we didn't sell many copies. So Cornell Gunter, our lead vocalist, looked through his favorite records and saw that many were on the Modern label. He called them up. The person on the other end told him to come down.

18

Our first record on Modern's Flair label was "I Had a Love" backed with "She Wants to Rock." The label renamed us the Flairs. We were just teenagers and didn't know the workings of the record business. We paid a price for that. The names that appeared as composers on some of our records had nothing to do with writing the songs. Whenever our Flair records came out, Hunter played them on his programs. We even went on his radio show, which he broadcast from his Hollywood office. Hunter was white but that didn't matter. Everyone knew he was white. We felt he was playing Black music because that's what he liked to do. We didn't give it another thought. When we went on his show, Hunter was good to us. His sidekick was a Black woman named Margie Williams. Everyone in the community was comfortable with him and he was comfortable with us.

Our first concert after we began recording as the Flairs was in 1953, at the Shrine Auditorium. We did four or five songs. There were others on the bill. Chuck Higgins, the saxophonist, led the house band. I remember it turned out very well. Other concerts and ballroom appearances in R&B vocal group revues followed. We also sang on local TV. Many of the people in the audience at these concerts were white. Years later, I asked someone who was white how he and his friends found out about our records. They weren't widely distributed outside of the Black community. The guy said their parents didn't allow them to listen to Black music, but they listened anyway. Then they snuck around and passed records back and forth among themselves. They found out about the music by listening to Hunter and other R&B DJs around L.A. who were inspired by his success.

When R&B first began being played on the radio, Black kids in L.A. didn't know that white kids were into the music. If you lived on the east side of L.A. then, where most Black people lived, you rarely got to the west side, where the white people lived. We knew there was a certain amount of segregation in L.A. and that there were distinct ethnic and racial neighborhoods. But that didn't matter to us, since we didn't need to go to them. The Flairs played all over L.A., up along the coast and even up in Washington State, where nearly everyone in the audience was white. These were mostly dance halls. We never thought that a white audience was shocking. We just thought of them as an audience.

Art Rupe
(Specialty Records founder and producer of Fats Domino, Little Richard, and other R&B artists)

I never produced any concerts on behalf of my L.A. label. For promotion, I concentrated on obtaining radio airplay. Concerts weren't as effective as radio play. It's important to remember that the white DJs who played R&B records were not necessarily social justice advocates. They were merely creating and supplying the growing demand for this music. Both Hunter and "Huggy Boy" Hugg played many Specialty records. And with no payola. Gradually, more mainstream DJs in Southern California began to play R&B records that they felt would suit their mostly white audiences. With radio dramas moving to television, they had plenty of airtime to fill. Before long, stations playing R&B records began to reach the adjoining L.A. suburbs as the audiences for this music grew. Many of these listeners were the kids of white parents who, like the parents of Black listeners, had migrated to the region in search of jobs.

Big Jay McNeely

As Hunter Hancock's R&B revues became more popular in L.A. in 1951 and early '52, there was a backlash. More and more white, Mexican, and Black teens were attending his midnight concerts. This caught the attention of the Los Angeles police, who tried to discourage future attendance by harassing teens leaving in their cars. Inside the arenas, I'm sure the police didn't like what they were seeing—interracial couples and friends getting wound up while I was playing and other Black artists were performing. I'm sure their parents started complaining when they heard where their kids had been the night before and how excited they were. The police also got rough on businesses that catered to young white and Black friends. At Dolphin's of Hollywood, John Dolphin struggled under police intimidation. The police would block the store's doors and warn white customers that being in a Black neighborhood at night placed them in danger. Still, a growing number of white teens in the Los Angeles area had other ways to access R&B, like on their radios.

By 1952, I was barred from playing in L.A. Since the police couldn't stop white kids from coming to the concerts, they made it hard for Black artists to be booked into venues. After I signed with the booking agency General Artists Corporation (GAC), they got me jobs in other cities up and down the West Coast. I guess audiences for Hunter's concerts fell off, since he, too, had to find theaters outside of the city where he could promote his concerts. Hunter's support for R&B and his ability to attract white audiences to his radio shows and concerts did not go unnoticed by independent record labels and disc jockeys throughout the country. The music was drawing fans and making money—not necessarily for the artists but for the record labels, radio stations, promoters, and concert halls. In my experience, when music makes money, these people start talking to each other.

Chapter 2

CLEVELAND THEATERS

Once small independent R&B labels gained a foothold in the Los Angeles radio market, R&B record promoters and pluggers quickly fanned out to visit top record stores around the country and disc jockeys in major markets seeking exposure for their artists. One of the most significant record stores in the Midwest that straddled working-class Black and white neighborhoods was Record Rendezvous at 300 Prospect Avenue in Cleveland. It's where the term "rock 'n' roll" was first applied to R&B.

Lance Freed
   (son of radio DJ Alan Freed)

When Record Rendezvous first opened in 1939 in Cleveland, Ohio, owner Leo Mintz would drive down to Columbus to buy used jukebox 78s at a deep discount and sell them in his store. By the end of the 1940s, Mintz featured a pretty wide selection of R&B records that attracted not only teens but also adult consumers from nearby cities and states. In 1950, one of those adult customers was my father, Alan Freed, a disc jockey then at WAKR in Akron. He began making the forty-mile trip north to the Rendezvous to keep up with what kids were listening to.

Though my father played jazz on his show in Akron, he had become increasingly curious about R&B. The number of R&B record ads and articles in *Billboard* was growing. Over the course of several visits to the

Rendezvous, my dad and Mintz struck up a friendship. Mintz didn't know much about R&B, but he had a soft spot for the many R&B record promoters and distributors who pleaded with him to carry their records. They'd show him the charts in Los Angeles and other cities as evidence of sales potential. Mintz also was encouraged by the large number of teens who came into his store and danced in the aisles to the R&B records he played on the shop's phonograph. They also played R&B records in the store's soundproof listening booths. Over time, my father began to develop a sense of which new R&B records would resonate most with his young customers.

Lesley Trattner
(eldest daughter of Leo Mintz)

My father knew a lot about music. He was skinny and tall—six foot four—and knew how to dress and enjoy the good life. He always had a cigarette and a drink in his hand. I have no idea why he opened Record Rendezvous. Like anyone who runs a record store, I assume it was because he loved music and loved being part of the entertainment world.

The store was downtown at 300 Prospect Avenue, a main drag. That's where all the fancy stores were. The store was a block from the bus terminal, which is how white families and kids reached the store from the immediate suburbs. The Black neighborhood was just a few blocks away. Inside, the store was long and narrow with a lot of record bins. In the back were six listening booths with doors and glass windows. Kids would take a record they wanted to hear back there and listen and dance. The booths were pretty revolutionary, since no other store in Cleveland let you do that. In other stores, records were behind the counter and you asked a clerk for help.

My dad played music in the store and had a speaker mounted outside to pull people in. Many kids came into the store to look for the records they'd heard the night before on the radio. They typically came in humming a few bars to a riff or a few words written on a scrap of paper. My father would help them figure out the record. Distributors of independent R&B records came in regularly urging him to take on their product. My father didn't know much about R&B. It was new. But

23

he listened for the beat, which is what got kids dancing and spending. Anytime there was a party, I'd bring the records. I was very popular.

When Alan Freed began visiting the store regularly in 1950, my father saw an opportunity. As Alan's visits increased, my father floated the idea of sponsoring him on a Cleveland radio station. Freed would play the R&B records and my father would have an easier time selling them. My father also knew early that the true market for R&B records was kids. In the store, he watched kids dance the bop and jitterbug in the aisles and in the listening booths after school and on the weekends. He watched in awe and referred to what they were doing as "rockin' and rollin'." Freed later picked up on the term.

Lance Freed

In April 1951, my father took a job at Cleveland's WJW as the host of a classical music show. One night in June, the disc jockey who normally hosted a show from 11:00 p.m. to 2:00 a.m. called in sick. The station manager asked my dad to fill in. But rather than spin the records the ailing DJ planned to play, my dad went down to his car and grabbed a stack of Mintz's R&B records from his trunk. After the show, the station manager reprimanded him for breaking with the show's existing format. When my dad told Mintz what had happened, Mintz called the station and offered to sponsor an R&B show—but only if my dad was the host. Two other local businesses joined Mintz's sponsorship—a furniture store and Erin Brew, a local beer that my uncle said tasted like piss.

My dad played records and announced ads live on the air with the same intimate "you and me" delivery he used to announce the records. The show quickly developed a following. My dad called his program the *Moondog Show*, after one of his favorite obscure R&B records, "Moondog's Symphony," which came out in 1950. My dad decided to use the record's mysterious, hypnotic instrumental as his theme to set the show's exotic, clubhouse mystique. He also began calling himself the Moondog and his listeners Moondoggers. I think opening his show with a song that embraced the sounds of the wild stirred the imaginations of many young listeners. As a friend and the show's sponsor, Mintz was often in the studio with my dad, handing him records that were distinct or popular with kids in his store.

Tommy LiPuma
(record producer and winner of five Grammy Awards)

In the early 1950s, I couldn't wait for the Moondog—Alan Freed—to come on at 10:00 p.m. I grew up in Cleveland and loved R&B and pop music. There was no one else like Freed. He was broadcasting to the Black community and he created this nocturnal world, an alternate universe where things were hip and happening and the music was filled with all of these secret messages. If you were a Black listener, he was completely in sync with your culture and up-to-date on emerging Black artists. If you were a white listener, you were being introduced to all this stuff. You knew nothing about it, but it was fascinating and exciting.

The music's energy was unbelievable. Blues shouters, horn sections, honking saxophones, a big beat—all of it. The music was addictive because it never fit into a rigid formula the way pop did. If you were a kid, Freed was your best friend, and he created an atmosphere separate from parents and teachers. It was a secret world of the night, with its own music, dances, and language. On the air, Freed referred to the Record Rendezvous as the 'Vous. Early on, it was hard to separate Freed and Leo Mintz, who owned the Record Rendezvous. Freed created this make-believe world on the radio, but the Rendezvous is where your imagination hit reality. You could go down there, listen to what was playing, and leave with records in your hands. The next natural step for Freed after radio and records was a concert.

Lance Freed

I don't know if my dad was aware of disc jockey Hunter Hancock in Los Angeles or his Midnight Matinee concerts there. What he did know is that he was broadcasting in Cleveland largely to a Black audience. By the end of 1951 and into the winter of '52, my dad held a series of dances at small local venues where he played R&B records that were featured on his show. These were called record hops. By February 1952, he and

25

Mintz—along with Mintz's associate, Milton Kulkin—planned a large dance and concert. They found a local concert promoter, Lew Platt, who was willing to put up the money to sponsor the event that was going to feature five R&B acts. The concert would be called the Moondog Coronation Ball and tickets were $1.50 each, or about $15 in today's dollars. It was to be held on Friday, March 21, 1952, from 10:00 p.m. to 2:00 a.m. It was a coronation because at the concert, my dad planned to crown himself King of the Moondoggers. A permit was secured and 8,600 tickets were printed for the Cleveland Arena, which held 12,500 people sitting in the stands and standing on the main floor.

As the concert date neared, Platt began to worry aloud about making back his money. So my dad promoted the concert aggressively on his radio show. According to posters for the coronation ball, the promised attractions included baritone saxophonist Paul "Hucklebuck" Williams, guitarist Tiny Grimes and His Rockin' Highlanders, the Dominoes, Danny Cobb, and Varetta Dillard. The four partners in the Moondog Coronation Ball had little or no experience accounting for tickets sold in multiple locations and were winging it under the assumption that too few people would show up to make the event financially worthwhile. The big mistake they made was making the tickets general admission instead of reserved seating. By 9:30 p.m. that Friday night, the Cleveland Arena was filled to capacity, with an estimated 6,000 people milling around outside unable to gain admission.

The concert wasn't oversold. It was a cold night and thousands of people showed up who didn't have tickets. My dad told me they came hoping to buy tickets at the door, but the event had already sold out. By 10:00 p.m., the streets were a sea of people. Most of those inside and outside were Black teens, the primary audience for my dad's radio show. The crowd gathering outside the arena unnerved the Cleveland police department. It didn't take much. After Paul Williams and His Hucklebuckers took the stage, those outside began to force open the doors. The twenty-five off-duty police officers hired by the promoter for the arena clearly weren't sufficient, so forty additional police officers and thirty firemen were rushed in to maintain order and protect the building. The crowd inside wasn't happy either. The arena was jammed, making it impossible to dance, let alone hear the live attractions on the primitive speaker system. When the fire department had the lights turned on at 10:45 p.m. and announced that the concert had been canceled, people were urged to leave in an orderly fashion. Many refused at first. According to the papers back then, one person inside was stabbed in the pushing and shoving that followed.

My father's radio station, WJW, was livid. Management felt the botched concert, near riot, and nonrefundable tickets tarnished the station's reputation with its audience. The next day, on Saturday, my dad was called into the station manager's office and told that his show later that day would be his last. When my dad went on the air that afternoon, he had nothing to lose. He opened with a goodbye monologue that became an apology to his audience and wound down with a plea for listener support. It lasted about a half hour. On the radio, as captured on tape, my dad threw himself on the mercy of his audience and launched into one of the great speeches in rock history.

Dad's mea culpa worked. Satisfied with his apology and distrustful of attempts by the station and the police to blame him for the concert's failure, listeners rallied to support the Moondog. Dad, Mintz, Kulig, and Platt were lucky. Had there been a stampede or had the police overreacted and triggered a full-blown riot, they and possibly the station would have been liable for deaths, injuries, and civil unrest. From that night forward, after being rescued from the brink of unemployment, my dad realized he owed his audience. He also knew rock concerts could be profitable if safety and security were priorities.

After the coronation mess, Dad immediately set to work planning another Moondog Ball for May. The Cleveland police chief protested. But as the city told the chief, Dad's request could not be legally denied by the city provided all of its requirements were met. This time, tickets at the Cleveland Arena were for reserved seating. Precautions were taken to limit attendance and protect concertgoers inside. A matinee and an evening performance that started at 8:00 p.m. were scheduled, and ticketing was taken out of the hands of promoters. What's more, only 6,000 tickets were allowed to be sold for each performance, despite greater capacity, and up to fifty special police were hired to

27

keep order. His follow-up concert, the Moondog Caravan of Stars, was held on May 24 and was highly organized. The two shows were held at the Cleveland Public Auditorium and featured the Mills Brothers, Woody Herman, Dinah Washington plus singer Tommy Edwards, and comedian Herkie Styles—a lineup probably selected to make city officials comfortable.

Once my dad proved he could be trusted to put on a safe show, he began to make a name for himself in the local concert business. In 1952, he staged Ohio "Moondog" events in Akron, Youngstown, Lorain, and Canton to sizable crowds. But by the end of the year, his experiments in Cleveland-area concert promotion began to fizzle. In December, one of his concerts was capped at 850 tickets, the maximum capacity at the city's Play Mor Auditorium. But fewer than 500 tickets were sold. When my dad arrived at the auditorium and saw the small size of the crowd, he said it would likely be the last of the Moondog concerts. But throughout his career, failure often led him to try again on a bigger scale with greater financial risks. In January 1953, he and Platt planned on putting on R&B shows throughout the Midwest and in Southern California. My dad also diversified. He partnered with Lew Platt and LCL Productions of Canton, Ohio, to put on a show at the Cleveland Arena in August 1953 that featured former heavyweight boxing champ Joe Louis. About 10,000 people filled the venue. Artists included Ruth Brown, the Buddy Johnson Orchestra, the Clovers, Lester Young, Wynonie Harris, and others. By then, his *Moondog Show* had become Cleveland's #1 radio program, catching the eye of radio stations in larger markets throughout the country.

Up until this point, his use of the term "rock 'n' roll" was only in passing. More often, he referred to the music he played as "blues and rhythm records," and the phrase "rock 'n' roll" never turned up in his radio show's title in Cleveland or on the posters for his concerts there. His concerts did become more integrated. At his Moondog Birthday Ball on June 25, 1954, at an armory in Akron, the audience reportedly was one-third white. In September 1954, my dad was hired away from WJW by New York's WINS, a station with much greater reach and prestige.

Tommy LiPuma

I didn't go to the Moondog Coronation, but I remember when it was all over the Cleveland newspapers. That's when everyone began to realize how big this R&B thing could be. Thousands of kids loved it, and Mintz was selling those records like crazy. When we heard that Alan was hired away by WINS in New York, everyone I knew in Cleveland was hugely let down. It felt like a baseball team was moving to another city. I remember in the *Cleveland Press*, this editorial cartoonist Bill Roberts had this thing called *Week's Wash*. It was a multipanel cartoon reflecting local news events. When Alan announced his move to WINS, Roberts drew a cartoon of a guy standing at the end of the Ninth Street Pier waving to a boat, like good riddance to Freed. It was funny.

Lance Freed

At WINS, that's where my dad built a name for himself as "Mr. Rock 'n' Roll." His use of the term that Leo Mintz had come up with to describe teens bopping in the aisles of his record shop began almost immediately. He called his WINS show *Moondog's Rock 'n' Roll Party*, likely at the urging of management. They wanted to appeal to a wider range of young listeners and differentiate from his Cleveland show. I know my dad was already familiar with the term from records or maybe from Leo Mintz, who helped deliver the "baby" and gave the music a name. But there were a bunch of folks contributing to the movement, so you can't really say one person invented the term. My father certainly was best known for exploiting it perfectly.

In the summer of 1955, my dad faced another crisis. Louis "Moondog" Hardin, that New York street performer who made the record my dad used as his theme, sued him for the unauthorized use of his name on WINS. Hardin wound up with a $6,000 settlement, and the judge told my dad he could no longer use the Moondog name. Dad told me he was panicked when that happened. He didn't know what to do. He had to go on the air to do his show but could no longer use the name so closely associated with him. When he went on that first night, he said, "This is the big beat and the music we're playing is rock 'n' roll." He even tried to copyright the term, but it was too generic. Dad just

29

dropped "Moondog" from the original title of his show and called it "The Alan Freed Rock 'n' Roll Party," referring to himself as "the old king of the rock 'n' rollers." From that moment on, the music would be known generically as "rock 'n' roll."

But regardless of intent and no matter what the music was called in 1955, the music at concert revues that crisscrossed the country was still being performed largely by Black R&B artists. For rock 'n' roll to cross over to the pop charts and ignite a national movement among all teens, a white artist would have to emerge who could record the music convincingly. That began with Bill Haley and His Comets in 1953, who combined the jumpy rhythm of R&B with the twang of Western swing. Haley's live performances onstage and on early television had plenty of visual energy. His first hit, "Crazy Man, Crazy" in 1953, featured an instrumental break during which Haley onstage played the guitar down on his knees while the tenor saxophonist played with honking touches, the bassist twirled his upright instrument and climbed up its side while continuing to snap the strings, and the slide guitarist gave the music a country-and-western flavor. The group borrowed from the physical R&B shows they had seen, and "Crazy Man, Crazy" became the first rock 'n' roll single by a white artist to become a *Billboard* hit, reaching #12 in June 1953. My dad loved Bill Haley.

Chapter 3

CHICAGO CLUBS

Performing in Chicago in the early 1950s meant playing the electric guitar at the city's many blues clubs in the Black neighborhoods on the West and South Sides. The intimate nature of the blues and the sonic limitations of guitar amps ruled out theater concerts by small R&B combos. Besides, many Black adults who had migrated from the South preferred to unwind in intimate clubs as they listened to music that reminded them of home. Chicago also was a major recording city where labels were constantly looking for new discoveries. One of those blues guitarists looking for a break in 1955 was Chuck Berry.

Marshall Chess
(son of Leonard Chess, cofounder of Chicago's Chess Records)

In 1950, my father, Leonard, and my Uncle Phil started Chess Records in Chicago. That year, the first Chess record they released was "My Foolish Heart" backed by "Bless You" by jazz tenor saxophonist Gene Ammons, who was friends with my father. I was at the first recording session. I was eight and fell asleep on two metal folding chairs.

Up until 1955, Muddy Waters was Chess's biggest star. He played acoustic guitar. In 1950, his first 78, "Rollin' Stone," was an acoustic side. Muddy used to say he made Chess Records and Chess made him. And he was right. We were so close with him that he used to call me his white grandson. The first time I met him was when he came over to our house. He had a nice car and a bright-green suit on. What blew me away were his shoes. They had the hair of a cow or a horse. My father and Muddy loved each other. They were good friends, and both were excited that his records sold so well.

My father was motivated by money. His love of music came from osmosis. In fact, my father and Muddy both were motivated by making money and improving their lives. That was their deep connection. They both just wanted to make it. Clearly, by the early 1950s, the blues was selling better than jazz. What changed everything was the rise of the electric guitar. Chicago was full of Mississippi Delta blues people. They all came up the Illinois Central Railroad from Memphis. It was a cheap ticket. They started making money in places without electricity. These were party houses—people having fun. The blues wasn't an art form yet. The early blues places I can remember had men and women drinking and grinding. Music was a sexual thing. Dank, dark clubs—a lot of them in basements and union halls. Within a few years, electricity was cheap, so guitarists began playing electric models with a portable amp.

Chuck Berry came to Chicago with his wife in May 1955. He came up from St. Louis carrying a tape of himself playing with a group called the Sir John's Trio. Johnnie Johnson was Chuck's piano player. Chuck wanted to be a blues singer, so he went to see Muddy Waters perform at a club on a weekend. After the show, Chuck told Muddy he had a tape and wanted to be a singer. Muddy told him to see my father. That Monday morning, Chuck came to Chess Records. Chuck said to my father: "Muddy sent me." My father and Chuck listened to the tape. One song was a twelve-bar blues called "Wee Wee Hours." The other was "Ida Red," inspired by a Western swing record by Bob Wills and His Texas Playboys in 1938.

My father wasn't crazy about the country lyrics to "Ida Red." He said to Chuck: "There's something really special and different about your guitar playing: the rhythm and the beat." My father knew this stuff instinctively. People who worked in the studio called him the Foot Stomper, because his foot constantly came down on the backbeat. My father said to Chuck: "Go back to St. Louis and rewrite the song." But before Chuck left, they came up with a less rural title for the song: "Maybellene."

For some reason, there was an empty box of Maybelline mascara on the floor. They altered the spelling of the name to avoid legal trouble.

Ten days later, Chuck returned to Chess with his piano player, Johnnie Johnson. He had written a new lyric for "Maybellene" about a drag race and a love interest. They recorded "Maybellene" on May 21, 1955. But after Chuck played it back, my father told me, he wanted a bigger beat and stronger bass line. I wasn't at the session, but the record was one of my most memorable listening experiences when my father brought it home. That song marked a big change not only in rock 'n' roll history but also in our family's life and finances.

Up until 1955, Chess only had minor hits by Black blues artists. My father and Uncle Phil would sell a few hundred copies to the Mob for a nickel each. The Chicago Mob controlled the jukebox business then. There wasn't any crossover to the white charts, and there wasn't any real Black radio except for Sam Evans's *Jam with Sam* show each weekday night on WGES. There also were a few shows featuring Black music on local foreign-language stations. Back then, you could buy three hours of airtime on those stations and play whatever you wanted. In exchange, you'd keep all the revenue from the airtime you sold to advertising sponsors.

Chuck Berry's "Maybellene" changed all of that. His record crossed over to the white pop charts largely because DJs and listeners at first thought he was white. Back in the mid-1950s, white stations didn't play Black artists. They played records by white artists who covered Black hits. When white stations found out that an artist whose record they were playing was Black, they pulled it out of rotation. But as demand for "Maybellene" grew, my father had problems pressing enough copies. He knew what a backbeat was, but he had no idea how to meet demand and how to generate big volume fast.

Once enough copies were pressed, my father drove to New York. He went up to see DJ Alan Freed, who by then was working at WINS, and brought him copies of "Maybellene." Payola was legal then. Without payola, most independent record companies wouldn't have survived, including Chess. My father gave Freed a writer's credit on "Maybellene." That was the payoff then, to play the record extensively, and Chuck Berry was well aware of what my father did to get his record played. On his drive back to Chicago, my father stopped in Cleveland and called Phil. My uncle said to my father: "What's going on? Everyone is screaming for that Chuck Berry record." Evidently, Freed had played it nonstop, all night long during my father's drive.

There was total racism in Chicago radio. Only after Freed played the record over and over did Chuck catch on. That's when white kids started hunting the dial for local Black stations to hear more music like Chuck's. The record made it onto WIND, the #1 white drive time radio station in Chicago. The DJ was Howard Miller. That's what broke "Maybellene." Miller had the biggest white audience in the city. I was thirteen then, and up until that point, I had never heard my father say the words "rock 'n' roll." And yet "Maybellene" was the very birth of the whole thing, crossing over from Black to white audiences.

Meanwhile, Bo Diddley, a street musician, was recording on the electric guitar on my uncle's Checker label. Same company but different distributors. Bo's records in 1955—"I'm a Man" backed by "Bo Diddley" and "Diddley Daddy" backed by "She's Fine, She's Mine"—caught on. Even with Chuck's and Bo's success on the radio, there weren't large-scale integrated rock 'n' roll concerts in Chicago. Zero. The city was fiercely segregated. All of the R&B performances went on at blues clubs, bars, and union halls. There were early local TV jukebox shows, but they played mostly white artists and groups who knocked off records by Black artists. And there were sock hops in schools where they'd play records. The only large-space concerts I can recall were at the Regal Theater in Chicago. But they were for Black kids.

WLAC in Nashville was very important to Chess Records. WLAC was a 50,000-watt station that played R&B and reached twenty-eight states and parts of Canada at night. A lot of artists didn't go on the road much. They played locally in Chicago. When their records wound up on WLAC, they were heard in Black and white homes in more than half the country. Also important is that Chuck Berry pioneered the electric rock 'n' roll guitar. For some reason, the electric guitar appealed much more to the white market than the saxophone or harmonica. Maybe because kids could buy a guitar and take lessons. The saxophone was expensive and wasn't as easy to learn and play. Chuck's sense of rhythm was addictive. With Chuck, it was all about the beat. It was a very tribal thing. He didn't just focus on playing. He teased out an audience. He knew how to get them wound up.

Byther Smith
(Chicago electric blues guitarist)

I was born in Monticello, Mississippi, in 1932. In the early 1950s, I went out to Prescott, Arizona, and drove a truck hauling timber. Soon my wife, Etta, and I had a child and we needed more income. So Etta took our child and went up to Chicago to see if she could find work. Her cousin lived there. When she got a job cooking at a barbecue house, I took the train up a month later in 1956 with my guitar. I was twenty-three. I wasn't a guitar player yet. I was just trying to learn while I worked for a candy factory. At some point I bought an early Fender Precision electric bass. There were more playing jobs for electric bassists, since it was new and so few people had one. I didn't take lessons. I just figured out how to play it on my own. The music was in me.

One day I met Roy Buchanan, a blues guitarist and the guy who pioneered the Fender Telecaster sound. His bass player was going on vacation and he needed a replacement. I took the job and wound up playing with Roy for about three years. I quit the candy-factory job. All kinds of music was being played in Chicago in the mid-1950s. Most of it was at clubs on the West Side. The music there was better than what you'd find at fancy nightclubs.

I saw Muddy Waters, Elmore James, Howlin' Wolf, Memphis Slim, Chuck Berry, and others. I was digging Chuck Berry's music. He played faster than everyone else on his guitar. It wasn't called rock 'n' roll yet. It was just faster than most of the Southern blues played around town. Then kids started to like him. I went to see Chuck quite a bit at a big club on State Street. Chuck was exciting. Unlike most of the blues players then, he didn't sit still on a stool. He was a showman. He could really put the screws to it. It was really something for a farm boy to see him do that duckwalk. He was no sit-still guy.

There weren't many theater concerts for Black audiences then and no integrated concerts at all. Chicago was strictly segregated. The police in

Chicago enforced it. Eventually, I decided to switch to the electric guitar. I wanted to start my own band. So many guitarists had switched over to the bass that it was hard to find guitarists. As a musician, it was the money I was after. When I played the blues onstage, I was listening to myself. I was thinking how I could change a song. The music that was inside of me just came out.

Jimmy Johnson
(Chicago R&B and electric blues guitarist)

In Chicago in the early 1950s, I wasn't really into playing blues music. My thing was doo-wop, playing and singing like the Ravens, the Orioles, and other "bird" vocal groups. That's what I'd do with my friends. In 1958, when I was thirty, I bought myself a Kay electric guitar and amp at Sears. It was a budget package. My first professional gig was at Turner's. I played every night of the week when I started. I also had gigs at Big Duke's Blue Flame Lounge, the Coil, Happy Home, and others. Chicago was a relief from the South in terms of racism. Eventually, economics turned me to the blues. There was a market for me to play it. I worked at clubs and got gigs at events held in halls—places you rented to throw a party. I enjoyed being onstage because I was making people happy. My life was always about helping someone or making someone's day. If I could make a person smile in the audience, it was a good night's work.

Chapter 4

MEMPHIS FAIRS

In 1954, Memphis was one of the country's most diverse music cities. Country music pressed down from Nashville and up from Shreveport, Louisiana, Western swing moved in from Texas, the blues migrated from the Delta region, boogie-woogie came from the cities farther up the Mississippi and on the East Coast, and gospel leaned in from the rural churchgoing areas ringing Memphis. If you were a singer who performed in Memphis, you couldn't help but be influenced by one or more of these many genres. Elvis Presley was one of these hybrids—a combination of white rural country music, Western swing, honky-tonk, gospel, and R&B singers such as Jimmy Sweeney and Arthur "Big Boy" Crudup. Presley's good looks, his ability to move suggestively onstage, and his deep voice made him a natural performer and a hot stage act, particularly with girls. But not even Presley could anticipate what would happen when rock 'n' roll met national television in January 1956.

Wanda Jackson
   (early female rockabilly singer-guitarist and performer)
   My parents moved us from Maud, Oklahoma, to Los Angeles in 1942. Work had dried up for my daddy in Maud. Out in L.A., he took odd jobs. At night, he'd play his guitar and teach me to play. On weekends, my parents didn't have any money for babysitters, so we'd go as a family

to dances to see Western swing stars like Spade Cooley, Bob Wills, and Tex Williams. But in 1948, we moved back to Oklahoma City.

By 1950, I had become quite a good singer and guitar player. When I graduated from high school in 1955, my father became my manager. That June, Daddy was reading *Billboard* magazine when he found an ad for a Memphis promoter named Bob Neal. Daddy called him on the phone. Bob said he was managing a young guy named Elvis Presley who was getting popular real fast. Bob said he was looking to book a girl on the live shows. So we signed with Bob. In 1955, most country songs on the radio were about hard times and adult life. Rockabilly was a new wind. It was about kids and their lives in school, on dates, at home, in cars, and everywhere else. The electric guitar was steadily replacing the fiddle, and the music was about the backbeat and the excitement of being young.

I first met Elvis on July 20, 1955. I was due to join his show in Cape Girardeau, Missouri, that night as his opening act. In the afternoon, we were on a radio show together to promote the event. Heck, I was seventeen and Elvis was nineteen. As I looked him up and down, I realized he looked very different from other guys his age at the time. He was a good-looking guy, and his hair was still sandy blond. But he had this aura. He was very charismatic. He didn't wear those customized Nudie's of Hollywood suits yet that he'd be dressed in a year later. Instead, he dressed his own way. He didn't copy anyone else. He wore slacks. I don't think he ever owned a pair of jeans.

The concert was a two-day run and featured country singers Bud Deckelman and Charlie Feathers, among others. Dancing started at 8:30 p.m. and then the acts went on at 10:00. Dancing pulled in the young crowds, since it let you get close to the person you were there with. After I arrived that night with my daddy at the Cape Arena Building in Cape Girardeau, I went on just before Elvis. There were a few hundred people out there. When I returned backstage to my dressing room, I heard the audience screaming. My daddy thought a fire had broken out. He said, "Get ready to get out of here," and left the room to see what all the fuss was about. When he came back a few minutes later, he said, "Wanda, there isn't a fire but you have to come see this for yourself." He took me into the wing.

Elvis was so cute out there. No drums, just a trio then—with Elvis on acoustic guitar, Scotty Moore on electric guitar, and Bill Black on acoustic bass. Elvis was having a lot of fun. I'd never seen anyone perform like that and flirt with the audience while saying funny things. That was unusual. It also caused the girls in the audience to get up and move forward to the stage. There Elvis was, inventing Southern rock 'n' roll, but I didn't realize it at the time. No one did. Elvis was already pretty popular down South among the girls, even in '55. Word of mouth had spread in spots in West Texas, Arkansas, and Missouri. And at state fairs, particularly in Tennessee. We did ten or twelve regional tours together.

Elvis and I had a lot in common. We were just two kids hoping to make it big. But we had no idea what big meant then. Big to us was a hit record. On our tour, I opened for him. In August '55, we were in Camden, Arkansas, at the Western Jamboree performing two shows starting at 7:00 p.m. There were around sixteen country-and-western acts on the bill. I was the only girl and had a hit out then, "You Can't Have My Love." We didn't get out of there until nearly 1:00 a.m. Elvis and I got encore after encore from the 1,200 people. The local paper said we stole the show.

These were package shows, so there were always four different artists, depending on where we were. Sets were short—about thirty or forty minutes. By the fall, we had Johnny Cash, Floyd Cramer, Jerry Lee Lewis, Carl Perkins, and Buddy Holly at different points. I didn't find it hard to be the only girl at these auditorium concerts. Most of the guys were doing standard country songs, which probably was boring for the kids. It finally got to a point where male stars wouldn't tour with Elvis. He was always the star girls were screaming for. There was no competing with him for that kind of attention.

I was lucky to work with Elvis as much as I did. I think Bob signed me so there was something for the guys in the audience to look at. If a guy had a date with a girl and Elvis was performing anywhere within driving distance that night, the girl wanted to go see him. Guys would take their girls without a fuss because they'd get to see me. Elvis was for the girls. I was for the boyfriends to keep them occupied. For the first few months we toured, I performed as a country singer-guitarist.

But Elvis kept raising the stakes with his act. I was transfixed. The kids were just loving it and him. We didn't call it rock 'n' roll or rockabilly yet. We just called it Elvis's kind of music.

A year later, in 1956, I signed with Capitol. Elvis had a talk with me and my daddy. He said, "Look, if you want to sell records, you need to record and perform what kids want to hear. Young people have money to buy records now and they call radio stations and make requests. You have to record their kind of music." Daddy said to me, "Wanda, I think he's right. You have to get in on it." But finding songs was tough. No one was writing Elvis's kind of songs for girls to sing. Most of the records were for guy performers to sing and appealed to girls' dreams and fantasies. Onstage, I was out on a limb by myself, so I began writing my own songs, such as "Mean, Mean Man," "Right or Wrong," and "Rock Your Baby."

By then, Elvis and I were dating. One day, Elvis drove me to his parents' home on Audubon Drive. His mother was home. We spent an innocent afternoon in his bedroom. He played me a record and then picked up his guitar and said, "See if you can do this," and gave the song his twist. He helped me with the feel and beat. He said, "You can do this and you need to." He really took an interest in my little ol' career, when his career was exploding around him. What songs did he put on his record player? I'm a seventeen-year-old girl sitting in Elvis Presley's bedroom. You think I'm going to remember what songs he played? I'll tell you this: He was a good kisser, but I don't know what he looked like up that close. I had my eyes closed.

That day at Elvis's parents' house wasn't a formal lesson, but he illustrated what he was doing by playing songs one way and then playing and singing them his way. He gave me what I needed: the courage to try his style onstage. So I began performing the way he did—freer, with more teenage attitude and that vocal hiccup. From the wings at concerts, I picked up other tips. Elvis never took himself seriously onstage and just had fun out there. I couldn't do what he was doing physically or I'd get in trouble. But the way I sang songs and how I dressed made the boys sit up and take notice. Even the girls liked me. I thought the girls might be jealous when I came out dressed the way I did. Instead, they were very cordial. No screaming for me, just polite.

My stage outfits broke the country code. I dressed to look like the date guys wanted to take to the prom. All the other girls who performed wore the full country-and-western Dale Evans thing. My mother made me a form-fitting fuchsia dress with lace on top with a halter neck and sweetheart neckline. It came down to just above the knees and then flared out. Clothes were one of the first things I was passionate about. I wanted to be a good entertainer, not just a singer of songs. Elvis and I realized early that to sing rock 'n' roll, you had to look the part out there.

Kay Wheeler
(president of the first Elvis Presley fan club in 1955)

In 1954, when I was fourteen, my older cousin, Diana, came over to our house in Dallas and told me about all this new music she'd been listening to. She brought over some records and a little suitcase record player. In my room, we closed the door and listened. I instantly loved what she played for me. She had records by Hank Ballard and the Midnighters, the Clovers, and other Black vocal-harmony groups. The beat was predictable, but the music and singing were fresh and exciting. I especially loved the saxophone. It was emotional and hot. As the music played, Diana also showed me the basic dance steps to the bop.

Listening to those R&B records was like jumping on a magic carpet and being transported to a whole new world that was ours. There was an energy and sensuality in those records that was overwhelming. Before long, my fourteen-year-old friends and I were buying R&B 45s at record stores in Black neighborhoods in Dallas. Sometimes I'd skip school with my younger sister, Linda, to see a movie. After, we'd go to King's Record Store in downtown Dallas. By the time we left, my sister and I had bought three or four singles.

One night in September 1955, when I was sixteen, I was rolling the radio dial and came across singing I hadn't heard before. My sister, Linda, and I listened wide-eyed. The announcer came on and said, "You

41

just heard Elvis Presley on the Big D Jamboree." I'd never heard music quite like that. And I had no idea what the singer looked like. This was before he was in the papers or on TV. What made his singing different was this vulnerable twangy sound in his voice. I loved it. I could only wonder who this Elvis Presley was. I wanted to meet him.

A short time later, I came across his flyer in a record store. From that moment on, I was Elvis crazy. My cousin, sisters, and a few of our friends talked about Elvis all the time. Fortunately, my aunt was an assistant to the owner of KLIF, a Top 40 radio station in Dallas. She was younger than my mom and wasn't married yet. One Saturday in late 1955, she took me and Linda to the station. Bruce Hayes, a DJ, came out of the studio, saw us, and offhandedly said, "I can't believe how ridiculous this guy Elvis Presley's name is." I protested: "That's not true. I have a fan club for him. He's going to be the biggest thing ever." The truth is the fan club consisted of me, my sisters, and my cousin, Diana. Hayes seemed amused. But more than likely he sensed the inflated reality of the situation. He said goodbye and left. My aunt later told me that Hayes had asked her for my address.

As a gag the following weekend, Hayes played an Elvis record and then announced that if listeners wanted to join the Elvis Presley Fan Club, they should write to me, the club's president. Then he read off my address. That station and show covered a lot of little towns in Texas. On Monday, I played hooky from school and stayed home. Around midday, my mother came running in. The mailman had dropped off boxes and boxes of letters on our front porch. I opened an envelope. The writer said she was listening to Bruce Hayes's radio show and wanted to join my fan club. I received hundreds of letters that day just like it.

I wasn't sure what to do next. So I took the Elvis record-store flyer out of my notebook. Bob Neal's address in Memphis was on there. Neal was his official manager. I wrote Bob telling him that I had hundreds of kids writing me to join my fan club. I asked him to please send me an address so that I could send him the letters.

Four weeks later, in November, I heard from Carolyn Asmus, Colonel Parker's secretary. She said that Colonel Parker now represented Elvis and that my letter was forwarded to her. She said they didn't have the facilities or the staff to handle a fan club for Elvis, that he was only one of their minor acts and that Hank Snow was their main focus. I was on my own. As a thanks for my effort, the Colonel's office sent me one glossy photo of Elvis.

I started by having membership cards printed. At school, my teachers hated me. I was a leader of the cool girls. Colonel Parker valued me enough that he had his secretary send me a telegram that would get me into Elvis's concert in San Antonio on Sunday, April 15, 1956. I remember holding the note and saying to my mother: "It's really going to happen." San Antonio was over two hundred miles away, so I took a Greyhound bus. My family had lived in San Antonio for a while when I was a kid, and Teena, a lifetime friend, lived there. I'd stay with her.

After I arrived—and before Teena and I left for Elvis's afternoon show—I tried to dress as grown-up as I could. I wore a beige sheath dress, high heels, and dangling earrings. "Heartbreak Hotel" had become a #1 hit, and I was totally taken over. Every day before school, we'd listen to ten Elvis songs. We were hooked, and here I was on my way to see my idol. At the Municipal Auditorium in San Antonio, I showed the telegram to the guy standing at the stage door. The telegram was like a magic wand. He opened the door, and Teena and I walked through and entered the backstage area. I had never been backstage anywhere before. Elvis's road manager, Tom Diskin, pointed to a door and said, "Elvis is in there. Just go on in." I thought I'd faint. For my generation, fame at this level was completely new and incomprehensible. What made it so exceptional was that Elvis was singing for teenage girls, not our parents. Teena waited outside the room.

When I walked in, Elvis was sitting in front of a mirror. He was carefully smoothing down his hair's ducktail. We were the only ones in the room. He wheeled around and walked over to me. I was in total shock. I said, "I, I, I'm Kay Wheeler. I'm president of your fan club." He said, "My fan club? I didn't even know I had one. What, what do you want me to do?" He wasn't one of those guys you see on TV who's much shorter in person. Elvis was six feet tall. And there was a lot of him. As he approached me, he got really close and started flirting around. I started getting nervous. He asked again how he could help me with my fan club. I pulled out photos I had made from the original one the Colonel had sent. Elvis signed them all.

After Elvis handed the signed photos back, he held me close and kissed around on me. It was all very sweet. Then someone knocked on the door and said it was time. We walked out of the dressing room door. Dozens of press people were there shouting questions. As they took pictures of us, Elvis held me tight. I felt I was no longer in control of myself. I always had a lot of confidence and self-respect. I got both from my parents. At some point he said to me: "You're my brunette type." But his arms were about friendship, hugs, and puppy love.

I'm a Southern girl, so we had that connection and instant friendship. And we both loved rock 'n' roll, which was brand-new. When all the fuss with the press was done and it was time for the show, Elvis asked me to watch the concert from the wings. Teena didn't like Elvis at all. But she did a great job with my Brownie Hawkeye flash camera. When they announced him, he couldn't wait to get out onstage. He knew who he was. He went on with vigor and excitement.

From the minute he put one foot on the stage, the screaming started. All he had to do was show up to get that kind of response. There was no crowd manipulation, no girls paid off to shriek. It was brain chemicals and hormones running wild. As soon as the audience saw him, pandemonium broke out. There was an instant explosion. This wasn't yelling. It was screaming to the point that you could hardly hear, an explosion of emotion by young girls. My sense from seeing the audience's faces from the wing was that the guys were threatened by the screaming. As for the girls, it wasn't up for discussion. Most of them forgot about who had brought them there in a split second.

Concert security was in its infancy then. Fortunately, in San Antonio, the stage was high. To further discourage any thought of trying to climb up there, about fifteen cops lined the skirt of the stage. When Elvis started singing, I started bop dancing to the music in the wing. At the break, Elvis asked what I was dancing. I said, "That's the bop, my dance." Elvis said he wanted to learn it. Backstage, Scotty Moore played the guitar and I danced. Elvis took a shot at it as well. Before I headed home, Elvis asked me to come to his concert on Friday, April 20, at the North Side Coliseum in Fort Worth. I said I would. He arranged for me to get in.

I asked Elvis why he wasn't performing in Dallas, a much bigger town. Elvis said that Colonel Parker couldn't book him there because he didn't think he'd be able to fill the seats. I said, "How can that be? That's crazy. That's your biggest spot in terms of fans." Elvis was smart. By telling me, he immediately got me started thinking: "What can I do to get him enough fans so he could perform in Dallas and I could go see him again."

Back home, I told my aunt. She said, "Let me talk to the station's owner." He told her that if I could get enough teens to go to the concert, the station might be able to sponsor him. "Get a letter-writing campaign going," he said. So I did. KLIF received tens of thousands of letters from fans vowing to attend the concert. So many letters came in that KLIF had to book the concert at the old Cotton Bowl. That was 26,500 tickets sold. It was Elvis's largest paid venue up until that point and probably rock's first stadium concert. And I promoted it with the fan club—not the Colonel.

I was on top of the world. My efforts had helped bring Elvis to my hometown. On Thursday, October 11, the day of the concert, they put up a ten-foot-high cyclone fence between the seats and the field. I was the only teen allowed on the field. It was just me and a few photographers. At 8:00 p.m., Elvis was driven out onto the field sitting on the back of a white Cadillac convertible. He was wearing a billiard-green sports jacket and buckskin shoes that just blew me away. His performance was pretty much the same concert he had been doing all over the place, plus songs that had just been released. But the screaming all but drowned out his singing. A day later, Elvis performed at the Heart O' Texas Coliseum in Waco, Texas. The place held 11,000 but only 5,000 showed up and they weren't too enthusiastic.

I was irate and told a reporter that Waco had hurt his feelings. I said, "Waco is the squarest town in America." Papers all over the country ran the article, and the publicity attracted more fans. Even though Elvis was a huge national star by late '56, you still had to win over every city and build advance buzz. Who knows why so few had shown up to see Elvis? What I did know is that I hadn't established a fan club in Waco yet. So much for Colonel Parker shrugging off the power of a fan club to fill concert venues. By December of '56, Elvis had become a different person. Whatever shyness he had was gone, and he had grown into his role as a superstar.

Barbara Hearn Smith
(Elvis Presley's girlfriend from 1956 to 1957)

I was born in Memphis and grew up there. I first met Elvis briefly in 1952 at a birthday party. We started dating in early 1956. Elvis loved to kiss. You know the old saying, practice makes perfect. He was a perfect kisser long before I met him. He was very tender and kind and affectionate. The word "girlfriend" back in '56 just meant someone you went with to events and then kissed. The truth is Elvis never went steady with anyone. He loved women, and that was all right with me. I didn't want to get married. My family didn't have many happy marriages. Besides, I wasn't a jealous type, so friendly sweethearts was fine with me. I really didn't expect anything to come of us. I felt I was better off being single.

Our relationship lasted about a year. While Elvis and I were dating in 1956, I was with him at many of his concerts during that pivotal year. Before performing and while onstage, he never seemed nervous. None of it seemed to bother him. At least that's how he made it seem. He just went about his daily routine. When it was time to go on, he'd just do it. I remember one of his early concerts on a flatbed truck at a newly opened shopping center in Memphis. Even then, in '54, he was pretty good-looking. Not nearly as good-looking as he'd become later, but plenty good-looking.

By '56, he was a wonderful performer. Before a concert and during the first couple of songs, I usually watched from the wings. Before he went on, it was quite boring. He'd mill around backstage and pal around with people and shake hands, probably to ease the stress. I'd stand back, out of the limelight. But the minute it was time for him to go out, he took these urgent steps to the stage, sort of running. That's when he became a different person. Personally, I never understood the frenzy over him. And it was a frenzy. Back then, it was unusual for girls to be uninhibited in public. Girls weren't allowed free rein. You cared what people thought because it reflected on your reputation and how people spoke of you in social conversation. So the fact that girls dropped all that and went wild in the audience was remarkable. Elvis thought the screaming was cute. He'd laugh onstage and reach out and kind of tease the girls in the audience.

For the rest of a show, I'd often sit with his parents in the audience. Elvis was so happy to be performing, but he was never overly excited about it or anything. He didn't have to do much to make fans crazy. He just had to be there. I talked to his mother, Gladys, about the frenzied girls a bit. She worried. She thought they might hurt him, either by grabbing his hand and yanking him off the stage or climbing up there and mobbing him. The concert that stands out was the Mississippi–Alabama Fair and Dairy Show in Tupelo, Mississippi, in late September of '56. Before we left his house in Memphis for the fairgrounds, he handed me a dry cleaner's bag. I walked around with the bag for about an hour before finally laying it down on the sofa.

When it was time to go, we got into Elvis's white two-door Lincoln Continental Mark II that he had bought in Miami that August. Elvis's friend, Red West, drove down with us and a couple of the other boys. I was the only woman. Tupelo was about a two-hour drive. When we arrived, the backstage area was a little building adjacent to the fairgrounds stage. Lots of people came back to talk to him. At some point, he turned and said to me: "Where are my shirts?" I said, "Shirts? I don't know. What shirts?" He said, "The ones I asked you to hold."

I suddenly realized I'd left them lying across the sofa in the family room. Instead of being angry with me, Elvis calmly called his house to see if anyone was still there. The person who answered his call broke all speed limits to get the shirts down there before his first matinee show at 2:30 p.m. Even after the shirts arrived, Elvis never became angry with me. He just teased me after he got dressed: "You didn't want me to wear the shirts because Natalie Wood gave them to me." Wood had bought him two fine shirts, one red and the other blue. Elvis gave a long matinee performance. The evening performance was at 7:30. Between shows, he walked around talking to people. Photos show me sitting and talking with Mrs. Presley. She had on a heavy brocade dress and I was wearing

47

a wool-blend dress. We were photographed melting and drinking ice-cold Cokes to keep cool.

A month later, toward the end of October, Elvis went to New York to appear on *The Ed Sullivan Show* for the second time. A couple of days later, Natalie Wood came down to Memphis for a few days with actor Nick Adams. Wood seemed to have a crush on Elvis. She stayed at his mother's house. In the morning, Wood waltzed around in a negligee while workmen were there. From then on, Mrs. Presley didn't like her. Wood was too modern and sophisticated. The next day, Elvis came over to my aunt's house. She lived downstairs and my mother and I lived upstairs. My parents had divorced when I was very young. Elvis seldom called to say he was stopping by. He just appeared. My aunt left the room, and Elvis and I talked for about a half hour. Then he left.

When my aunt returned, she said, "Natalie Wood was sitting out in front of the house on a motorcycle the entire twenty-five minutes he was here." At this point, I think fame confused and frightened him, especially as he became exposed to Hollywood. With national TV appearances and the film *Love Me Tender* in '56, he seemed torn between his new life and his old one and the people he knew and those he was meeting. Performing was no longer about winning fans and a following. Concerts and movies were now necessary to keep his income coming in, and a lot of people were depending on that income, including Elvis. His father was worried it was all going to fall apart. He had been very poor and he knew that with success came the risk and disappointment of being poor again.

Though I didn't travel with him, I often went to his regional concerts. After performing, as soon as he came offstage, he instantly returned to himself. He was strictly a performer. The stage gave him freedom, and people paid to see him be free. It opened up a better way of life for him and his family, which is what drove him at first. But by late '56, I think they all wound up with way more than they expected or even knew how to handle emotionally. Elvis's concerts were different than anything anyone had ever seen before. Audiences were awestruck by his confidence and his good looks. Many rock 'n' roll singers then sounded good on records but when they showed up, they weren't particularly good-looking onstage. I had been to a few concerts by other big artists, including Bill Haley and His Comets. I never saw an audience react much to them.

Elvis was different. Everything about him was astonishing and sensual. Maybe the fuss he caused onstage was due to the fact that TV sales had reached a critical mass across the country and audiences saw him perform in their living rooms. Or more radio stations were playing his music and record stores seemed to be everywhere. Or that he was starring in movies. Today, virtually everyone has seen rock stars live in concert. Back in '56, seeing someone as big as Elvis perform made you hyperventilate. The excitement was overwhelming. Add Elvis's larger-than-life good looks and his sexuality, and you couldn't believe what you were seeing or hearing. All of this made people take notice and feel the way I did—that he belonged to you but also to everyone else.

Throughout 1956, Elvis called me once or twice a day. But by '57, he called me every couple of days and then once a week. When he met Anita Wood, a Memphis disc jockey, she was everything he wanted. There was never any big breakup between us. Our relationship ended slowly. Elvis would call all the time asking if I could go out. But I had college studies to complete. He wanted someone to travel with him on tour. I wouldn't do that. I couldn't do what he wanted me to do one time too many. I knew our days together were numbered and that I had to focus on me and my future. But it was a great year.

Chapter 5

Northeast Fests

Disk jockey Alan Freed didn't waste time when he arrived at WINS in New York in 1954. By April 1955, he began holding large-scale rock 'n' roll concerts at Brooklyn's Paramount Theatre during the weeklong school breaks over Easter, Labor Day, and Christmas. Meanwhile, up in Boston in '54, nightclub owner George Wein launched the Newport Jazz Festival in Newport, Rhode Island, becoming the first to promote the multiday outdoor popular music festival. Like Freed, Wein sought to unite audiences of all races and expose them to exciting new music. Both would lay the foundation for the rock festivals of the 1960s.

Lance Freed
(son of disc jockey Alan Freed)

Soon after his arrival at New York's WINS in 1954, my father was introduced to Morris Levy, a New York club owner and record entrepreneur who saw the potential of exploiting R&B. Levy set up Sieg Music Corp., with himself, Dad, WINS, and concert promoter Lew Platt as partners. The partners planned a live show—the Rock 'n' Roll Jubilee Ball. Levy put up the money and booked the concert into the St. Nicholas Arena, a 4,000-seat boxing venue on Sixty-Sixth Street and Columbus Avenue. The two-night event was scheduled for Friday, January 14, and Saturday, January 15, 1955. Dad promoted the show relentlessly on the radio, and both shows sold out a week ahead of the event. After the strong, integrated turnout at the arena, a large venue was needed that could be booked for up to a week at a time and would feature films and stage shows.

Levy turned to his contacts at ABC's entertainment division. Levy wanted the show at ABC's Paramount Theatre in Times Square. But the idea of an integrated R&B crowd milling around on Broadway in the heart of Manhattan's entertainment and theater district surely didn't sit well with ABC management at first. So the executives offered up their Brooklyn Paramount Theatre on Flatbush and DeKalb Avenues. No dancing was allowed in the 4,100-seat theater, aside from the small space in front of your seat. To sweeten the deal, ABC offered Levy the Brooklyn Paramount at a reduced rental rate. By then, the entire record industry had jumped on the term "rock 'n' roll," making it ubiquitous and impossible to copyright.

R&B had always been code for music by Black artists. By contrast, rock 'n' roll was race neutral, which record companies viewed as easier to sell in segregated parts of the country. But if rock 'n' roll was going to be a generic term, Sieg's goal was to put Dad at the head of the DJ parade and make him the originator of the term. Sieg signed the Paramount deal, and the first weeklong concert event in 1955 was called Alan Freed and His Rock 'n' Roll Easter Jubilee. It ran daily during the Easter school vacation, from Friday, April 8, to Thursday, April 14. A movie was sandwiched in between each of the five music revues. The first screening started at 9:30 a.m. and the music shows began at 11:30.

I was at Dad's first Brooklyn Paramount concert that Easter week. I stayed backstage during the movie and watched the show from the seats out front. My sister, Alana, and I spent all seven days there, watching all of the shows each day. The movies generally lasted about an hour and fifteen minutes. Nobody in the audience had time to leave and have a meal or hang out. If you left, you weren't admitted back in. But backstage, food was brought in for the artists. Someone started a fried chicken business bringing food back there.

Marshall Chess
(son of Leonard Chess, cofounder of Chess Records)

In Chicago, I didn't see white and Black kids at concerts sitting together. At Alan Freed's shows at the Brooklyn Paramount, I did. I went

51

to my first concert there in 1955, which also happened to be Freed's first Paramount extravaganza. It blew me away. On the bill was tenor saxophonist Red Prysock, who played on his back like Big Jay McNeely. Also, LaVern Baker, the Moonglows, and the Moonlighters—all of whom were on Chess Records. I'd never seen anything like that. Kids were dancing in the aisle. Soon I was up dancing. Chuck Berry's first concert was at the Brooklyn Paramount in September 1955. I was there.

Chuck wore a white tuxedo with black lapels and played a cherry-red Gibson. When he did his signature duckwalk, the integrated audience went crazy. He was never nervous about the audience. Onstage, he knew how to connect with Black and white teens and make them dream. They responded to his confidence and his guitar. He wasn't playing the blues in the old style. He made kids feel cool.

Lance Freed

Over the next five years, Dad held these rock 'n' roll revues during school holidays. Dad's radio shows continued, sometimes abbreviated, but he would show up at the radio station at the end of each day and tape his show. It would be broadcast the following day. The music had become so popular that some of the live shows at the Brooklyn Paramount lasted ten full days. Lineups would vary. My favorites were Frankie Lymon and the Teenagers, Buddy Holly and the Crickets, Little Richard, and Jerry Lee Lewis. All of the performers had little areas backstage. In his area, Fats Domino played checkers with Frankie Lymon. Frankie taught me how to play and then beat me every time. Even before he went onstage, I'd be losing. Everyone had a good time back there.

There were always arguments over who would close the show and who would get more than one song to perform. One day, there was friction between Chuck Berry, Jerry Lee Lewis, and Little Richard over this. Dad went back and talked with them. He worked it out so one closed one day, the other closed the next, and the third closed the day after that. If you closed the show, you got to perform two or three songs, and each of these guys could bring down the house. The kids went nuts. These were the first large integrated rock 'n' roll concerts for teens. If you look at photos, you see kids of all backgrounds waiting in line to get in. As Little Richard used to say to me looking down at those lines from backstage, "Chocolate and vanilla together."

Fats Domino wore a lot of diamond-encrusted jewelry. He had this diamond stickpin for his tie. One day it went missing backstage. He said, "I can't find my diamond stickpin anywhere. We have to shake everyone down. I can't go on without it." My dad pointed out that there were only so many people back there and that everyone respected each other. The comradery was amazing. The artists knew they were at the birth of something big. You could hear it in the audiences. Eventually, my dad produced Fats's tiepin with a smirk on his face. He had taken the pin and hidden it just to shake things up. It was boring otherwise waiting to go on. People were going stir-crazy. At one show, I was standing with Little Richard in the wing. The Chantels were finishing before Dad went out to announce the next act. He turned to Richard and said, "You're doing a fabulous job." Richard said, "Thanks, Mr. Freed." Dad said, "Stop calling me Mr. Freed." Then Dad pulled out a bunch of hundred-dollar bills and stuck them in Richard's suit pocket.

I was really excited about the concerts at the Brooklyn Paramount. I was in awe that my dad had put them together. I remember being in his dressing room one day and looking out the window. Four stories below were about 150 kids standing in line. Kids outside spotted me and waved up, shouting that I should get them my father's autograph. So I had him sign lots of pieces of paper and I threw them out of the window like confetti. During the movie in the late afternoon, my dad and I would grab something to eat. We had to time it just right. We knew it took ten minutes to get downstairs. Out front, my dad liked to talk to the kids at the head of the line for the next show. He'd ask how long they were standing on line and if they were cold. Sometimes he'd tell his assistant to take the kids at the head of the line to the front row, which thrilled them. He was empathetic.

Little Richard was always funny. Jerry Lee Lewis kept to himself. So did Chuck Berry. Frankie Lymon was closest to my age. But none of these guys ever seemed nervous to go out onstage. Jerome Green played maracas in Bo Diddley's band. One day he was in the wrong place backstage and the stage manager smacked him with a rolled-up newspaper to shoo him out. My father heard about it and fired the stage manager on the spot. My father detested treating anyone that way. For him, music was about talent, not race. He had enormous respect for the underdog.

In 1959, my father was swept up in Congress's six-month payola hearings. A major election year was coming in 1960 and parents were angry about the sexually explicit lyrics in rock 'n' roll songs. Parents also were unhappy about the sassy attitude of their kids, and integration at concerts was rattling senators and representatives from many segregationist states. When the hearings were over in 1960, the House drafted a bill to eliminate payola from radio, but the regulations in the bill were watered down in the Senate. Many major disc jockeys escaped prosecution.

My dad had no choice, financially, but to plead guilty in New York to accepting bribes to play records. He was fined $300 and given a six-month suspended sentence. Though he saved money on legal fees by avoiding a lengthy trial, his reputation was badly damaged. ABC fired him, and he couldn't find a steady job to cover his bills. Months before his death in 1965, he was indicted on charges of tax evasion, owing the IRS more than $35,000 in back taxes.

My father wasn't willing to cut a deal to testify against others the way many caught up in the scandal had done to save their skins. The decision cost him. My father had a talk with me about it in 1964. Sitting on the sofa, sipping a scotch, he said, "I just want you to know, because you may hear stories about me later on in life. People will say I took money in exchange for playing records. I never took money to play records."

In the 1990s, when civil rights pioneer and my former college roommate Willis Edwards was president of the Rosa and Raymond Parks Institute, he lobbied the White House to honor Rosa with the Presidential Medal of Freedom for refusing to give up her seat to a white passenger on a bus in Montgomery, Alabama. I planned a dinner for Willis at my home in Santa Monica. At one point, Willis told me Ms. Parks was coming. I couldn't believe it.

When she came over, we talked. As she was leaving my home, she noticed a poster of my father. "Are you related?" she asked. I told her I was his oldest son. She knew all about my father. She said, "I wouldn't give up my seat on the bus, but your father helped desegregate this country with music." I said, "Ms. Parks, that wasn't his intention." She said, "I understand. But it was the music that brought everyone together. He was the pied piper who led the charge. You should have a lot of respect for him."

Seymour Stein
(cofounder of Sire Records)

I grew up in Bensonhurst, Brooklyn. In 1954, I began listening to Alan Freed on the radio. The following year, Freed began talking up his rock 'n' roll revues at the Brooklyn Paramount. I started going to his shows in 1955 during Easter week, around Labor Day, and over the December holidays. I was thirteen then so I took the subway to Flatbush Avenue and walked to the Paramount. Some of my friends were interested in music but not nearly to the crazy extent that I was, so I went to the Paramount by myself. I knew I could stay from 9:30 a.m. to around 6:00 p.m. and see all three shows. Before I left for the Paramount, my mother packed me three corned beef sandwiches with mustard and enough money to take the subway and buy a ticket.

I arrived pretty early at the Paramount, around 8:30 a.m., which ensured a good spot on line. I always had a great seat up close to the stage, since tickets were general admission and I was toward the front of the line. Entering the theater was amazing. It was larger than any other theater I had been in, and it was ornate. So long as you remained in the theater, you could stay all day. When the show started, Freed came out onstage and talked up the artists, extolling the excitement of rock 'n' roll and reminding everyone that even though people said the music was a fad, it was growing in popularity.

I loved seeing Buddy Holly, the Moonglows, the Penguins, the Platters, Frankie Lymon and the Teenagers, the Five Keys, the Heartbeats, the Cleftones, and the Five Satins. But there were many more artists. Everyone was screaming throughout the shows. Seeing the music up close was much more exciting than just hearing it on the radio. It was very emotional for me. Tears were often running down my face during performances.

I particularly loved Fats Domino. He was a great performer. He'd move the piano with his stomach and turn his head away from the keys to smile at the audience while he played. He was lovable, and you wanted to hug him. When Chuck Berry began appearing at Freed's shows, he had it all. Berry played guitar unlike anyone else. I choke up today just talking about Alan Freed's rock 'n' roll shows at the Paramount. They had a profound effect on me and my career.

Jimmy Merchant
(original member of Frankie Lymon and the Teenagers)

The Teenagers began playing the Brooklyn Paramount in Alan Freed's rock 'n' roll shows in March 1956. Our hit "Why Do Fools Fall in Love" had been released that January. By March, our single was #12 on *Billboard*'s chart. We were the first rock 'n' roll group made up of teenagers singing for teenagers about love. We started rock 'n' roll's youth movement. Groups that came before us were mostly adults, and we became an inspiration for nearly every teen group that followed us.

I grew up in the Bronx and started my first vocal group in 1952 with a friend. We sang songs by the Chords, the Mellows, and other Bronx vocal groups. I met Sherman Garnes in 1954, on my first day in junior high school. Sherman was already six foot four and had moved from the Bronx, like me. The only thing I was interested in was his deep voice. In the days that followed, we called ourselves the Earth Angels and developed a repertoire. We sang songs by the Penguins, the Fi-Tones, the Harptones, Robert and Johnny, and Clyde McPhatter and the Drifters. Soon we added lead singer Herman Santiago and baritone Joe Negroni. The four of us rehearsed in Sherman's building at 631 Edgecombe Avenue. We harmonized after school in a hall off the lobby. The echo amplified our harmony and made it sound like a record.

One day, a guy who lived on the first floor came out of his apartment. He had been listening to us for several weeks. He handed us a batch of love letters and said we could keep them. He said they were written by a young woman, and he thought we could turn them into song lyrics. I'm not sure if he found them or he had to get rid of them before his wife found out. We never asked. We were too busy laughing at him. We were stupid teenagers and laughed at everything. I took the letters home and read them. That's when I realized the lines in the love letters rhymed. Based on one of the letters, I came up with an idea for a ballad that wondered why fools fall in love and why birds sing so gay. At our next rehearsal, I introduced the song to the guys.

In the summer of 1955, after graduation from junior high school, we were all looking forward to attending high school. We knew Frankie Lymon from the neighborhood. He was two years younger than us but he was a smart, talented boy. Our group was due to appear at an August talent show at our old junior high school. Frankie followed us around as we rehearsed when he wasn't working at a corner grocery on 155th Street and Amsterdam Avenue.

Once Frankie joined the group, things changed. Richard Barrett of the Valentines had moved into a building on 165th Street and Amsterdam. As we sang on the street corner, Richard watched us from his window. One day he came down and said, "I'm gonna take you downtown to meet George Goldner at Gee and Rama Records. He told us to sharpen up. Not long after, he took us downtown. We stood in front of Goldner and sang a couple of songs. Goldner liked Frankie for our lead singer. He said to him: "What can you do?" Frankie said, "What do you want me to do?" "Let's hear you sing." Frankie sang "I Want You to Be My Girl." Goldner said, "Good. Richard, take the boys. We're going to record them. The kid is their new lead singer." We didn't mind. We had been discovered and it was like something spiritual from God. I always dreamed of becoming a professional singer.

Goldner wanted Barrett to break in two songs. So he worked with us on our "Why Do Birds Sing So Gay," which Goldner and Barrett changed to "Why Do Fools Fall in Love," and "Please Be Mine" for the B side. Barrett suggested we sing "Fools" up-tempo, not as a ballad. And in keeping with how the record business worked back then, Barrett's name wound up as a songwriter on "I Want You to Be My Girl" while Goldner's went on "Fools" with Frankie's name. Guys like Goldner and Barrett gave out opportunities and then took a songwriting credit as payment without any real songwriting input. They knew the value of royalties and we didn't.

Jimmy Wright's band backed us. Jimmy was the label's musical director and saxophone soloist. After we recorded the song, Goldner came up to us in the studio and said we needed a better name. Jimmy said, "Call them the Teenagers. Everything is teenager today." A bunch of seconds went by and Barrett added "featuring Frankie Lymon." So it was Frankie Lymon and the Teenagers. Along the way, "Teenagers" got smaller and smaller in print.

We recorded "Fools" in late 1955. Afterward, they sent us home in a car. Goldner said the single would come out after the Christmas holidays. He didn't want the song crushed in the rush. By then, I was a sophomore and Frankie was in eighth grade. When we appeared at the Brooklyn Paramount that March, the screaming by girls and boys in the audience was unbelievable. We came out onstage in white sweaters, white bucks and white socks, black pants, waved up hair, red bow ties. Goldner and Barrett came up with the outfit. They took us to a sporting goods store near Thirty-Fourth Street. A tailor put a red varsity letter T on the front and red "Teenagers" on the back.

A line of cops stood in front of the stage to keep the kids from rushing us. The kids were all waving their hands and singing along. Then the sax solo hit and Frankie did his dance, followed by Frankie and Herman doing a split. Joe and I walked over and put our hands on top of their heads and it seemed like we were lifting them up and down to the song's beat. What a scene.

The audience had the same response at all of our Paramount appearances over the coming year. The song was great, our singing was passionate, but most important, we were teens just like them. They identified with us—the fun we were having onstage, the harmonies we sang—and we asked in the song why kids like us fell in love. Teens cared about a handful of things then, and love was a big part of life in and out of school.

Up in our neighborhood, the five of us didn't let fame go to our heads. The record company gave us a small allowance—$12 a week. We did three one-nighter tours that lasted up to three months each. We also were on TV shows and in two movies. We even appeared at the Apollo

Theater. To make sure we were getting an education, Goldner put us in a private school for young professionals

I have no idea whether the guy who handed us the letters that day in Sherman's hallway or the woman who wrote them heard our song and put two and two together. All the words I used in the song were in those letters. Neither the guy nor his girlfriend came forward. They couldn't, when you think about it.

George Wein
(Newport Jazz Festival founder)

I opened Storyville in Boston in September 1950. The nightclub's audience was mostly made up of professors from different local colleges. We didn't draw many kids because they didn't drink, and most were under twenty-one, the legal age limit then. If Boston had allowed drinking starting at age eighteen, I might still be in business up there. The club attracted Black patrons when I had certain artists booked, but for the most part the audience was white and middle-class.

The pressure I faced was having to get different attractions every week. That was very tough. There just weren't that many great artists and groups. Remember, I needed forty different attractions because we were open forty weeks a year. But booking artists with hit records wasn't the basis of what Storyville was about. I had a love for what I was doing. I wanted to do things that people would be proud of. I didn't want a joint. I wanted them to have a nice place to play and hear jazz.

By 1953, I wanted to find a way to stage jazz during the summer. But the city was dead on the weekends. That fall, one of the professors who regularly came to the club introduced me to socialite Elaine Lorillard. Elaine and her husband, Louis, a tobacco heir, lived in Newport, Rhode Island. I sat down at their table at Storyville. Over drinks, Elaine spoke about how she and her husband months earlier had brought the New York Philharmonic to Newport for a concert series. The problem was the symphony drew far too few listeners, and the investors lost much of their $30,000.

As Elaine talked, she asked if I thought Newport could stage live jazz the following summer. I said I thought so and asked for some time to put together some ideas. Elaine, it turned out, loved jazz, and I was looking for a way to generate business and raise my profile over the summer. Weeks later, I drove down to Newport to visit with Elaine and her husband. I had figured the easiest way to make a Newport event successful was to base it on the Tanglewood Music Festival. The festival was held outdoors in Stockbridge and Lenox, Massachusetts, every summer since 1937 and featured multiple concerts with different types of classical groups.

I told the Lorillards about my idea for a series of day and evening concerts featuring different types of jazz. Elaine and Louis said they loved the idea and agreed to finance it. I had to put together the acts, the schedule, and the promotion. Going in, I knew which artists would sell tickets based on how they did at Storyville.

I also knew what I wanted to do with the festival. I saw it as an opportunity to promote jazz on a large scale and expose people of all ages to the music. For the first time, people who didn't go to clubs or couldn't get in because they were too young now could see and hear the music and musicians live, outside, in a relaxed, laid-back setting. The most important thing about the first Newport Jazz Festival in '54—and probably one of my greatest contributions—was not sticking with one kind of jazz. Whether it was traditional jazz or swing or bebop or modern jazz, everyone's taste would be covered. Even if the others weren't your favorite, you could see what those other forms had to offer. That had never been done before.

In 1958, John Hammond urged me to include Chuck Berry in the festival program. John was on the Newport Jazz Festival board, and I had respect for him. So I put together a good group of jazz musicians to accompany Chuck. But they were all the wrong musicians—Jack Teagarden, Jo Jones, Buck Clayton, and others. They were wonderful blues players, but they didn't play country blues or funk blues. They played jazz blues. I was thirty-three then and still a jazz purist. I cringed when Chuck Berry did his duckwalk across the stage during "School Days." This wasn't right for the purity of our jazz festival. I wasn't cringing for the audience or the other jazz musicians. I was cringing for myself and the critics. Jazz fans hung on their every word.

If we were accused of selling'out by powerful jazz critics, we might have a serious drop in attendance the following year. When I listened to Chuck play that Saturday evening, I enjoyed it. The music was fun. But whether it was the right thing to do is another story. Chuck Berry at the Newport Jazz Festival? You have to be crazy.

Newport changed the whole presentation of popular music outdoors and paved the way for outdoor rock festivals starting in the 1960s. At the time, I had no idea I was doing that. I just wondered if we could put up a stage here and another one there and feature different styles of jazz. I was motivated to create something different. I just wanted to draw all kinds of people to the music that I loved and for them to bring their families, spend a few days, and make some friends.

PART 2

THE 1960s

Once the House of Representatives completed its six-month radio payola hearings in May 1960 and drafted a bill, 1950s-style rock 'n' roll was damaged goods. The record and radio industries were cast as negligent or complicit in bribery schemes, and rock 'n' roll was viewed as a wildcat enterprise in need of restraint. Though the House bill was watered down in the Senate, which felt the onus was on stations to alter business practices and weed out "bad apples," the hearings resulted in the prosecution and fining of DJs. They also ended the on-air careers of a good number of radio personalities cited in Congressional testimony, including Alan Freed. Left shaken, the radio and record industries immediately took steps to make rock 'n' roll less slippery and the music more wholesome.

Songwriters got the message, and a new conservatism took hold in the industry, resulting in softer messages in music marketed to preteens and teens. Rock 'n' roll quickly gave way to pop rock and pop soul. "Long John Blues" and "Work with Me, Annie" were out, and "The Twist"(1960) and "Please Mister Postman" (1961) were in. Starting in the mid-1960s, the music changed again thanks to Bob Dylan's electric tour in 1965, the emergence of FM radio in the late 1960s, and the growing popularity of the rock album. Rock bands went on longer tours, and concerts were held in larger ballrooms and theaters and at outdoor festivals.

Throughout the decade, rock bands aligned themselves with a new generation advocating for peace, civil rights, the ecology, and the sexual revolution, among other issues. Rock's shift to original songs that addressed issues of the era had its roots in the folk revival movement of the late 1950s and early 1960s and in folk's alignment with political causes and civil rights.

Chapter 6

Folk at the Mall

Launched in 1959, the Newport Folk Festival in Newport, Rhode Island, was an extension of the popular Newport Jazz Festival, which had begun five years earlier. The outdoor folk concert series represented a high point in the folk music revival and attracted a wide audience of college-age fans. Artists such as the Kingston Trio, Bob Gibson, Joan Baez, Odetta, Earl Scruggs, the New Lost City Ramblers, Tommy Makem, and Barbara Dane all gained greater visibility at the festival. By August 1963, several leading folk artists were invited by organizers of the March on Washington to join gospel singers and perform before Martin Luther King delivered his "I Have a Dream" speech. For the first time, young popular music artists performed before an outdoor audience that extended to the horizon. Serious rock musicians took note.

George Wein
    (founder of the Newport Jazz Festival and Newport Folk Festival)
    In the mid-1950s, I went down from Boston to New York to visit various jazz clubs and began to notice that hip cabaret singers and folk groups were being mixed into their weekly schedules. So I had folk musicians play my Storyville club in Boston—including Josh White, Pete Seeger, Odetta, and others. Diversity was the key to survival in the jazz club business.

Folk made sense to me for another reason. Politically, I had a leftist background before, during, and after World War II. In 1948, I played piano for Henry Wallace rallies and accompanied activist singer Laura Duncan. I wasn't a Communist and never became one. But I was simpatico with the left. They fought against racial injustice. My whole life has been devoted to that cause, because I was in love with my wife, Joyce, who was Black. That led me to folk music, which was political.

But I didn't think of folk as political when I started the Newport Folk Festival in 1959. I had already held specialty mini festivals within the Newport Jazz Festival the year before, including afternoon showcases of tap dance, gospel, and folk. There was such demand for the folk afternoon that I realized we could stage a separate stand-alone folk festival. So I talked the Newport board into holding one.

The first folk festival was held on July 11 and 12, 1959—a week after the jazz festival. It was an instant hit, not because of the folk music but because we put the Kingston Trio on. Parents brought their kids to hear the group, and we had a huge crowd. The appeal of folk then was the songs. Song communicates more effectively than instrumentals and speeches. Kids who were brought to the concert by their parents learned the lyrics to folk songs to sing along. In this regard, our first outdoor folk festival groomed a young audience for the rock festivals that followed nearly a decade later.

If you look at the audience in *Jazz on a Summer's Day*, the documentary about the 1958 Newport Jazz Festival, you can see that the jazz and folk festivals were attended by the same sort of crowd, just different generations. The folk festival was younger and comprised mostly of college intellectuals and thinkers. But the demographic spread was high school to people in their midthirties. Younger concert promoters also were paying attention to Newport throughout the late 1950s, particularly our folk festival. Many of the guys who worked for me at Newport went on to work at Woodstock and other rock festivals.

Our '59 folk festival was successful. The problem I faced, however, was the popularity of the Kingston Trio. They were scheduled to go on last, but by midnight, many people who had been waiting up for them would be tired. So festival cofounder and president Louis Lorillard suggested moving the trio earlier and having Earl Scruggs close. Earl played a five-string banjo with three fingers and had deep roots in traditional folk-country music.

But when the Kingston Trio finished their set on Sunday and left the stage, the audience felt deprived and carried on with applause for about ten minutes. Finally, Dave Guard of the trio came out and urged the audience to quiet down and respect the brilliance of Scruggs. They did, Scruggs came out, but the trio had to return to close out the show. The audience insisted. Traditional folk critics hammered me for the switch that seemed to cater to a more commercially successful group at the expense of a legend. To them, it was an insult.

But folk, like everything else, was changing fast. Between 1959 and 1963, sing-alongs became less popular. For the younger demographic group, Bobby Dylan was becoming increasingly meaningful as a generational voice that resonated. They were looking for folk songs that addressed the times and how they felt about everything rather than mirroring the scratchy sing-along albums of their parents.

Peter Yarrow
(folk singer-songwriter and member of Peter, Paul and Mary)

In June of 1963, entertainer and activist Harry Belafonte called our manager, Albert Grossman. Harry said the Council for United Civil Rights Leadership was organizing a march in Washington, D.C., on August 28. He said there would be speakers and performers and that he wanted Peter, Paul and Mary. We told him we'd be there, but privately we didn't know what to expect. We weren't sure if the event was going to be a peaceful situation or one with anxiety, animosity, police, and confrontation. The event began in the morning with a rally at the Washington Monument, where we sang Bob Dylan's "Blowin' in the Wind" and Pete Seeger's "If I Had a Hammer." A week earlier, our version of Bob's "Blowin' in the Wind" reached #2 on the *Billboard* pop chart. A year earlier, our cover of Pete's "If I Had a Hammer" hit #10.

After the performances at the Washington Monument, the crowd of about 250,000 marched a mile to the Lincoln Memorial. There, a three-hour program was held on the steps that included speeches and performances. We sang the same two songs. But before we went on, actor Ossie Davis, who was emceeing, so to speak, said to me: "What do you want me to say when I announce you?" I said, "I want the audience to know that we're not here as performers. We're here to participate as activists. So just say, 'Now, here's Peter, Paul and Mary to express musically what this gathering is all about.'"

Paul, Mary, and I weren't nervous about being accepted by such a large, diverse crowd. By this point as performers, we weren't anxious onstage. We were old hands and had each other to inspire us. What happens when you sing is you listen to yourself. When people join you, you find you're listening to the audience sing, and that happened in Washington. We felt uplifted by the wave of spirit and collaboration. Later, on the steps of the Memorial, when we heard Martin Luther King's speech, Mary slipped her hand in mine and said, "We're watching history being made." She knew it right away. We all did. His speech was so inspiring that we made an internal commitment never to stop being part of the movement.

Paul, Mary, and I felt only love and acceptance by the crowd. It was euphoric and extraordinary for us, especially when the audience sang along. That's what really galvanized us. As a group, we were looking at a quarter million people, so it obviously was a singular moment. But singing together with so many people bonded us to them. It wasn't just seeing, but feeling. The songs we sang can be sung in an embracing way, but they also were songs that weren't written to make money. There's an authenticity and a motivating quality about them that transcends songs that are meant to entertain. Our intention wasn't to entertain, but to inspire.

Looking out on the crowd as we sang, I felt the love was so thick you could scoop it up and eat it for lunch. It was beyond overwhelming. It was a spiritual transformation. Before we arrived, we didn't have any doubt about how people would receive us, but we had no precedent in our experience for what took place and the sheer scale. Remember, there was no precedent for the songs we sang that day in terms of changing music considered a Top 40 hit. The Kingston Trio had a lot of hits, but none of them were political.

I'm not sure if we had an influence on rock 'n' roll that day. The change was more than that. What Joan Baez, Bob Dylan, and everyone else was doing was putting out a web of music that people began to hear on mainstream radio. A lot of the change had to do with a reevaluation of the culture we were handed—one that was hierarchical, where success was measured by your wealth and came with prejudice and bias. In part, the civil rights movement was about bringing greater social justice, but it also sought a society that respected the idea of the individual having a right to his or her own perspective, identity, and place of value without conforming.

Inherently, pop rock performances at the time were incapable of producing the kind of chemistry and mutual participation that folk could with an audience. Folk is traditionally acoustic music, and acoustic music has that kind of inclusive flavor and capacity. You used to hear audiences singing at rock concerts all the time, but it was even more pronounced with folk music. Folk was considered an act of faith. Singing along to folk was an act of support for music that was intended to be an expression of a united commitment to making the world a more just and authentic place.

Joan Baez
(folk singer and political activist)

Standing on the steps of the Lincoln Memorial that day, my initial emotion was surprise that I was there. I remember looking out at the crowd's expanse and being overwhelmed. I was grateful that I was part of it. I felt lucky. I recalled that when I was thirteen, one of our assignments was to write our life history in a page. In my notebook, I wrote: "If there's an underdog, I'm always for the underdog." In junior high school, I sang in the choir. But I had a problem. My voice was as straight as an arrow. I needed vibrato for warmth. One day, in the bathroom, I wiggled the flesh around my Adam's apple. As I sang, a vibrato emerged. That exercise taught me what my voice had to do.

69

In 1958, my family moved from Stanford, California, to the Boston area after my father took a position at MIT in Cambridge, Massachusetts. At Boston University in the fall of '58, I started singing for money. The guitar was never out of my hands. I sang around town and developed a following. One day in early 1959, I was performing at a coffee shop in Cambridge when manager Albert Grossman saw me. He had me appear in Chicago, where I met folk singer Bob Gibson, who invited me to the first Newport Folk Festival that summer. I was eighteen and Bob was ten years older than me. We sang two songs together at Newport. After the concert and the media coverage, my career took off.

At the March on Washington in '63, when it was my turn to move to the microphone with my guitar at the Lincoln Memorial, I wasn't worried about the two songs I was going to perform. I had some stage fright, which was common. My stomach would ball up in a knot and the only way to get rid of it was to get out there and sing. My first song was "Oh Freedom." Then I led the crowd in "We Shall Overcome." When you take "We Shall Overcome" in increments, the way I did with the crowd, it has a different meaning than if you just sing it through. I was expressing what we all wanted—the end of segregation and freedom from oppression. But you can't sing "We Shall Overcome" and expect world peace.

By singing the song that day in Washington, it helped remind us all that the struggle we faced was doable. Steps were being taken every day in the civil rights movement to help us overcome. I had already hung around with Dr. Martin Luther King enough that I felt part of the movement. I had sung with him and for him and people in the churches. I was in touch with the audience. To me that day, the crowd felt very dignified. In my mind, it was a large outdoor church and King was the congregation's orator. He had spontaneity. Without much encouragement, he took off in that speech and just let it go. Some people have that ability, to just take off.

I remember moving all over the place on the Lincoln Memorial for a while as the event unfolded. At one point, I was up high on the steps. There weren't many people with me up there. I remember seeing King and a bank of reporters. I had never seen so many before, which reinforced what a significant day it was. Just being in such close proximity to him and knowing him from the time I was sixteen, when I first heard him speak, was so moving. Now here I was in Washington, when I was twenty-two. When I hear recordings of his speeches now, I just well up with tears. I was in tears during his speech in August 1963.

Like everyone else who was there, I was hearing King's "I Have a Dream" speech for the first time. As King's cadence built, we all knew it was a tour de force. Over the previous years, I had been in the Black churches and neighborhoods. At the march, I felt myself in a different way. I felt more Black than white. I was comfortable there, and being with King was a positive feeling.

The artists there that day were singing speakers evoking the spirit of the struggle with song. There were several hundred thousand people there, so I suppose what all of the artists did was really conversational, even though we were called on to sing. That's what music does. It was inspiring and uplifting in a way that was different from the speakers. I'm sure many of the people in the audience preferred to hear the singing than some of the speeches. The music was personal and emotional and filled the crowd with hope. On that day, folk was sorting out its commitment to the civil rights cause. The crowd's reaction showed that our voices mattered and could make a difference.

The Bob Dylan phenomenon had already become so strong it took on a life of its own. Protest songs had become a thing of the day and they passed from the counterculture into the mainstream. After August 1963, some artists believed in what they were singing while others sang these songs because it was trendy. Some people were fully into it and others were out to make a dime or were just halfway there or not really part of it at all. What we were pushing for, as folk's leading young voices, was for all folk artists to go all the way and walk the talk.

At the March on Washington, I was already there. I was so far into the civil rights movement that I viewed the day as an amazing chapter in an ongoing story. I didn't feel I had turned a corner. The day was simply an extension of where I was to begin with. I don't think my appearance was a landmark performance, but it was as special as everyone else's. And just as moving and influential.

Noel Paul Stookey
(folk singer-songwriter and member of Peter, Paul and Mary)

For me, the March on Washington was a combination of amazement and confirmation. I was astonished by the event's scale and purpose. Clearly, society was changing. The number of people who gathered to march proved that. But the march also confirmed that since our trio's inception three years earlier, folk music was inspiring people and making a difference. What we had inherited from our folk elders like Pete Seeger, Woody Guthrie, Cisco Houston, and Josh White had great potency. In this regard, the march was an underlining of our hopefulness.

Looking back, the most curious part of the day was that it happened twice. In the morning, before the march, a dress rehearsal took place with all the artists performing on a lawn at the staging area near the Washington Monument. The iconic photo of Peter, Mary, and me taken from behind as we sang to an expanse of people was shot at the morning rehearsal. The photo appeared on the back of our *In the Wind* album when it was released in October 1963. After the rehearsal, we all marched arm in arm through the streets to the Lincoln Memorial with a dedication that came from that earlier focus of purpose.

Up on the Lincoln Memorial steps later that afternoon, standing on the side as we waited our turn to go on, it was easy to get nerved up. But honestly, when Ossie Davis introduced us, my only concern was how I would get my guitar past the person standing on the third step so I could arrive at the right-hand microphone before Peter struck his first chord. I was thinking logistically, not emotionally. As we performed our two songs, the audience's first six or seven rows became touchstones for me and probably Peter and Mary. Folk has a subtlety and intimacy that louder forms of music don't have.

That day, we knew we were mostly preaching to the choir and that all of the performers and those in the audience were on the same page. But there is an effusiveness, a surety of purpose that when songs are shared, the result becomes even more exciting than just agreement. It's a bond. As we performed, we were reminded that we had become the articulation of what the audience had gathered for. You feel as if you're part of a larger movement and that the songs you're performing are part of a larger force for change.

There's no doubt that the civil rights movement had its first national expression at the March on Washington. Images of the march reached print, radio, and TV media and had an impact on music fans and musicians who weren't there. The emergence of folk on popular radio in the 1950s and early '60s began benignly with the Weavers and the Kingston Trio. From 1959 to 1961, there was a battle between a rococo rock 'n' roll rooted in the 1950s and a folk revival that reflected what was going on around us. People suddenly became aware that the rock 'n' roll they had been listening to had an artificial sentiment or no longer had context in the real world. Suddenly there was room for realism and responsibility in the early '60s. People sensed there was more to life than conformity and the fairy-tale life promulgated by advertisers.

By 1961, the Eisenhower era was over and we were stuck with some really hard facts. Part of the reason for the emergence of the blues and Black music in the late 1940s was a growing desire for truth-telling. White radio listeners began to tune in and question the status quo. They wondered, "Are we deluding ourselves?" Out of that abandonment came this hearty band of folk musicians who said, "Hey, you know what? We all share some of the same concerns about our society." The rising number of college students who became fans between 1959 and 1963 were thinkers with sophisticated tastes and an ambition to make a difference. The civil rights movement was entering a new phase, the free speech movement was heating up on campuses in California, and students were starting to question the truthfulness of government institutions.

At the march, with the speakers and the performers, the message was: "We're all in this together. Let's take off the chains of oppression and put everyone on equal footing." Then throughout the 1960s, the message kept shifting. First came the civil rights movement; then let's get out of the Vietnam War; let's concern ourselves with ecological issues; hey, the United States is supporting oppressive regimes all over the world; and, finally, the world is a crazy place, so let's get stoned and all that matters is love.

The March on Washington was a large-scale starting point and gave us permission to view social ills in a musical context that hadn't been taken seriously before. As folk songs became mainstream hits, music executives who had relationships with 1950s pop singers were trying to get them to sing folk songs, sometimes with embarrassing results. The youth culture demanded conviction and authenticity. Singing the words to folk songs without belief in the lyrics came off hollow.

Joe Boyd
(production manager of the 1965 Newport Folk Festival)

What was impressive about the March on Washington's folk and gospel performances was that artists could command the attention of hundreds of thousands of people. If I had been a young folk artist or any artist back then, I would have looked at those performers and said to myself, "Wow, that's really something." There wasn't any gimmickry, there wasn't any stagecraft, and there wasn't a light show. It was just the artist playing an acoustic instrument and singing into a microphone to a sea of captivated people.

Undoubtedly, performing for such a large crowd comes with great exposure. But many younger artists then weren't watching the march on TV and thinking of the event in terms of a career move. The music was a footnote, an asterisk, a kind of nice augmentation of the event's centerpiece: Martin Luther King's speech. From the artist's perspective, the march showed that doing what felt right creatively was as important as the movement itself. Those seeds were planted there.

Noel Paul Stookey

I'm sure the march got a lot of rock musicians thinking about a new direction and awakened a lot of hearts. This was especially true as the culture's stakes escalated rapidly. The Birmingham church bombings took place in September 1963, just weeks after the march. Then came the assassination of President Kennedy in November followed by the Vietnam War's escalation and the horror of the draft.

It's hard to imagine that any serious musician didn't comprehend the impact of the march's performances. Photos and articles appeared in the nation's magazines and newspapers and footage ran on TV news.

CBS covered the march live and PBS broadcast it. All folk and rock artists saw the same thing. In addition to Martin Luther King's moving speech, musicians were performing in front of 250,000 people. The March on Washington performances redefined what an outdoor concert meant and could be. It would take another six years before musicians performed in front of 400,000 people at Woodstock.

Chapter 7

POP'S ENDLESS SUMMER

Folk advocated for social and political change on college campuses, at civil rights marches, and at coffeehouses, but not all popular music then was on the same page. In the early '60s, dance songs dominated the charts, captivating those who had mastered the twist, the mashed potato, and the watusi. Then came beach movies, which led to romantic vocal harmony groups in 1963 like the Beach Boys and the Four Seasons, followed by girl groups such as the Ronettes and the Supremes, and then the Beatles and the Dave Clark Five in 1964. Pop rock had become a national sensation as groups performed on television variety shows, in revues at auditoriums and theaters, and, in the case of the Beatles, at stadiums.

Ronnie Spector
(cofounder and lead singer of the Ronettes)

I was brought up in Manhattan's Washington Heights, on West 151st Street. There were people of all ethnic backgrounds in our neighborhood, including kids like us, from multiracial families. My mother, Beatrice, was Black and Cherokee. My father, Louis, was white. My mother would do anything for the three of us—me; my older sister, Estelle; and our cousin, Nedra.

We started performing for others in 1961, when I was in my late teens. We had been singing in front of mirrors since we were five. Along the way, we took singing lessons and sang at local dances and bar mitz-vahs as the Darling Sisters. One night, Estelle, Nedra, and I went to the Peppermint Lounge, a New York discothèque on West Forty-Fifth Street. We stood on line to get in, but Nedra and I were underage. To look older, we stuffed Kleenex in our bras, dressed in the same outfits, and held cigarettes.

When the club manager came out, he spotted us on line and shouted, "Girls, you're late. Get in here." He thought we were the dancers he hired to do the twist. The dance was all the rage then after Chubby Checker's hit "The Twist" came out in 1960 and Joey Dee and the Starliters followed with "Peppermint Twist" in '61. Estelle said, "No, wait, we're not the—" Before she could finish, I elbowed her in the ribs. We followed the manager inside. We were told to dance behind Joey Dee and the Starliters, the house band. But when we were up there, the group's lead vocalist, David Brigati, handed me a mic and said, "Sing!" That's all I had to hear.

We sang Ray Charles's "What'd I Say" and were hired on the spot. The Peppermint Lounge was relatively small, but in 1961 it was the hottest club in town. Before the Beatles arrived in New York in Febru-ary 1964, the city was twist crazy. Young adults twenty-one and older danced freestyle at clubs to records and live acts. That in itself was a revolution. Freestyle dancing freed women to shake away without worrying about the roaming hands of men who asked them to dance. Soon, the Peppermint Lounge became popular with famous writers, models, socialites, actors, and singers. It was exciting, and everything there was happening.

The club had a forty-foot bar along one side, mirrored walls, about twenty tables near the stage, and a small dance floor in the back. While performing at the Peppermint Lounge, I saw so many movie stars and celebrities—Marilyn Monroe, Jackie Kennedy, Judy Garland, and others. The place in the early '60s was like Studio 54 in the late '70s. You never knew who would show up. There was just one dressing room backstage at the Peppermint Lounge. When we had to get in there, Joey Dee's wife said, "OK, everyone, out! The Ronettes have to change." Nedra and I were so young we had school the next day.

The three of us dressed alike when we performed, but we looked different than all the other acts. People who came to the Peppermint Lounge were curious about us. I was so hungry to be onstage singing. Nedra and Estelle liked performing. I loved it and couldn't wait to get out there. In mid-61, our manager, Phil Halikus, worked out a deal with Colpix, and we started recording records as Ronnie and the Relatives. But none of our eleven sides for the label charted. That didn't stop our manager. When we weren't at the Peppermint Lounge, he booked us into nightclubs and supper clubs all over the New York region, especially on Long Island. The places were jammed, but we couldn't check out the scene. We were underage. After performances, we had to go straight backstage. We weren't allowed to mingle or hang out.

We didn't perform concerts in theaters back then. We needed hit records for that. In the fall of '61, the owners of the Peppermint Lounge opened a Peppermint Lounge in Miami. We went down there to perform. That's where we met Murray "the K" Kaufman, the popular New York disc jockey on WINS. He was in Miami on vacation with his wife, Jackie. After he heard us, Murray said, "I wish I had some girls like you who lived in New York." I said, "What are you crazy? We live in New York!" So he had us on his radio show and then invited us to be on his rock 'n' roll revues at the Brooklyn Fox Theatre starting in 1962, during the long school holidays. We were paid $200 per girl per show at the Fox. By then we were going through cans of hairspray.

Murray the K was so great. He loved the way we looked. Even his wife looked like us, with her big hair. Onstage at the Fox, I'd do a lot of skits with Murray. That began as an accident. After a show, I threw up my arm to wave goodbye to the audience and knocked off his trademark golf hat. The audience went nuts. Backstage, he said, "That was great! Knock my hat off after every show." Going forward, everything I did became part of a routine we had. Murray loved us, but it was strictly fatherly. Despite our streetwise image, we were good girls. With Murray, we worked with the Temptations, Smokey Robinson, the Marvelettes, Little Eva, the Four Seasons—all those acts. Murray was a very smart man. He used us to liven up his shows. We did about six sets a day. You did your two songs and went backstage until the next show. We were in the dressing room all day and kept our makeup on. I wanted to be the girl who sounded most like Frankie Lymon. I wasn't afraid of the stage. Murray knew I was hungry.

In 1962, we were the only ones on Murray's shows who didn't have any hit records. But we looked like we did. We wore tight dresses with Chinese slits up the side. My sister's best friend was Chinese and that's what she wore. My aunt Helen made our outfits. The kids at our shows went crazy for us. They were emotional and just went nuts screaming. The whole point was to lose control. They also could relate because we had a New York attitude but were so down-to-earth. They responded because what we did onstage seemed natural. We were them—or who they wanted to be in school. We didn't have professional choreography, like the Motown groups. We had a different act. We came up with our own steps and stuff before shows. As I sang, one of the Ronettes would do the twist while the other did a different dance, like the mashed potato. That's what worked for us. The kids in the theater loved it.

By January 1963, we still didn't have a hit. We decided we needed a new record producer—and a new label. A good producer matched you to songs that would connect with your audience who, in turn, would buy your records. From the radio, we knew Phil Spector was a big deal. His name was on all these records that were hits as cowriter and producer. He also had his own label—Philles—that he started in 1961. And he was just twenty-one. But we didn't know how to reach him. So Estelle and I decided to cold-call him at his office from our bedroom.

Estelle had a more polished grown-up voice, so she called and I watched. When Phil's secretary answered, Estelle asked in her measured voice to speak with him. Miraculously, the secretary put her through. Estelle spoke to Phil for a minute or two. From my end, all I heard were one-word answers from Estelle. When she hung up, she freaked out. She said Phil wanted to see us at Mirasound Studios on West 47th Street in Manhattan the next night.

In July 1963, Phil recorded us singing "Be My Baby" at Gold Star Recording Studios in Los Angeles. The record was released in August. We finally had our hit. And what a hit. The song went to #2 on *Billboard*'s pop chart and #1 on *Cash Box*'s chart. It also was a big hit throughout

Europe. "Baby, I Love You" was next in November and went to #24 in the United States and #11 in the U.K. One of our biggest live appearances during this period was at the Surf Party concert at San Francisco's Cow Palace on September 28, 1963. There was no headliner. It was sponsored by a local radio station. On the bill were Stevie Wonder, the Beach Boys, Dee Dee Sharp, Dionne Warwick, the Righteous Brothers, and so many others.

In January 1964, we toured in the U.K. Our records did so well over there that we were the headliner. The Rolling Stones opened for us. I know, right? My mother came along. If someone had a birthday, we celebrated with cake and soda. It was all so innocent then. The Beatles hadn't arrived in America yet. Everyone on the tour wanted to be stars and hear themselves on the radio. Our appearances over there were more exciting than here. We were foreigners, we looked exotic, and U.K. kids wanted to see what we looked like. We also met the Beatles in London, before they came to America in February. They told us they were coming. I knew right away they were special. Murray the K had been going nuts on the radio in New York plugging them all day long. He was obsessed.

When we met the Beatles, I told them they had to go to the Peppermint Lounge when they came over. It was my first time overseas. John Lennon and I became close friends. He was so helpful, showing me around London, taking me shopping. When the Beatles arrived in America on February 7, they went to the Peppermint Lounge just hours after their Pan Am jet from London touched down. We were back in the States by then and spent time with them. They hadn't changed. They were just under a lot more pressure.

While the Ronettes epitomized the urban sound of girls in love, the Beach Boys sang about what California boys prized most—cars, the surf, and going steady. In July of 1963, two cultural events combined to remake the beach's image. First, the Beach Boys released "Surfer Girl," a love song that linked sex and the surf. It climbed to #7 on the "Billboard" pop chart. Also that summer, the film "Beach Party" was released in theaters. The movie, starring Frankie Avalon and Annette Funicello, blended silliness and sexuality, kicking off the beach-party film craze that would last until 1968. The Beach Boys and beach-party films fed off each other, transforming Southern California into a region of teenage bliss. By the end of '63, the Beach Boys were among the country's most popular surf rock bands. The following year, they became the first pop rock band to release an album recorded live in concert.

Fred Vail
(first concert promoter of the Beach Boys, from 1963 to 1965)

In March of 1963, after I graduated from El Camino High School in California, where I booked talent for events, the head of the senior class called. He wanted me to book their graduation party that June. He said their budget was $750, which was enough for a duet act and backup band. However, it wasn't enough to rent a venue, print invitations and tickets, and provide catering and security if they wanted money left over for talent. He was devastated. Then I came up with an idea: Why not take the $750, hire one popular band, and have the band put on a concert? That was rare back then. Most bands didn't have enough material, and audiences were accustomed to seeing many acts in a revue for the price of a ticket.

The high school committee liked my idea. At this point in 1963, music had shifted from the twist to surf music. Every independent record company seemed to have a surf band signed to their label: Dick Dale and His Del-Tones, the Lively Ones, the Challengers, and the Ventures were among the most popular. I zeroed in on the Beach Boys. Their first single, "Surfin'," was a hit in Sacramento in early 1962 on Candix, a small indie label in L.A. But the song had only reached #75 on the national *Billboard* pop chart. The label couldn't afford a follow-up single.

The Beach Boys' manager, Murry Wilson, father of the three Wilson brothers—Brian, Dennis, and Carl—got them signed to Capitol in July '62. They still weren't a national act at this point, but they had a solid following on the West Coast, where surfing was popular. The Beach Boys' second single, "Surfin' Safari" on Capitol, came out in June '62 and reached #14 in October. Their third big single, "Surfin' USA," was out in March '63 and would ultimately hit #3 later that spring. The difference between the Beach Boys and all the other surf bands was that

81

they not only played great instrumental music but they also had great vocal harmonies, and many of their songs were originals.

I called the William Morris Agency and was transferred to Marshall Berle, Milton Berle's nephew and a junior agent. I told Marshall I wanted to book the Beach Boys on May 24 at the Sacramento Memorial Auditorium. He said they'd cost $400. I told him to pencil me in. When Murry Wilson called me back the next day, he said they were available but that Carl, the youngest Wilson brother, didn't get out of school until 3:00 p.m. They wouldn't make it in time if they drove up, so they countered with two options: either $400 plus six round-trip airline tickets or a flat $750. I opted for the latter.

On the afternoon of May 24, I borrowed my folks' 1954 Chevy station wagon. My friend Mike Davidson drove his '57 Chevy, and we went to the old Sacramento Municipal Airport to pick up the Beach Boys. When the plane landed and the stairs rolled up to the door, Murry and five Beach Boys emerged—Mike Love, Dennis Wilson, Carl Wilson, Al Jardine, and a neighbor, David Marks, who played rhythm guitar. Brian Wilson didn't make the trip.

In the car, Carl asked who the Beach Boys were opening for. I told him they were the headliner. In early 1963, the Beach Boys typically opened for Dick Dale, Jan and Dean, and Ike and Tina Turner. The Sacramento concert would be their first headlining performance in a major market. Carl asked if the concert promoter was going to do all right, financially. I told Carl that I was the promoter. "But you're just a kid, like us!" he said. I told him I had broken even with the advance sales. How much I'd do at the door would make the difference.

Onstage, the Beach Boys opened with a forty-minute set, performing a handful of their hit singles at the time. The crowd went crazy. Backstage after the set, the group was ecstatic. They were all congratulating themselves. I reminded them that it was just intermission, that they had to perform a second set. The problem was that they had just played most of their repertoire. I told them to mix their extra songs with the ones they had just played and test new songs they were working on. I told Carl to do longer guitar solos and Denny to work in a few more drum solos. The second set went over as well as the first.

After, we went back to the Mansion Inn just a few blocks from the auditorium. At the hotel restaurant, Carl asked Murry how much the band had made. Murry said I paid them $750, but after the William Morris commission, the hotel rooms, the six airline tickets, and money put aside for meals, each of the Beach Boys would make about $55. Carl looked over at me and asked how the senior class and I did. I was honest and told him we made $4,000 and that my deal was 15 percent of the net, so I had made around $600. Carl said, "You made more than we did!"

That's when I decided to become a concert and dance promoter. My next concert with the Beach Boys would be in Sacramento in September. This time, I'd have two shows—one in the afternoon for preteens, where a parent would be admitted free with each child, and one in the evening for the general public. It didn't hurt that by then, the Beach Boys had a few more original hits—"Shut Down," "Surfer Girl," and "Little Deuce Coupe." They also mixed in covers, including "Long Tall Texan" and "Papa-Oom-Mow-Mow."

Brian was there at the September concert singing his distinctive high falsetto. The audience, particularly the girls, seemed to scream at every gesture, at every song. They were screaming from the time the curtains opened until they closed. Girls were crying. It was the height of the surf era, and summer love songs and beach ballads were big. I was the emcee at all the concerts. I usually stood in the wings.

At the concert, Murry was more about business. That afternoon and night, we did about $8,000. William Morris booked the major markets, and I did the secondary markets. As I had told Murry, concerts were becoming a major part of their revenue. The Sacramento concerts were so successful I decided to hold a Beach Boys dance in Marysville on November 22, about fifty miles north of Sacramento. That day, after President Kennedy was shot and killed in Dallas, parents wanted their kids out of the house, where the TV was on and conversation was dominated by the horrible event.

That afternoon, I drove out to the Sacramento airport to pick up the Beach Boys, and we drove to Marysville. Before the Beach Boys went on, I went out and asked the audience for a moment of silence. It lasted for about ten seconds, which felt like an hour. Then I brought them on. They were great.

After the show, we stuffed all the box office cash into shopping bags and drove back to the El Dorado Hotel. In one of their rooms, Murry and I were on one of the double beds counting the cash. On the other bed, Mike and Brian were putting the finishing touches on a new song they had started that morning. They called it "The Warmth of the Sun." I drove them to the airport the next morning. I also discussed the idea of recording a live concert album in Sacramento, perhaps their most receptive market at the time.

Murry and Brian weren't high on the idea. They didn't think anyone would buy a live album, since a concert was about seeing the band perform live. I told them to think of it from a kid's perspective, that they'd want the record as a souvenir, to relive the concert. Also, since we still had many markets we hadn't appeared in, a live album would energize ticket sales there. The album would give kids a taste of what it's like to attend a Beach Boys concert. Murry and Brian decided I was right.

The album concert was held at the Sacramento Memorial Auditorium on December 21, 1963—five days before the Beatles released "I Want to Hold Your Hand" in the United States. We decided to hold just one evening show at 8:00 p.m. It would be billed as a "gala Christmas concert and recording session." The engineer, Chuck Britz, set up the console in the custodian's supply room. He ran cables out to the stage. Just before their opening song, "Fun, Fun, Fun," I went out and announced: "And now, from Hawthorne, California, to entertain you tonight with a gala concert and recording session, the fabulous Beach Boys!" *Beach Boys Concert* was released by Capitol in October 1964, and was the band's first #1 album and the first live rock album to top the pop charts.

By early '65, the Beach Boys had become so popular nationally and internationally that William Morris took over booking their concerts with promoters all over the country. Murry never told me it was over. It happened organically. I was promoting Beach Boys concerts less and less and supplementing my Beach Boys income with radio station appreciation shows and working with other acts. I didn't feel bad. The Beach Boys had become so big so fast that it was physically impossible for me to do it nationwide, so I pretty much concentrated on the West Coast.

During those early years, I was close to the Beach Boys. I remember attending a concert with the Beach Boys at San Francisco's Cow Palace in '63. Denny and I took my cobalt-blue Corvette Stingray up to the event; Denny drove. As we pulled in, girls hanging around the parking lot went wild. After the concert, we came out and found my car completely scratched up. I couldn't believe it. When I looked at the surface, I saw that girls had used their keys to carve notes, names, and phone numbers into the fiberglass body. They also stuffed notes into the car's windows inviting Denny to stop by their house, promising that they'd leave their windows unlocked. The scratches ruined my Corvette's surface, which had to be completely sanded and repainted. I eventually traded it in for a lavender '65 Chevy Malibu SS convertible. Now I wish I still had the Stingray—with all those crazy scratched notes to Denny.

As big as the Beach Boys had become as a pop rock group in 1963, they would soon find themselves eclipsed by the Beatles. Late that year, New York concert promoter Sid Bernstein cut a deal with Beatles manager Brian Epstein to bring the English group to America. They performed in Washington, D.C., on February 11, 1964, and twice at New York's Carnegie Hall on February 12. Those performances would be accompanied by live performances on The Ed Sullivan Show *on February 9 in New York and on February 16 in Miami, followed by a taped performance on February 23. The first* Ed Sullivan Show *appearance was viewed by nearly 73 million people and primed the market for the Beatles' monthlong North American concert tour in August and September of 1964. When it was over, a new concert business model had emerged that depended on image, promotion, hype, strategic ticket pricing, venue size, transportation, DJs, record sales, hysteria, and stamina. Powering it all was Beatlemania, which began in London in 1963.*

Tony Barrow
(Beatles' publicist between 1962 and 1968)
Beatlemania was a bit of an accident. Up until their London Palladium TV concert on Sunday, October 13, 1963, the Beatles were on a roll but

hadn't really captured Britain's imagination yet. Certainly, performing at the Palladium that night was a big deal—much like your *Ed Sullivan Show*—since it was televised live, nationally. But what happened hours earlier played a big role, too.

By mid-1963, the Beatles' popularity in the U.K. was growing but hadn't attracted the London newspapers yet. Brian Epstein, the boys' manager, had been going around saying they were going to be as big as Elvis, but that was about it. I spent days that summer trying to get the press to pay attention, but they wouldn't take my calls. Meanwhile, young audiences in theaters around the country where they performed were getting pretty wound up.

Screaming girls weren't new. That had started in Liverpool, at the Cavern, where the boys regularly played. The space there was so tight that John, Paul, and George could reach out from the stage for a girl's half-smoked ciggy, take a puff, and hand it back to her midsong. It was a cozy setup. Girls at the club screamed when things like that happened. By October 13, the expectation of seeing the Beatles on live TV heightened the excitement around London.

That afternoon, the Beatles were driven to the Palladium for a rehearsal and sound check. The London papers typically sent photographers to Palladium rehearsals to take pictures of performing artists to make the next morning's early editions. But the photographers weren't there to take pictures of the Beatles; they wanted American singer Brook Benton, who shared the bill with them. While they snapped away, you could hear a commotion outside. Teens had descended on Argyll Street in front of the theater to catch a glimpse of the Beatles. Some of the photographers went outside to see the fuss.

As the rehearsal wrapped up, Brian heard that the crowd had shifted to the stage door on Great Marlborough Street. Bringing the car there would have been trouble. We started thinking about different ways to get them out—using decoys or having them cross over the roof to another building. We decided to just have the car pull around the front, since no one would expect that. But the car sat out front too long and fans figured out what was going on. When road manager Neil Aspinall brought the Beatles through the front doors, fans swarmed them. They rushed forward to touch them—to be with them and be one of them. That was all new to us, and the press took photos of what was happening. I thought, "Hey, that's going to be great stuff. I'll be able to build momentum on that tomorrow."

That night, on live TV, the Beatles performed four songs as 15 million TV viewers in the U.K. watched. Many were teens who knew their hits but hadn't seen them in action, just in photos. The following morning, the London newspapers were filled with photos of hysterical teenage girls besieging the Beatles outside the Palladium the previous afternoon. In the days ahead, copycat fans grew in number outside concert halls in the U.K. and in Sweden, where the Beatles toured during the final week of October.

On Friday, November 1, 1963, the Beatles were booked to perform onstage at the Odeon Cinema in Cheltenham. The next day, London's *Daily Mirror* featured an article with the headline: BEATLEMANIA!—IT'S HAP-PENING EVERYWHERE . . . EVEN IN SEDATE CHELTENHAM. That was one of the first uses of the word "Beatlemania" in print. Ten days later, Brian agreed to have the boys appear on *The Ed Sullivan Show* in February.

Bob Eubanks
(Los Angeles producer of three Beatles concerts)

Prior to the Beatles arriving in the United States in February 1964, there was no organized touring rock concert business. Dick Clark had his Caravan of Stars road show, but that was it. Producing large-scale concerts in multiple cities wasn't a moneymaking enterprise yet. Brian Epstein and the Beatles started the business in August and September of '64.

In earlier years, you'd see a concert pop up once in a while, but you didn't have bands touring North American cities on a regular basis. Elvis did a couple of tours in the late 1950s but gave up on it for the stability and comfort of Hollywood. Then he was in the army. The Beatles in '64, '65, and '66 showed what was possible. They also exposed the risks. But those were easy to fix or mitigate. The big challenge for rock promoters was finding other highly talented bands and making them popular enough that tens of thousands of kids would do anything to see them in multiple cities.

When the Beatles arrived in the United States in February '64, New York was the first stop on a two-week East Coast tour. Then they returned to the U.K. and announced plans to come back for a monthlong North American tour in late August and September. At the time, the only other concert promoter of note in L.A. was Lou Robin. But he turned them down because he was used to paying Ella Fitzgerald and Frank Sinatra $10,000 at the Hollywood Bowl. The Beatles wanted $25,000.

I was a radio DJ, so I knew the Beatles were going to be huge in August and beyond. I could feel the phone jumping off the hook every time I played their records on the air. It was obvious the Beatles were changing the music world and bringing a generation of record-buying kids along with them. But guys who weren't on the radio didn't catch on until a year later. In '64, I was determined to produce a Beatles concert in L.A. I had my Cinnamon Cinder teen club, but I clearly needed a much bigger venue. I called Brian Epstein in London and asked him where he wanted to play. His reply was the Hollywood Bowl—the most prestigious venue in Southern California.

So I called General Artists Corporation (GAC), the Beatles' talent agency in the United States. I told them I wanted to bring the Beatles to the Hollywood Bowl. They said, "But you've never done a concert before." I said, "Yeah, but I'm a club owner and a talent buyer." They said they'd let me book the Beatles only if I had the Hollywood Bowl. So I went to the Bowl. They said I could have the venue if I had the Beatles. I finally got everybody together and closed the deal.

The problem was I didn't have $25,000, so I had to borrow it. I went to Security Pacific Bank for a loan. They said I was crazy and kicked me out. Next, I went to a storefront lender called Trans-World Bank. I told the manager what I wanted and why. She had no problem with the Beatles. Her son was a big fan. Trans-World loaned me the $25,000 with my house as collateral. Which was a miracle, since I was earning only $12,500 a year as a DJ.

Brian needed to be paid in full the night of the concert. The pressure was on to sell seats. I also knew the Beatles came with a lot of fans, but with fans came Beatlemania and chaos. Further complicating things, the group didn't want ticket prices to exceed $7. I was hoping to charge $10 for a top ticket. To promote the concert, KRLA took out a full-page ad in the *Los Angeles Times* announcing that tickets would go on sale on April 25. Worried, I asked the box office guy: "Can we sell this thing out in one day?" He said, "You'll be lucky if it sells out in a week." About two hours later, he told me we had sold out.

The Beatles flew into LAX on the morning of August 23, the day of the Bowl concert, after performing the night before in Vancouver. They wanted to hold a press conference before the concert, so we had it at the Cinnamon Cinder. But they would only do a half hour, which made everything frantic. The place was a zoo. We had something like 800 people in a 440-person-capacity space. Even worse, security for the Hollywood Bowl in '64 was a line of cops at the front of the stage. Everyone assumed the worst.

Getting the Beatles into the Bowl wasn't tough. There was no back or side road into the venue, just a main driveway. There was a ramp under the dressing area that allowed artists to gain access to the facilities under the bandshell. So we brought the Beatles in on the main drive in a limo and brought them to the back door. I knew that getting them out was going to be much more problematic when the audience was hysterical. I had a plan.

I devised a way to get them away from the Hollywood Bowl quickly. We parked a couple of limos behind the dressing area where everyone could see them. But when the Beatles came off the stage, they weren't sent to the limos. Instead, we took them along a path near the stage to a clearing where a new white Plymouth Barracuda was waiting with a driver. A local dealer had loaned us the two-door car with hopes we'd get a photo of the Beatles climbing out or posing next to it. The Beatles piled in, and the car took off. Cops down at the Bowl's exit at the bottom of the hill stopped the traffic. We had them off the premises before anybody knew anything.

About a mile away, at a gas station on Sunset Boulevard, they switched to a limo. As for the limos at the Bowl, they crawled through the crowd with several hundred kids pounding and jumping on the roof. The cars were ruined. It was just awful. As for the photographer, everything happened too fast for him to get the shot. Instead, he wound up with pictures of the backs of the Beatles' heads in the car. The local car dealer wasn't happy. When everything was said and done, I only made $4,000 and had to split it with my three partners.

The Beatles' sold-out crowd at New York's Shea Stadium on August 15, 1965, marked the start of a new phase in the rock concert's evolution. While Elvis Presley at the Cotton Bowl in 1956 and the March on Washington in 1963 featured marquee artists performing in front of sizable audiences, the 55,600 hysterical fans at Shea was the first sign that hype and mania could result in considerable box office revenue. From the promoter's standpoint, the sky was the limit. The Beatles also proved that the music was secondary, since few in the stands at stadiums during the Beatles' North American tour could hear the band sing or play. As Beatlemania intensified between 1965 and '66, security procedures and sound systems had to adapt to keep up.

Tony Newman
(drummer for Sounds Incorporated, a Beatles opening act in 1965)
In 1961, I got a gig in London with a group called Sounds Incorporated playing behind Gene Vincent. Sounds Incorporated was an instrumental sextet that became quite popular, since we became the go-to backing band. We crisscrossed all over Britain playing gigs. In 1962 we backed Little Richard at the Star-Club in Hamburg, Germany. That's where we first met the Beatles, who played there regularly. We also wore suits like the Beatles. It was all very straight up. Back in England, we began backing Cilla Black, who, like the Beatles, was from Liverpool and was managed by Brian Epstein. Before long, Brian signed us, too.

In the summer of 1965, Brian called and said he wanted us to open for the Beatles on their first North American stadium tour. The initial concert would be on August 15 at Shea Stadium in New York. We flew over to the States a day before. On the afternoon of August 15, we went out to the stadium and had a walk around. I remember being concerned that the planes arriving at LaGuardia Airport were coming in so low.

Shea was the first time we played a stadium. Sounds Incorporated was Griff West on tenor sax, Alan "Boots" Holmes on baritone sax and flute, Barrie Cameron-Elmes on baritone sax and keyboards, Johnny St. John on guitar, Wes Hunter on bass, and me on drums. The six of us were blown away by the size of the place. We were traumatized by the magnitude of the gig, but we didn't show it. At some point, we walked out to the stage at second base to do a sound check.

Rather than have roadies swap out gear, I used Ringo's Ludwig drum kit. It was a cool set. I noticed that his black cases said RINGO STARR / LUDWIG in white lettering. Even the head of his bass drum facing the audience was lettered with THE BEATLES. Before we went on, roadies put a circular cardboard placard over Ringo's bass drumhead that said SOUNDS INCOR-PORATED. Then before the Beatles came out, the cardboard would simply be removed to expose the Beatles' logo.

I brought my own snare drum, since the head was set to the tautness I liked. I also wanted Ringo's tom-tom to come up a bit higher. I didn't use the drum key to loosen the stand first. I just wrenched it up. Mal Evans, the Beatles' road manager, saw me and was pissed. He asked me not to do that again during the tour. A year earlier, we introduced the Beatles to Dougie Millings, a tailor in London. He made our suits and theirs. Our camel suits that night were collarless and zipped up the front. They looked like Beatle outfits. We also wore black Chelsea boots. I can't recall, but I'm sure Brian Epstein wanted us to wear the suits to give the crowd a visual preview of what was coming.

When we finished our set, the crowd was screaming. It was incredible. Then they began chanting: "We want the Beatles, we want the Beatles!" We left the stage and headed to the dugout doorway leading to rooms under the seats. We had played a twenty-minute set, but we felt subdued because of the magnitude of kids in the stands. No one was particularly interested in us. Everything was the Beatles. As we reached the hall beyond the dugout door, the Beatles were already making their way along the corridor to the door we had just come through. They paused, waiting for the signal to run out.

Seeing them, it was impossible not to stare at their faces. They were like gods. Their eyes were like saucers. I don't know whether it was because of the anticipation or they were stunned by the sound of the audience above them or they were just excited. Then Ed Sullivan announced them from the stage and off they went. When they emerged, you could see them look around as they ran across the infield. It was as if what they saw was overwhelming, even by their standards. What I remember most was the explosion of sound rushing through the door. The screaming was so loud you couldn't hear yourself breathe. I'd never heard anything like that. It was a tidal wave of screaming.

Looking back, we now know how momentous the first Shea Stadium concert was. But in '65, it was just another day at the office for us and probably for them. We didn't go out to the field to watch and listen. We had been working with them since Hamburg and we'd been through Beatlemania in Britain. This was just more of the same on a grander scale. When the Beatles came off, they were as happy as can be. They mopped themselves off with towels before leaving the stadium in the armored truck that shuttled them to their helicopter.

Touring with the Beatles involved a lot of flying. On board, they kept pretty much to themselves. They were classy like that. They never went over the top with the ego business. They took everything in stride and were measured. During the tour, on August 22, the Beatles held a press conference at the Minneapolis–Saint Paul Airport and then boarded our plane to Portland, Oregon. As we neared Portland, I was up in the cockpit talking to the pilots. That's when we saw smoke coming from one of the engines. Everyone on board saw the problem and took pictures of it. Fortunately, the pilot was able to bring the plane down. When we came to a halt on the tarmac, John jokingly shouted, "Beatles, women, and children first." It was nerves more than anything else.

The final concert on the '65 tour was in Daly City, California, on August 31. For Sounds Incorporated, the tour was just us passing through. We were hoping to get a fan base, but we were a background band. We had hoped to be accepted by audiences. That happened for the Beatles, not us. It was bittersweet.

Bob Eubanks

Shuttling the Beatles in and out of the Hollywood Bowl safely and creatively in 1964 put me first in line for their 1965 appearance in Los

Angeles. Dick Clark and Disney tried to take the Beatles away from me and put them in the Los Angeles Coliseum, but Brian wanted to go back to the Hollywood Bowl. When Brian called to ask if I wanted them again, I told him I did but only if I could get them to do two shows. He agreed. So we did two shows at the Hollywood Bowl, on August 29 and 30 in '65. But I was smarter by then. The Beatles had made KRLA, where I worked as a DJ, the #1 radio station in Southern California. So I asked Brian if I could promote the Beatles' appearances by adding: "KRLA and Bob Eubanks present the Beatles." I also asked if I could do the same when introducing them at the Bowl. Brian agreed, and KRLA paid me $100,000 for securing that. We had the same deal in '66. Funny, I made more money than the Beatles did the second and third year in L.A.

Bill Hanley
(designer of the Beatles' stadium sound system in 1966)

For whatever reason, Sid Bernstein either didn't want me to do the '65 Shea concert or had promised it to someone else. I never could figure out who that person was. Whoever did the sound at Shea placed thin speaker columns along the first- and third-base lines. The sound didn't carry, especially when 55,600 people started screaming.

The following year, I designed a system for a Boston-based band called Barry and the Remains. They were opening for the Beatles in Chicago on August 12 at the indoor International Amphitheatre, the first stop of the Beatles' 1966 tour. I trucked the sound system I designed for the Remains to Chicago. Once Beatles' manager Brian Epstein saw the system the Remains were going to use that night and compared it to the inadequate public address system the Beatles had to use, he had the Beatles use my system. Brian then hired me for the Eastern portion of their '66 tour.

By the time the Beatles came to New York to perform at Shea in August '66, I had designed a system to overcome the sound problems I witnessed a year earlier at the stadium. For the concert, there was no black backdrop behind the stage. Instead, the stage at second base was simply a platform exposed on four sides, with the sound and mixing boards behind the stage. Sid and his partner, John Drew, told me about the shortcomings in '65, so I doubled the speakers and sound capability.

Sid was hoping for 55,000 people in '66, but they only wound up selling around 45,000 tickets, which is still huge. I decided on twelve monster Altec 210 bass horns and a range of Altec midsection horns and cabinet speakers and woofers distributed around the field. I also had a 300-pound RCA amp, Shure 546 microphones, and other gear. I trucked it all to Shea early in the morning of August 23 from my Medford, Massachusetts, office and workshop. It took six hours to set up everything.

I placed speakers in front of the stage and at the corners of the field to bounce the reverberation out of the stadium. I pointed other speakers up at the seats. We didn't have a sound check. I just avoided turning up the volume on the soundboard too high. You could blow them out by doing that. So I turned them up until I saw the oscilloscope start to turn bright blue. Then I turned them down slightly. But as soon as the Beatles climbed out of the armored car that delivered them to the stage, all of my hard work was a bust.

Tens of thousands of girls started screaming, and that was the end of it. The volume and pitch were deafening. But the acoustics at Shea were fascinating. Shea was designed so it was wide open in the outfield, as if someone had sliced a huge piece out. The sound of the girls' screams coming from the stands went across the field and out through that gap and into the parking lot. The people in the highest seats could actually hear the Beatles coming through my sound system perfectly. A bunch of musicians who attended the '66 concert told me this a few years ago. Looking back, though, I wish I'd had ten times the amount of gear that night, but I didn't have the budget.

Henry Diltz
(photographer at the Beatles' Shea Stadium concert in 1966)

In August 1966, I was shooting the Lovin' Spoonful in New York for an album cover. The five of us went to the Beatles' concert at Shea to take pictures out there, too. We arrived early, and our seats were way over in the side bleachers. Lead guitarist Zal Yanovsky had on a monk's robe with a hood and one of the other guys was wearing a cowboy hat and sunglasses. I was standing away from them taking pictures.

At one point, girls closer to home plate started pointing at us and screaming, thinking the Lovin' Spoonful were the Beatles hiding out in the stands before the show. We watched as about a hundred of them started running toward us in the stands. We were close to the field and must have looked panicked. Someone on the field knew who we were and said, "Quick guys, jump down here." We all jumped down and followed the guy into the dugout. We went through these little narrow hallways.

Light bulbs on strings were hanging down as we ran by. Someone shoved us in a little room and said to me, "No photographs." There in the room were the Beatles looking at us bewildered. We were in their dressing room. They recognized the guys in the Lovin' Spoonful. John Sebastian sat with John Lennon and talked at a table. Paul was walking around playing the bass with a harmonica in his mouth. He didn't talk to anyone. I sat at a table with Ringo. I asked him what he did with all the stuffed animals people threw onstage. He said, "I give them to me son, Zak."

They got dressed and eventually someone popped in and said, "OK, boys, let's go. Out this way." The Beatles went out first and we were herded behind them with a bunch of others. We all went onto the field. We stopped and the Beatles kept going to the massive stage at second base. It was my first year of photographing. I tried to take a couple of images but the film I had wasn't fast enough for the low level of light. They all came out blurry. So there I was on the field with the Lovin' Spoonful watching the concert.

After the concert, we were sent through the dugout to the stands so we could leave through the exits. As everyone was heading out, I remembered seeing the Beatles on *The Ed Sullivan Show* in February '64. Back then, I was on the road playing banjo with the Modern Folk Quartet. We were on our way to play at some New England university but wanted to see what all the fuss was about. We pulled into a motel and paid for a room to watch.

When the Beatles sang, we listened to them play this happy music. I wondered why we were singing stuff like "Ox-Driver Song" when we could be singing fun stuff like that. After the show was over, we turned off the TV and the lights and left. The next day we bought an electric bass and electrified acoustic guitars. I bought an electrified five-string banjo. We even did the unthinkable for a folk group. We hired a drummer.

Chapter 8

DYLAN INVENTS ROCK

When Bob Dylan returned from Britain in May 1965 after a seven-city tour, he was fed up with folk's denim-clad egalitarianism. The Beatles had changed the pop landscape by standing out and taking artistic risks. In the studio in June, Dylan recorded "Like a Rolling Stone" with an electric guitar and other electric instruments and drums. He also decided to remake his image, appearing in mod King's Road attire at the 1965 Newport Folk Festival. His band's high-volume electric set on the evening of July 25 resulted in some audience outrage. But Dylan's break with folk's past outweighed the audience's discomfort and scorn. That night in Newport, Dylan invented rock—without the roll. His electric crossover, longer songs, and lyrics critical of love and the culture at large raised the stakes for the Beatles and all other rock 'n' roll groups. His concert and the one that followed at the Forest Hills Tennis Stadium in Queens, New York, on August 28 would end the folk revival movement.

Joe Boyd
(production manager of the 1965 Newport Folk Festival)

To understand what went on at the Newport Folk Festival in 1965, it's important to understand the contrast between the New York and Cambridge folk scenes of the early 1960s. One of the big differences were the sing-alongs. New York folkies often got audiences to join in. Cambridge artists rarely did. There was a joyful reverence for archaic folk styles in Cambridge. It didn't matter whether the music was a Tin Pan Alley ragtime ditty or a Delta blues. Audiences there were conditioned to listen keenly.

To me, New York folk was what Pete Seeger and the Weavers were about. They'd sing a South African miner's song, an English seafaring ballad, a Spanish Civil War song, and a Southern spiritual and play them all with the same strum. The music was meant to make all songs sound related. They also wanted to make the music democratic, in the sense that everybody could sing the songs around a campfire or at demonstrations.

The left in America basically used folk music as its own soundtrack. There's nothing wrong with that, but New York folk just wasn't my cup of tea. In Cambridge in the early '60s, while at Harvard, I found all these new, younger artists who were doing the opposite of what was happening in New York. That's why Dylan was in Cambridge in '63.

Peter Yarrow
(folk singer-songwriter and member of Peter, Paul and Mary)

On the afternoon of Saturday, July 24, 1965, at the Newport Folk Festival, Bobby [Dylan] performed three acoustic songs at a songwriters workshop: "All I Really Want to Do," "If You Gotta Go, Go Now," and "Love Minus Zero/No Limit." That same afternoon, Alan Lomax was emceeing a blues workshop. Lomax was a traditionalist who favored acoustic folk, and he belittled the Paul Butterfield Blues Band onstage during his introduction. Word spread. His remarks were viewed as a generational jab, that younger white blues artists with electric instruments had less value.

When Bobby heard about Lomax's knock of electric instruments, he wasn't happy. Then he heard that the festival was putting him on Sunday night between Cousin Emmy and the Georgia Sea Island Singers, two acoustic folk acts. He was upset. He felt he should have been the closer, the most natural place for him. That's when Bobby decided he was going to play an electric set on Sunday night. It was something of a personal statement aimed at Lomax and the festival's older, more traditional hierarchy who favored acoustic folk music. To top it off, Bobby was going to use members of Paul Butterfield's electric group who Lomax had chided Saturday afternoon.

They rehearsed Saturday night. The decision to schedule Bobby in the middle of the Sunday-evening lineup was made by Lomax. Instead of scheduling acts so that a concert built to a climax, with the obvious headliner going on last, Lomax decided he would do it Dadaistically, using an illogical, haphazard order. That really angered Bobby. He said people coming to the concert to see him would be angry because they might miss him perform. He also felt it was insulting.

But something else happened at that blues workshop where Lomax had chided the Butterfield band during his introduction. When Lomax came off the stage, Bobby's manager, Albert Grossman, who also represented Butterfield, called him on it. Tempers flared, shoving started, and they were on the ground punching away. That lasted only a few seconds before it was stopped and they got up. It was just a dustup. At some point that day, Grossman told Lomax that Lomax's programming decisions were screwing up the festival, that concerts weren't flowing properly. Lomax's response was that they were going to get rid of the star system, which was anathema to folk's ethos.

Personally, I don't think the friction between Grossman and Lomax was triggered by a shitty Butterfield introduction on Saturday afternoon, but it may have started there. It was really about the tensions building over Lomax taking things into his own hands and attempting to eliminate any sense of status or stardom among the folk artists. But Grossman managed stars, including Bobby and us, so he was set on edge.

After his scuffle with Grossman, Lomax left in a huff and approached festival founder George Wein about banning Grossman from the rest of the festival. An emergency board meeting was called and held that night. I was a member of the board, but I wasn't at the meeting. I wasn't invited, probably because Lomax knew that if I had been there, I would have said, "Are you crazy?" I would not have gone along with what he wanted to do. I was never told about the meeting, even after they met. Had I known, I would have been irate that they held one without me and I would have quit the board. Which is probably why no one told me about it after. At the Sunday night concert, I did the mix on the soundboard.

99

When Dylan performed his electric set, he was backed by guitarist Mike Bloomfield, drummer Sam Lay, bass guitarist Jerome Arnold, organist Al Kooper, and pianist Barry Goldberg. Bloomfield, Arnold, and Lay were in Butterfield's group. Bloomfield and Kooper had recently played on Dylan's recording of "Like a Rolling Stone." All of them had practiced with Bobby on Saturday night in a nearby mansion.

Once Bobby started "Maggie's Farm" on his Fender Stratocaster and continued into "Like a Rolling Stone," it was clear the music's volume was loud. The problem we faced is that the mics couldn't tolerate too much amplified sound onstage. If you contain the amount of sound coming out of a speaker from an electric guitar with the musician standing a reasonable distance away from the mics, we would have been OK. But that's not what happened.

We had multiple mics up there, and they weren't the kind you saw used in rock 'n' roll concerts. If you turn up the sound on the electric guitar and amps, the way they did onstage, you'd hear the singing voice and electric guitar and bass blended together. They wouldn't sound distinct. There was nothing that could be done at the mix board. If the dials were turned down, the mush would just be softer, without much clarity among the instruments. So we did our best.

George Wein
(founder of the Newport Jazz Festival and Newport Folk Festival)

I was on the side of the stage when Dylan walked off after his third electric song, "Phantom Engineer." As he came toward me, I said, "Bob, you have to go back and sing or there's going to be a riot." Bob said, "I don't have an acoustic guitar." I shouted backstage: "Anyone have a guitar here for Dylan?" Someone gave him one. The screaming and booing that night was hectic. But the whole thing has become a myth. In retrospect, the sound was horrible. Dylan and the other musicians onstage had turned up the sound on their amps so it would be as loud as possible.

This story about Pete Seeger asking for an axe so he could chop the main electrical wire was bullshit. Pete did say, "If I had an axe, I'd cut the line," but that was just metaphoric talk. Before Dylan finished his electric set, people came to me and said I should go see Pete, that he was very upset. So I went out into the parking lot where he was in a car to avoid the volume. I got in. Pete said, "George, can you do something about that sound?" I said, "It's too late, Pete."

Of course, we'd had electric guitar players before at the folk festival—different blues players like B. B. King and Muddy Waters. But they didn't make their sound that loud. They were just amplifying their instruments. The sound coming from Dylan's band was pushed to the point of annoyance, probably on purpose, as a political statement against the folk establishment.

I think those who booed were voicing their feeling that Dylan had sold out to pop and was using the loud sound as an excuse. After Dylan went electric that night, that was the end of the Newport Folk Festival. The festival lasted a couple more years, but attendance kept going down. The Beatles had left this impact on the musical soul of young people. Dylan that night put an end to the traditional acoustic sound of folk music. In the years that followed, the folk festival's attendance dwindled.

After Dylan went electric, the focus turned to the messages in the words of new songs or the meaning between the lines. Concerts became a happening for young people, especially the ones held outdoors, and drugs were taken to enhance the experience. When rock arrived, drugs were part of the rebellion against the mores of society. Concerts gave them an opportunity to escape their schools and their mothers and fathers.

Noel Paul Stookey
(folk singer-songwriter and member of Peter, Paul and Mary)

I remember hearing that Phil Ochs was really upset with Dylan's performance at Newport in '65. I suppose Phil felt that what Dylan had introduced with "Blowin' in the Wind" was squandered for commercial and egotistical gain. But Dylan's decision to take politics from public to personal in 1965 was huge. He didn't really abandon the larger political spectrum but instead said, poetically, "The answer is within each of us. It's not the corporation or the government. It's you, babe."

Each of us has a responsibility to find out who we are and how we can be better. That was the door he decided to go through, and I think the world is richer for it. When you close your eyes at night, you're all alone. You're the one who's got to make a difference and make the choice whether you're going to contribute to the world or just take away from it.

Joe Boyd

I thought Dylan was great that night in '65. I wasn't as excited as some people, but I was excited. There was a feeling that Dylan was never going to be a footnote again. I had spent the second part of '64 in the U.K. and what was going on there was really exciting. A corner was being turned. From my perspective, Dylan's performance was as if America was overtaking England and showing them how to do it. The Animals, Eric Clapton, and the Rolling Stones had really seemed to understand something that America didn't about where the mother lode of musical adventure was. They appreciated American blues in a way America didn't.

But after Dylan at Newport in '65, you felt, "Oh, America kind of gets it now." Now we were trumping England. The intensity that Dylan brought owes a lot to the civil rights struggle. The political battles going on in America were life and death. America was at war in Southeast Asia and with itself in Watts in Los Angeles and in Mississippi. For all of Britain's sophistication, open-mindedness, and its embrace of American roots culture, they could never be that intense.

The differences between the Beatles and Dylan in '65 weren't significant. Both were very sophisticated and played a very evolved body of music. It's the audience that was different. By leaving that world of folk and left-wing protest, Dylan found a new audience in the middle class. Dylan, Grace Slick, Jim Morrison, and other early rock artists represented a well-educated bourgeoisie that was elbowing the working-class Johnny Cashes and Jerry Lee Lewises out of the way. They were saying: "We've got this now. We're going to take over."

I don't think any of us realized at the time that a major shift in music had taken place during Dylan's electric performance that night. Nobody had used the word "rock" yet. There was rock 'n' roll, but rock was something different. What Dylan did at Newport and what he would go on to do with his tour that fall was to create something called rock that was different than what the Stones and the Beatles were doing. They were playing pop music with electric guitars. At the same time, the Beatles' music was advanced, elevated, and sophisticated. The Stones were playing a kind of white version of R&B.

What Dylan did was to place the American singer-songwriter aesthetic in front of a very aggressive American blues band. And that's a model that became the icebreaking prow of the rock era. Rock soon sucked all the energy out of folk, out of jazz, out of pop, out of everything. With three electric songs, Bob Dylan shattered the New York folk power structure and introduced a new approach that became known as rock—not rock 'n' roll.

If you want to define rock as what we saw that night, it was about dressing the way you wanted, the end of formulaic guidelines for lyrics, and songs that weren't about male-female relationships. Rock was about anything you wanted to make it about without preconceptions about song lengths or anything else. Rock and rock concerts became this monster of two guitars, bass, and drums that swept up everything like some huge glacier. It moved the whole surface.

Chapter 9

BALLROOMS AND BE-INS

After Dylan's electric concerts in 1965, better rock bands began to take them-
selves more seriously. Instead of recording songs by professional songwriters
about puppy love, dead man's curves, and crying at parties, newly emerging
rock bands wrote their own material and relied on personal experiences, cultural
shifts, and drugs for inspiration. Bands such as Cream, Jefferson Airplane, the
Who, the Rolling Stones, and the Doors quickly filled the concert void left by the
Beatles' retreat to Abbey Road Studios in '66. Ballrooms and theaters sprang
up throughout the country. In San Francisco, Bill Graham opened the Fillmore
Auditorium (1965) and Chet Helms launched the Avalon Ballroom (1966). In
Boston, Don Law ran the Boston Tea Party (1967), while in Philadelphia, Larry
Magid opened the Electric Factory (1968). In each major city in the country,
college-age promoters were setting up shop to attract bands as savvy agents such
as Frank Barsalona began representing rock bands. The rock concert was about
to become a business.

Don Law
(New England rock concert promoter)

When I started promoting rock concerts in the late 1960s, we made
it up as we went along. Everyone did. That's how it worked. Rock was
uncharted territory. People have long assumed that a rock concert business existed from the very start—or at least by the 1960s, when pop

rock's popularity started to grow. In fact, there was no such thing. The first half of the 1960s was essentially the dark ages of the music business.

The turning point came in the second half of the 1960s, from about 1967 to 1969. Many people think the turning point was Woodstock in '69, but that concert was really late in the evolution. The big driver in the shift during those years was the rise of FM radio. Before FM, the pipeline for talent was very small. Most acts didn't develop much of a career. They might have had hit singles, but they often made records under usurious contract terms.

Tom "Big Daddy" Donahue deserves enormous credit for the rise of album rock and the concert revolution that followed. He was at KSAN in San Mateo, California, in the 1960s and was among the first DJs to decide that FM could be a terrific medium for the airplay of rock albums. Originally, in the early '60s, FM emerged as an option in expensive new cars and was positioned as the great hope for classical music. Donahue was the first to realize that FM could be a terrific avenue for rock, since FM was broadcast in stereo and rock sounded incredible when stereo albums were played on the air.

Other stations caught on to what Donahue was doing, and FM broke out as an album rock format. That's when rock concerts began moving into ballrooms, where bands could be booked over a series of nights or for an entire week. Before then, bars would put a stage in the corner, and acts were secondary.

The first rock concert I promoted was Vanilla Fudge in 1968 at the Commonwealth Armory in Boston. I also did a series of workshops on the history of the blues. I had Muddy Waters, Otis Spann, Buddy Guy, and others. I received very good press on my series, which is how Ray Riepen found me. Riepen deserves a lot of credit for reimagining the rock concert market in Boston. He had been in San Francisco and saw what Tom Donahue had been doing at KSAN and what Chet Helms was doing at San Francisco's Avalon Ballroom and what Bill Graham was doing there at the Fillmore Auditorium.

Riepen came to Boston in 1966 and decided he would try to do the same thing in Boston. While at Harvard Law School, he hooked up with David Hahn, an MIT grad student. They took over a late nineteenth-century

Unitarian meetinghouse at 53 Berkeley Street in the South End with a group called Film-Makers' Cinematheque, founded in New York by Andy Warhol and Mel Lyman. In January 1967, they opened the Boston Tea Party, the city's first rock club. The psychedelic sign outside said FILM-MAKERS' CINEMATHEQUE with the BOSTON TEA PARTY underneath. At first, the concerts were held on the weekends to help fund the avant-garde films.

At the same time, Riepen made a deal with entrepreneur Mitch Hastings to buy what was left of his Concert Network. It had been a series of five classical FM stations along the Eastern Seaboard. The last two stations remaining were WHCN in Hartford, Connecticut, and WBCN in Boston. I was hired by Riepen in 1968 to take over the Boston Tea Party just as he changed BCN's format from classical to album rock. At the FM station, the needle first dropped on the Mothers of Invention as people were sitting at home listening to their classical music. Our switchboard lit up with callers demanding to know what was going on.

Riepen was frantic because his investment in the two radio stations was a big risk. The fun part about being there during all of this was Riepen's idea to hire college students as on-air hosts. We would take students from Tufts and Emerson who had their FCC broadcast licenses and put them on the air. We also brought in Steve Segal, a West Coast underground radio DJ. Steve was brilliant. He understood the whole idea of the free-form, album rock format. We also had BCN broadcasting out of a back room at the Boston Tea Party several nights a week.

The move to have BCN broadcast at the ballroom fused FM with album rock and helped create a new rock culture. Part of what I did was go out and promote FM as a much hipper alternative to AM. At this time, album rock was flooding onto FM radio as a natural way to fill airtime and hold an audience. During these early years, there was plenty of airtime on FM stations, since mainstream advertisers still spent their money on AM stations. Playing entire rock albums, interviewing band members, and talking at length about what listeners had just heard made perfect sense.

Then came the stereo system component revolution in Boston. FM widened its reach considerably when new, affordable Japanese integrated receivers started to be sold in the growing number of stereo stores near college campuses. These Japanese makers probably had added the FM band to the radio built into the receiver as a way to maximize their list price and remain competitive in the U.S. market. At the Tea Party, we designed posters for BCN that said, UGLY RADIO IS DEAD! Essentially, we were going after WRKO-AM's and WMEX-AM's market share.

Also significant in the ballroom evolution during the late 1960s were people like Doug Weston in Los Angeles. Weston owned the Troubadour. If you played the Troubadour, you had to commit to three to five future dates when you played Los Angeles again. So if you played the Troubadour once, you were in servitude for a set number of years. At that time, you didn't really have a rock music industry, so the power was in the hands of the club owners. It was set up for pop rock.

With Frank Barsalona and his Premier Talent agency, the dynamic was reversed. The concert promoter had to prove himself or herself to the artist and show how he or she could help build the act. Only then would the artist agree to play the venue. It was an entirely different approach. With Barsalona's new model, success became a function of how plugged in to the market a club manager was. His instincts were outstanding. He essentially reinforced promoters who could do what was necessary to break acts.

Next in Boston came George Papadopoulos, who in the late 1960s opened two venues—the Unicorn Coffee House, a folk club, and the Psychedelic Supermarket, which was devoted to rock. Around the time that Barsalona started Premier Talent, he called up Papadopoulos and introduced himself. He said he had signed a bunch of English acts.

Papadopoulos stopped him and said, "Hey, I know you. You're the guy who has Herman's Hermits and Freddie and the Dreamers." Barsalona said, "That's correct. But I want to talk to you about—" Papadopoulos cut him off and proceeded to give Barsalona the bum's rush about the kinds of acts he played at his clubs and how important he was. Papadopoulos basically shut him down.

So Barsalona hung up and found me sitting at the Boston Tea Party. We talked about how he had wanted to be a country music singer as a young man and had toured as a singer under the name of Greg Mitchell. My father, of course, had been a Columbia Records producer who in the 1930s made blues artist Robert Johnson's only recordings and recorded top country artists. We hit it off, and the Tea Party booked Barsalona's acts and helped him break them. Soon, Barsalona wound up signing every major rock act coming out of England. Which was great for me.

In addition to Barsalona's creative agenting, what elevated the rock concert business was the confluence of FM radio and the ballroom circuit. This circuit became a network of ballrooms and theaters with promoters who dominated each region of the country. In addition to Helms at the Avalon and Graham at the Fillmore in San Francisco, Aaron Russo in Chicago had the Electric Theatre, which later became the Kinetic Playground; in Detroit, Russ Gibb had the Grande Ballroom and Bob Begaris had the Eastown; Larry Magid had the Electric Factory in Philadelphia and I had the Tea Party in Boston. Later, Graham came into New York with the Fillmore East. This circuit helped establish many rock acts. Bands would come into ballrooms and theaters without much of a following and wind up huge by the end of the weekend.

Alcohol wasn't served at any of them. That's one of the reasons they survived. By avoiding alcohol, we could admit kids who were younger than the legal drinking age. Rock acts were that significant. The goal was to book bands for multiple nights, since the demand to see them far exceeded our capacity on a per-night basis. The Tea Party's capacity was around 800, and we projected a light show onto a wall from a modest balcony. You could have a relatively unknown band play the first night and be sold out by the third. Word-of-mouth was extraordinary.

Remember, the mainstream culture back in '68 wasn't dominated by hippies. It was largely buttoned-down, like the *Mad Men* TV series. Young people with long hair were being harassed or mocked by the mainstream, the drug culture was surfacing in San Francisco, and the anti-war movement was full-blown. A huge cultural sea change was happening, and rock became the music of this shift. It all happened together and exploded as a phenomenon.

By 1969, the Tea Party needed more capacity. We moved into the space vacated by the Ark at 15 Lansdowne Street. This gave us a capacity of around 1,200—about 400 more than we had on Berkeley Street. The new space was standing only, no seats, but nothing changed about our mission. We were in the business of breaking new acts. Sometimes this was a long process.

Larry Magid
(Philadelphia rock concert promoter)

When I began working in the music business in the mid-1960s, the word "promoter" didn't really exist in rock yet, but the job did. Older people like George Wein, Sid Bernstein, and a few others put on concerts. The word "promoter" then was most often associated with people who booked boxing matches and circuses. Bill Graham on the West Coast was probably the first to be called a rock promoter, with all of the job's many moving parts and sophisticated responsibilities.

At the time, I worked for a top New York talent agency, but I wanted to be on the promoter side of the business—the buyer of talent, not the seller. I wanted to book and promote young acts before they were big and make them bigger so I could do bigger shows. In the months before leaving New York, I had returned to Philadelphia every two weeks to see friends and family. Invariably, I'd wind up at jazz clubs.

One of them was the Showboat, where I met the three Spivak brothers —Herb, Jerry, and Allen. They owned bars in Black neighborhoods along with the Showboat. Herb said they wanted to get into the rock business. I gave Herb a few tips and told him he'd have to cultivate artists. I also told him that if he wanted to be in that business, he should open a club. Our conversations developed, and the Spivaks decided I had the right idea about going into the rock business.

At some point in the fall of '67, the Spivaks and I agreed that I'd move back to Philadelphia and handle the bookings for a rock club they'd open. We found a warehouse that I said we should call the Electric Factory. The capacity was 2,500 people. On Thanksgiving of 1967, I quit my job and returned to Philadelphia.

About two months later, on February 2, 1968, we opened the Electric Factory. It was on the corner of Twenty-Second and Arch Streets, right off the center of the city. It was a great location. Our first act was the Chambers Brothers. We played them for three nights and did great business. A week and a half later, we had Jimi Hendrix and then Janis Joplin. I knew I was in the right place. I knew I could do this, that I knew how to sell and that my instincts and training about artists were correct.

If the Electric Factory was going to be a hot spot, we needed the right look before we opened. We found artists from art schools in Philadelphia to paint the outside psychedelic Day-Glo colors. When you walked in, we had machines blowing fog. It was like another world. After you walked twenty feet, you were hit by strobe lights. The interior walls also were painted Day-Glo psychedelic colors. Instead of chairs, we had about fifty of these things we called coffins. You could lay back in them at a thirty-degree angle. They had a place for your feet and you could relax and listen to the music.

Over the thirty months we operated there, we made design adjustments. The club had an open floor plan, meaning people stood to watch the bands or they danced. We put in little playground benches so people could sit. As the club's reputation grew, the psychedelic part went by the wayside. We didn't need it, and people who came didn't care about it. Instead, we became known for presenting good shows for $3.00 or $3.50 admission. We even had the American debut of the Who's *Tommy* in 1969. For that, we charged $4.00. We had played the Who before. Their manager, Peter Rudge, and I had become friends. Their agent was Frank Barsalona.

We didn't have FM stations yet in Philadelphia to run ads for us. At first, we used a simple strategy to get the word out. We bought staple guns, and we went to different neighborhoods and put up flyers on telephone poles and placed them in store windows. We also advertised in newspapers. When album rock began to spread on FM stations between 1968 and 1970, the promotion helped us tremendously. WMMR helped us the most, and we helped that station grow. We bought ad time and brought members of bands up to the station to talk about themselves and their shows at the Electric Factory. Two other FM stations began to follow the same format—WDAS and WIFI.

The only time of year that was a struggle for us was the summer. We didn't have air-conditioning, so we closed. During these months, a station asked me to be a DJ, which was a way to promote the Electric Factory and keep it top of mind while we were closed. I played the music of artists who were going to appear at the club when we reopened in the fall. In the fall of '68, I thought we had grown to a point where we could put on a rock festival indoors with five acts. That was a big deal then and the natural next step for us.

On October 19, 1968, we held the Quaker City Rock Festival at the indoor Spectrum sports arena, which had opened a year earlier. It became one of the first rock festivals and arena rock concerts in Philadelphia and the entire country. We sold over 19,000 tickets for one day and sold out. The bands I booked were Vanilla Fudge, Big Brother and the Holding Company, the Chambers Brothers, Moby Grape, and the Buddy Guy Blues Band. We held the concert in the round, with the stage in the center. We had just eight spotlights and a small sound system. The concert ran from 8:00 p.m. to 1:00 a.m.

We held another festival at the Spectrum two months later in December that featured the Grateful Dead, Steppenwolf, Iron Butterfly, Creedence Clearwater Revival, and Sly and the Family Stone. No one came to these concerts alone. There were some people coming on dates, but mostly it was a bunch of girls or guys coming together for a shared experience.

New York was different. Between 1968 and 1971, promoter Bill Graham turned the Fillmore East into an East Coast extension of his Fillmore Auditorium and then Fillmore West in San Francisco. The former Yiddish theater in New York would feature the biggest-name rock bands of the time. Not only was the Fillmore a last and first stop for bands leaving for and returning from European tours, but it was also the setting for some of the best rock concert albums by bands such as the Allman Brothers Band, Derek and the Dominos, Joe Cocker, Jimi Hendrix, the Grateful Dead, Jefferson Airplane, the Who, Sly and the Family Stone, and many others. The secret of the venue's success had a lot to do with Graham's eye for detail, his good relationships with talent agents and bookers, and his eclectic approach to programming on any given night.

Joshua White
(founder of the Joshua Light Show)

At first, Bill Graham didn't want to enter the New York market. He had been a failed actor in the city and at the time he was a successful, happy concert producer in San Francisco. But we persuaded him to come visit us at the Anderson Theatre on Second Avenue. The Anderson began holding rock concerts on February 2, 1968, that were sponsored by *Crawdaddy* magazine. Bill came to the Anderson on February 17, during Janis Joplin's sold-out concert. He also came to the next three concerts. We brought him out onstage each night.

I had set up the Joshua Light Show there, and we did this thing to make Bill's stage view possible. The Anderson had a curtain of lights. In order to change the bands, our rear projection screen had to be raised. But you didn't want to do all of this in front of a seated audience. So we had a set of blue lights that went across the front of our platform that was six to eight feet off the ground. They were a gentle blue and were pointed into the audience.

When the curtain went up, the blue lights would be turned on. You could see the audience from the stage but the audience couldn't really see you. When we flipped them on, Bill walked out on the stage each night over a four-day period in February and counted the house. That's when he realized we had four sold-out shows at $2 to $4 a head.

Bill did the math and bought the Village Theater two blocks north on Second Avenue at Sixth Street. The Anderson had around 1,700 seats. The Village was closer to 3,000. When he told us about the purchase, all of the tech guys and the Joshua Light Show quit the Anderson and went with him. We helped prep the theater in February '68 and helped him open in March. I painted the box office. I fixed the marquees. It was like summer stock. At the very last minute, he named it the Fillmore East. Someone already owned the Village Theater name and threatened to sue.

The Joshua Light Show began as the permanent light show at the Fillmore. Bill just turned us loose. He didn't have any concerns. The light show didn't get in the way of the rock acts. They couldn't see the light show or us. The light show was going on behind them on a screen. Behind the screen was my team creating the imagery. We initially used colored oil and water with overhead projectors but also mixed in dozens of other ideas including slides, light reflected off hand-manipulated mirrors, pure color, film loops, and even primitive video projection.

112

The artists all trusted us to get it right. We were like the house band for visual effects. During a performance, before we started, there would be a moment of darkness as we switched over from cartoons or some montage on the screen. Just when the band came out onstage into the darkness, Bill would announce the band. At that moment, we'd put a slide up behind them with the name of the act. The stage lights would come up and the act would be in place.

The moment the band hit the first note, the light show would begin. We'd continue until the very end when we knew they were finishing because the stage manager would tell us. We'd have a sudden blackout at the end and up again would come the slide with the name of the band. When Bill announced acts, he'd stand onstage and do it. When he wasn't in town, Kip Cohen did it. Before the final act went on, Graham would always say, "Let's give credit where credit is due. Please thank the Joshua Light Show." So we were acknowledged constantly.

What made the light show work so effectively in New York was that it was disciplined. I was really listening to what was happening onstage, so it was very tight. We never performed with oil and color when bands weren't playing. What we did was always in response to how we felt about what we heard. We understood that when you sat in a seat in the audience, it really was hard to do anything but look straight ahead. We kept a strong visual line going from the stage to the audience.

As bands became bigger, drug abuse among artists became a bigger problem, sadly. A year after the Fillmore opened, we began to see greater use of cocaine backstage. With the new drug came new attitudes. With cocaine, when people got angry, they got really angry. Bands of limited talent who were not finding their groove would get into screaming fights backstage between shows. Previously, it was mostly pot and drinking. By 1970, there was mounting hostility in the air, and that was certainly one of the things after Woodstock that made me not want to be around that environment anymore.

As for technology, in late 1968 the Fillmore's sound guys invented an intercom system that changed everything for us. Through the headset, I could talk to the stage manager and the lighting person, and they could talk to me. I could talk to everyone in my light show. It was a headset that you could put on and talk at your normal voice with colleagues. The system was one of the things that were invented at the Fillmore to solve unique problems. That's how good the Fillmore's tech guys were.

Jerry Pompili
(Fillmore East house manager)

At the Fillmore, I started as an usher. I was take-charge, which Bill Graham apparently noticed. So when they fired the house manager, Bill promoted me. For some reason, he knew I was more on top of details than anyone else they could bring in. As house manager, I ran all the security, all the ushers, all that staff, everything in front of the stage, indoors and outdoors. And I ran the concessions. And I was selling the advertising.

Security was hugely important. If you wanted to keep booking top acts, you had to prove that the venue could protect paying audiences as well as the acts. Graham's philosophy was if you piss off people early in the evening while they're on line outside, they're not going to have a good time, no matter who is playing. The people we used for security weren't hired for their brawn. We hired them for their brains. About 99 percent of your problems with people can be addressed and defused with information.

The first thing I did when I became house manager was to get rid of the orange jumpsuits for the security guys. They looked like a bunch of convicts. I set up security in a military manner: the captain, lieutenants, squad leaders, and privates. I was the captain. Then I had three lieutenants, four or five squad leaders, and the rest were privates. I didn't give them that nomenclature. It's how I thought of the organizational structure. Before every show, I'd have everyone sit on the stairs going up to the mezzanine. I'd tell them what we were going to do that night and how we were going to do it.

At this point, I had everyone wearing kelly-green football jerseys with gold lettering. I bought the jerseys at Paragon Sporting Goods in Union Square. Then I had FILLMORE EAST pressed on the front along with a number on the back, either a 0 or a 1. I didn't get different numbers for everybody on the back. Doing so would have become a tug-of-war over people who wanted this number or that number. That was one of the first rock T-shirts.

In-house, I never referred to these guys as security. They were "staff"—smart guys who used their brains to make sure nobody screwed up. The point was they worked as a unit, and they were really good at what they did. Their job was to first get everyone in their seats. This wasn't a raw ballroom space. This was a reserved-seats theater. The second thing was to keep the audience in their seats, not dancing in the aisles. You could dance at your seat but you couldn't clog the aisles because if you did, the fire department would have a shit fit.

In the late 1960s and early '70s, the best promoters could put together an interesting mix of bands for a bill. If you got the recipe right, you had a business. But this wasn't easy. It was an art. Look at the bills Graham put together: Jefferson Airplane, John Lee Hooker, and Led Zeppelin, or Santana, the Grateful Dead, and Miles Davis. Bill had a saying: "Don't give them what they want, give them what they should want." When Led Zeppelin played the Fillmore, Graham wanted people to know that it was John Lee Hooker's shit they were playing, so he put Zep and Hooker on the bill.

Amalie R. Rothschild
(Fillmore East photographer)

At NYU's film school in the fall of 1967, there were only six women in a class of thirty-four. I was the techy, nerdy one. I was buddies with the film-equipment technician Lee Osborne. In early 1968, when the Village Theater became the Fillmore East, Osborne began working there. He was the first sound mixing engineer who worked with Bill Hanley, who furnished the sound system.

One Friday afternoon at school, Osborne asked, "What are you doing later? Come over to the theater at five p.m. Here's a pass. I think you'll like this." So I did, two weeks after the theater opened on March 8, 1968. After that, Osborne gave me passes every week to come whenever I wanted to. So I just started hanging out with the tech staff, because that's what interested me and because those guys took my interests in the technical side of things seriously.

From the start, I was amazed at what a laboratory the Fillmore was for the theatrical presentation of music. It was a real test kitchen of innovation. Everything that became standard in the business was invented there in one way or another. That included rolling platforms for quick set changes, drum kit dollies, the headset and microphone intercom system, the first experimentation using live video projection of artists, the sophisticated light show, multichannel live mixing boards, the sound system, and the development of microphones that could clearly reproduce music at that decibel level without overloading the system.

John Chester, an electronics designer who was in the NYU theater tech program, became the chief sound engineer at the Fillmore East after initially starting to work with Hanley. Chester took over and in 1968 designed the in-house headset system. In 1969, he also designed and built the new in-house sound system and multichannel mixing console with sliders. It was one of the first in-house rock theater systems in the country.

So, back when Osborne gave me my first pass, I arrived at the Fillmore East with my cameras in tow, since I wouldn't leave them anywhere for fear they'd be stolen. On one of my free-pass visits, I was inspired and I just started taking pictures. No one stopped me and said I couldn't. I didn't know these groups initially, so the music was new to me. I quickly grew to love it with a few exceptions. I also was mesmerized by the Joshua Light Show. The staff got to know me, and there were no rules back then. I'd walk right down to the foot of the stage and shoot. Becoming the Fillmore's staff photographer wasn't an official job. It's just something I did and invented for myself.

The Grateful Dead and the Allman Brothers Band were basically the staff's most popular house bands. The Dead first, because they were around before the Allmans showed up. The Fillmore East was a theater with a proscenium arch and 2,654 numbered seats. It wasn't like the Fillmore West or the Fillmore Auditorium, where kids milled around. There were no seats out West, where everything was pretty hippie-dippie. At the Fillmore East, acoustics mattered. You didn't want to have an audience wonder what was being said from the stage or not hear the music in all its complexity. It wasn't just a matter of how loud it was.

Graham was an enlightened impresario. He knew when he had good people and he knew a good idea when he heard it. Underneath it all, he wanted to give the public a good show, the best show. It wasn't the money-grubbing thing that so many promoters were into. Graham was about top quality. He knew how to give the right people free rein and the financial support necessary to develop the bells and whistles as well as the solid underpinning to make a show superb.

As a photographer, I think I brought a female perspective to the images I took there. I don't believe photography is generic. I believe everyone has a perspective. I used Kodak Tri-X film for black-and-white images that I pushed to 800 ASA, and for color I used High Speed Ekta-chrome film, which I pushed one stop to 320 ASA. I also was very flexible and could turn and prop my 300 mm lens on my shoulder and shoot rock steady at 1/60 of a second using my body as a tripod. But I wasn't shooting all over the place and then cropping to get a picture. I was very deliberate in what I was photographing and how I was composing it in the viewfinder, which is why I leave the negative edges on my prints.

I also wanted my images to be very fine grain, so I used a special fine grain developer for Tri-X. I also wasn't rip-roaring high, stoned, or drunk like so many of the male photographers. I was sober and very serious. Looking back, maybe too serious, but it was my way of protecting myself from being hit on in that often-chauvinistic environment. My cameras were my shields and I tried to be the fly on the wall.

I wasn't the only woman working at the Fillmore, but I was the only woman on staff taking photographs. There were women there who were critical to the Joshua Light Show. There also were two women who worked on the stage crew. The real pioneer and most remarkable was Candace Brightman, who was the second lighting designer for the Fillmore. The only reason she didn't stay is because she got hired away by the Grateful Dead. She became their lighting designer for years. She was extraordinary and way ahead of her time in that environment.

All of the women had to put up with some really snarky, nasty stuff from the bands and some of the Fillmore's guys, particularly the stage-hands. It was chauvinism all the way. This was the end of the 1960s and the women's movement was just getting started. Women were having to deal with these kinds of experiences until finally a light bulb went off over enough of our heads that something wasn't right, something wasn't

117

fair. Women began organizing to change perceptions of our worth and right to be treated as equals.

That was a constant problem. Women were fair game. Back then, guys thought girls were there for the taking. It was sex, drugs, and rock 'n' roll. Either you were somebody's "old lady" or you were a sister or a relative or a secretary or a groupie. You were always considered available, especially if you hung out with the bands. So I kept my distance. I didn't want to put myself in a bad situation. The key was not to get cornered after a concert or you'd be hit on.

I only took photographs of artists whose music I liked. Joni Mitchell and Laura Nyro were standouts for me. The first time I heard Joni, I was just, "Wow." And I had no idea who she was when she played the Fillmore in April 1969. But her voice and her harmonies hit me. I can't put this in words. I would go back to see who this lovely young woman was in a red velvet dress on the stage who insisted on performing without the light show, just blackness, with amazing long white-blonde hair and a bell-like voice playing the guitar marvelously. She mesmerized me. And I took some of my very favorite color photographs of her.

There were other acts that performed specifically without the light show, among them Crosby, Stills, Nash & Young and Laura Nyro. She was onstage by herself with a grand piano. Her first time was in April 1970 and again in June 1970. Her lyrics mattered in a different way even if they were at times abstract, since her music was her voice, her melodies, her everything. She didn't need a band. As I photographed her, I saw her openness and vulnerability, and her soulfulness. She had that ineffable quality that produced enormous joy in me.

Joni and Laura had a presence onstage that was undeniable. It was magic. It's being in the presence of something that you can't define that transports you. They were women singing on their terms, not copying someone else. They were 100 percent original and unashamedly female. They were singing from a woman's perspective, and the strength of that was towering. They were saying, "This is who I am and that's the way it is. You either love what I'm doing up here or you don't, but I'm not changing." That's what was going through my mind and heart when I photographed them.

Chapter 10

FESTIVAL MANIA

In the late 1960s, while some rock concert promoters had the means and opportunity to rent and manage ballrooms and theaters, others followed in the footsteps of Tanglewood's classical concerts, the Hollywood Bowl's pop performances, and the Newport Jazz and Folk Festivals. These new promoters staged rock concerts outdoors for a day, over weekends, or during school and college breaks. All that was needed was a stage, speakers, lights, and access to electrical power. But any hope of making money on festivals was dashed by bad weather and large, surging audiences that believed live music should be free. Nevertheless, the outdoor rock festival became the concert format that most defined the second half of the '60s.

THE HUMAN BE-IN
(San Francisco, January 14, 1967)

Michael McClure
(San Francisco poet and Human Be-In performer)

Back in '66, I was living on Downey Street in the Haight-Ashbury district of San Francisco. I moved into my place before there was any sign of a hippie scene or movement there. The next thing I knew, a bunch of rock bands moved into houses on the street. We became friendly and got together to sing songs based on my poems. All the classics.

Poet Allen Ginsberg had introduced me to Bob Dylan when he was in San Francisco in late '65. Bob invited a whole bunch of us to his electric concert in December at the Masonic Auditorium. I knew Allen very well by then. The Hells Angels were there. Joan Baez was there. And everyone you can think of in the far-out elite, all sitting in the front row. It was a great concert. Allen and I hung out with Bob while he was here, and a famous photo was taken by Larry Keenan of Robbie Robertson, me, Bob, and Allen standing against a wall in Adler Place behind City Lights Books in North Beach on December 5.

Dylan knew I wanted to write songs or sing poems, so he asked me what instrument I wanted to play. I told him an autoharp. I didn't know much about the autoharp other than it was relatively simple to play. So he gave me one. The following year, in October '66, California banned LSD. Up until that point, it was legal. Seems crazy now, but it was. The new law pissed off a lot of people in San Francisco who enjoyed it. On the day the ban went into effect, an outdoor gathering was held in the Haight-Ashbury district called the Love Pageant Rally. It spilled into the Panhandle, a narrow, block-wide extension of Golden Gate Park that juts eight blocks into the neighborhood.

The rally was sort of a peaceful statement against the state's decision to ban acid. A few thousand people showed up, and many consumed LSD in protest. The Dead and Janis [Joplin] performed for free. At the rally the co-organizer and artist Michael Bowen thought another, even bigger outdoor event should take place in January at Golden Gate Park, sort of a sit-in for humanity. Rock concerts for causes and statements became a thing. So on Saturday, January 14, at Golden Gate Park's Polo Field, around 30,000 people showed up. Michael's posters for the event called it "a gathering of the tribes" and urged attendees to bring children, flutes, drums, gongs, incense, and feathers. It was perfect imperfection.

The bands performing were the regulars who appeared at the Avalon and Fillmore—the Grateful Dead, Jefferson Airplane, Big Brother, Quicksilver Messenger Service, and Blue Cheer. Allen Ginsberg and

Gary Snyder opened the Be-In chanting a mantra. I played my autoharp and sang words out of key to one of my poems, "The God I Worship Is a Lion." It was the first gathering of what we called at the time the young seekers—people looking for truth who were soon referred to as the counterculture or hippies. They came together in that field to celebrate peace, love, and community by listening to rock, dropping acid, dancing in place, and thinking about the state of the world. From the stage, looking out at the audience, I thought all of it seemed perfect, that this was really it.

Since the event had been publicized by the underground press in San Francisco, particularly Michael Bowen's *San Francisco Oracle*, the national wire services like AP and UPI were there. Which meant articles turned up in every major newspaper in the country. Young people read about it and many flooded into San Francisco that summer looking for meaning and music. And love.

Steve Miller
(Steve Miller Band founder, singer-songwriter, and lead guitarist)

I first went to San Francisco in the fall of 1966. The night I arrived, I jammed with Paul Butterfield at the Fillmore Auditorium. I stayed at a house with other musicians near Telegraph Avenue and Russell Street. The Jabberwock, a folk club and coffeehouse, was around the corner. Some of the musicians at the house were in the Instant Action Jug Band—instant because when the club was short on performers, these guys were ready to go at a moment's notice. I played with them and realized I kind of liked it out there.

That's when I decided to stay. Some of my musician friends from Madison, Wisconsin, came out. Some stayed and we formed a band. We had a steady gig at the Forum, another coffeehouse in Berkeley. But these jobs didn't pay, and I was running out of money. Fortunately, we got a paying job in December of '66 performing at the Avalon Ballroom. And at the Matrix. I formed the Steve Miller Blues Band and we had steady work at the growing number of rock venues all over the Bay Area.

The Human Be-In in January '67 was an odd affair. The event seemed to come out of nowhere to be imposed on the loosely connected San

121

Francisco music community, perhaps as a way to maximize the crowd size. It had an "out of town" momentum of its own. The press hyped the San Francisco bands as a draw, but in reality the affair was about Allen Ginsberg, Timothy Leary, Ken Kesey, and their pals doing an ad-lib poetry performance.

For our part, the Steve Miller Blues Band had been asked to play a concert that day at Grace Cathedral on Nob Hill. After our performance, we went over to the Golden Gate Park's Polo Field to wait behind the stage to go up and play. But it never happened. Ginsberg and Leary took over the whole event. They horsed around in front of the crowd for a while and then started chanting and reading poetry. Of course, everyone was deferential to them and it was interesting for a moment. Then it went on and on and became obvious they didn't have anything more to offer the audience, which was getting restless until the Dead and Quicksilver Messenger Service took over.

Free outdoor events had already been going on in San Francisco and were beginning to happen in New York in Central Park as well. San Francisco's Human Be-In was the first one with nearly 30,000 people but the least enjoyable of them all. It was more of a Me-In than a Be-In. We were amateurs in '67. Back then, the Jerry Rubins of the world were always lurking around the back of the stage ready to grab the micro-phone and start pontificating. I remember playing an impromptu free gig at Central Park and having to push him off our stage when he tried to interrupt our performance by taking over one of the mics. His basic approach was to act like a Communist disrupter at a political event, but in the rock world, he got kicked off the stage.

The Human Be-In would turn out to be the Beat poets' last stand. By the summer of '67, rock had won the tug-of-war for the stage. For a brief moment in '65 and '66, the Beats held sway over the folk move-ment as an influence, especially for lyricists. But once the Dead paved the way for rock and the rise of singer-songwriters, the Beats' grip on San Francisco began to loosen. When it came to captivating an audience, rock had a stronger connection with the audience than poetry. To remain relevant, the Beats tried to piggyback on the popularity of rock musicians by inviting them to events. By the Monterey Pop Festival in June of '67, rock could hold its own, rendering the Beats largely irrelevant.

Music performed outdoors was nothing new. Its roots can be traced back to ancient Greek amphitheaters where open-air performances were accompanied by a chorus and early string and wind instruments. In the late 1960s, the allure of the outdoor rock festival was a natural progression as the number of rock fans outstripped the capacities of ballrooms and theaters. The nationwide expansion of San Francisco's counterculture and its embrace of the ecology also placed a premium on the wilderness and the personal freedom and privacy it offered. But perhaps the most potent and seductive promotional tool for the outdoor rock festival was the release of D. A. Pennebaker's "Monterey Pop" documentary in December 1968. The film artfully captured the colorful counterculture that celebrated the live music. The film's portrayal of live rock and its connection to the hippie audience led to a surge in outdoor music festivals.

MONTEREY POP FESTIVAL
(June 16–18, 1967)

Steve Miller

In early 1967, John Phillips of the Mamas & the Papas and their manager, Lou Adler, planned a three-day concert at the Monterey County Fairgrounds in Monterey, California. Called the Monterey Pop Festival, it was a charity event, so most of us performed there for free, with proceeds going to a foundation. My invitation came from Lou Adler's office. In my mind, being asked was confirmation that we had become a legit part of the San Francisco scene. I was looking forward to playing with all of the other artists on the bill. Our band had already played lots of outdoor free concerts together in San Francisco's Golden Gate Park and at Stanford, Berkeley, and in city parks all over the Bay Area as part of the different cities' community outreaches. But Monterey was a big deal. We all knew about the Monterey Jazz Festival that jazz disc jockey Jimmy Lyons and jazz pianist Dave Brubeck helped start in

1958, so there had been large outdoor shows going on for nine years previously, just not rock shows.

Country Joe McDonald
(Country Joe and the Fish's lead singer and guitarist)

Performing at Monterey Pop was an opportunity for me to see and meet artists I'd heard of or listened to on albums. Jimi Hendrix and the Who stood out. I watched them onstage at Monterey Pop and was amazed by what they were doing. I also saw new music, like Ravi Shankar and Mike Bloomfield's Electric Flag. One of the great things about being a performer at a festival was that you got an all-access pass. I could just walk around. I had never taken part in a jam session or schmoozed with other artists. At Monterey, there was some of that going on.

I also took this incredible new psychedelic drug called STP, which stood for "serenity, tranquility, and peace." It was manufactured by underground chemists Owsley Stanley and Tim Scully and really stoned me out. I wanted to try some and told Owsley: "Make sure I get a good dose, so give me one and a half tabs." After I took them, I lived in a Monet painting for a week. It was a really, really amazing experience. That's another thing about the late '60s that was special. Color was invented then. More color TVs were out there, fluorescent Day-Glo paint and markers became popular, more color photos appeared in magazines, new colors emerged, and color varieties multiplied. Plain red no longer existed. By comparison, when I think of the '50s and early '60s, I think of black-and-white and pretty drab, flat colors.

The crowd at Monterey Pop was sitting in folding seats, which was a formal setting. That was unusual for an outdoor festival then, where people typically sat on blankets or tarps. The artists also varied. To me, the Mamas & the Papas were like the Weavers—pop music dressed up as rock. At Monterey, it became obvious to me that San Francisco bands had it going on compared to groups from L.A. Except for the Byrds.

The Monterey Pop Festival was a game changer for the music business. It put the artists who performed there on the map, especially as rock albums became popular. So from the artist's perspective, it became easier to pay the bills. I came from a family that didn't have a lot of money and was always worrying about it. Although I didn't go looking for money with my music, composing, performing, and recording became a way to make ends meet. Like me, many musicians back then came from working-class families. No matter your background, you brought your struggles to your art. Look at Janis Joplin's performances. The audience connected, probably because they had their own stuff from their pasts, and the emotional performances were real and touched them.

Steve Miller

During the performance at Monterey, there were mobs pushing at the back trying to break in, especially when the Smothers Brothers foolishly began spreading rumors from the stage that the Beatles were there. The Smothers Brothers reminded me of the Beats who showed up out of nowhere to capitalize on the crowd the festival had drawn. The Smothers Brothers were disliked by most in the crowd and were obviously out of their swanky showbiz element.

I also was disgusted by the Who's smashing of instruments at the end of their set. It felt like they had pissed on the stage, the audience, the recording equipment, and especially on the whole idea of peace, love, and happiness that they tried to embrace later. At that moment, they seemed to be on their last legs as a fading British pop act and this was their last chance to make it in America. It definitely felt to me as if they were only in it for the money. It took me years to appreciate their talent after seeing that. When Jimi Hendrix followed by kneeling on the stage, pulling out a can of lighter fluid and squirting it on his guitar and setting it on fire, I was even more disappointed, especially after seeing his defiantly phenomenal musicianship overshadowed by that kind of pandering.

It was a lesson in what happens when that kind of attention-grabbing is unleashed in front of a crowd and takes over. It also was sad to see the festival's musical highlights—people like Otis Redding—reduced to the lowest common denominator. On the bright side, Monterey helped the Steve Miller Band close our record contract negotiations with Capitol Records and established us as an underground progressive rock band from San Francisco. We also were able to expand beyond the city's main

125

concert venues. We started playing colleges up and down the West Coast and performing gigs at venues I called psychedelic dungeons.

D. A. Pennebaker
(documentary filmmaker and director of *Monterey Pop*)

In the early 1960s, Albert Maysles, Ricky Leacock, and I developed a portable 16 mm camera. It took us about two years to get the damned thing designed and built. Al and I had to do it ourselves because no company wanted to make a new camera then. There was no market for it. In 1963, Ricky and I formed Leacock-Pennebaker Inc., our own film production company. Not long after, in early '65, manager Albert Grossman appeared in our office and asked if I'd like to make a documentary about his client Bob Dylan during his upcoming tour of England. The tour would run from April 30 to May 10. I used one of my portable cameras and I called the film *Dont Look Back*, purposefully leaving off the apostrophe in "don't" in the title to simplify its look. This was about three months before Bob went electric at the Newport Folk Festival. The film's title was from a quote by baseball pitcher Satchel Paige: "Don't look back. Something might be gaining on you." I bought into the quote's sentiment. So did Dylan.

By 1967, we built five or six portable sync cameras. One day early that year, a guy from California called me in New York. He asked if I wanted to film a rock concert in Monterey, California, from June 16 to 18. I told him I wasn't sure, but I did want to get out to California. Back then, everyone who graduated from high school wanted to go to California. I thought that's where all the action was, and I agreed to do the film. I knew I needed four or five other people filming to bring it together. I knew nothing about directing them. I wasn't a director. But I was already committed to the project. So out I went with the portable cameras.

What I did was use the guys I worked with—Nick Proferes, Jim Desmond, Albert Maysles, and my partner, Ricky Leacock. Ricky was the only real cameraman. The rest were guys who had worked with us and knew how to operate the portable cameras. The only thing I knew for sure was that the cameras were going to allow us to go anywhere and shoot whatever we thought was interesting and relevant.

126

Each morning, the guys and I would go to this place to have waffles. I'd give each of them five or six rolls of film. That night they'd give them back to me. So I had no idea what most of them were doing. I wanted guys on the team who knew music. I could teach them how to operate the camera.

I had two guys filming at the front of the stage. I assumed they would shoot performers. Bob Neuwirth, who was part of the team, was onstage with a little red light. When he wanted them to shoot, he'd put the light on. When Hendrix was on, Bob's red light never went off. I was onstage, too, where I could shoot not only the performers but also audience reactions. You could do that with these portable cameras. I wanted the film to be like an album that you'd put on and listen to.

I didn't want to interview people, and I didn't want to talk to them about dope or anything that they thought was interesting about the festival. No major revelations were going to come out of that. I knew that if we did do interviews, we'd wind up with the same comments said hundreds of different ways. Instead, I wanted the film to be purely about the music and whatever it meant to you, the viewer. Maybe you'd see it as entertainment or you'd relate to it based on what you were going through in your life. I wanted it to be just that and nothing else.

The fantastic moment in the film for me was Ravi Shankar. Initially, I didn't even think he was going to be part of the film. I didn't even know who he was at the time. I thought nobody in the United States was listening to that kind of Hindustani classical music. But when I went to see what the other camera operators were up to and if they needed help, I saw Nick and Jim. They were right on Ravi. It was just amazing. They were as close as you could get with a camera. I felt I was watching two people learn about what you could film with these cameras.

When *Monterey Pop* was first released in 1968, it was the first concert filmed with portable sync cameras—a 16 mm shoulder-held camera with synchronized sound recorded on a Nagra tape recorder using a crystal clock movement to ensure that film and sound were in lockstep. The other thing with *Monterey Pop* is that for the first time, artists were conscious of the cameras and were playing to them. They were engaging the audience, but they also were treating our film cameras as a secondary audience. They

127

knew we were giving them an even wider market and that they had to put on a show for both the live audience and the one that would see them later in theaters. You see the emergence of rock narcissism in the film.

I grew up on showbiz music that came out of Broadway shows. The music said, "This is for people who are well-off," and told listeners that their life was good. Then suddenly in the 1960s, along came a new kind of music that Dylan and others were partly responsible for. It said, "Look out." That "look out" quality got me. I heard it in Janis and a lot of other artists. They were saying, "This isn't friendly music. It's a warning." Which is why the cameras in *Monterey Pop* gravitate toward the oddness at the concert with a childlike curiosity. The cameras weren't making a statement about whether what we saw and heard was bad or good, silly or serious, or right or wrong. The camera was operating as an independent inquisitor that wanted to learn more about what was going on, which is exactly what the camera operators were feeling.

I wanted the film to be a natural history of a warning. Like what I did with Otis [Redding] in the film. I didn't intend for that footage to come out the way it did. As I was editing that part of the film in December '67, someone told me that Redding had just died in a plane crash. I thought I should shuffle the edit to pay tribute. Then I decided I'd just leave his segment the way it was.

MIAMI POP FESTIVAL
(May 18–19, 1968)

Michael Lang
  (coproducer)

The first concerts I attended as a kid were Alan Freed's rock 'n' roll revues at the Brooklyn Paramount. I could feel the energy bouncing from the stage to the audience and the audience throwing it back up to performers. And there wasn't a parent or teacher in sight to tell you to turn it down. After high school, I went off to NYU, where I started out as a business major. I soon switched to communications. After two years, I dropped out and moved down to Coconut Grove, Florida, in 1966 to open a head shop. I wasn't into the dry approach of professors or the rigidity of college in general.

At the time, Coconut Grove was an artist community, and it was one of the only overgrown, tropical parts of Florida. It seemed like a great environment and there was plenty of music. Folk singer-songwriter Fred Neil was there, and people like Joni Mitchell and David Crosby would come down to play with him. I was always totally into music but most inspired by my interest in festivals. The film *Monterey Pop* in 1968 was of particular interest. My friend in Coconut Grove, Ric O'Barry, saw the movie, too. Ric trained dolphins at the Miami Seaquarium and became head dolphin trainer for TV's *Flipper*. He also was a stuntman.

One day that year, Ric and I were sitting in my kitchen talking about *Monterey Pop* and how cool it would be to put on a concert like that in Miami. At some point, we decided to go forward with Miami Pop. Fortunately for us, we didn't know any better. The difficulties of promoting an outdoor concert escaped us.

We got a couple of people together, put in some money, and approached Gulfstream Park, the horseracing track in Hallandale Beach, Florida, just north of Miami. We wanted to rent the track. Marshall Brevitz, who owned Thee Image Club in Miami Beach, came in with us with some money. But his funding was good only for six weeks. He had to return it then. So we put together a concert at Gulfstream on May 18 and 19. We made it up as we went along.

I flew up to New York and went to the William Morris Agency to meet with Hector Morales, a cool agent. I sat in his office for a week and booked the festival. We got the Jimi Hendrix Experience, the Mothers of Invention, Blue Cheer, Chuck Berry, John Lee Hooker, the Crazy World of Arthur Brown, Blues Image, Charles Austin Group, Evil, and others. We promoted the two-day concert mostly through radio ads. We also put together six flatbed trucks for the stages. This let us change acts without a break in the action. While one act played, another set up on the other flatbed trucks. When the first band was finished, the second one started.

It wasn't that hard, and in some cases we lucked out. Jimi Hendrix was finishing a tour, so we managed to get him. The first day of

129

Miami Pop was phenomenal. It was really inspirational. The second day it poured. Naturally, attendance plummeted on the second day. The only act I could get onstage was Mississippi Fred McDowell because he was acoustic. You couldn't have all those wires and electricity humming through amps while it was raining. Still, we managed to attract 50,000 people over the festival's two days.

Ric O'Barry
(Miami Pop coproducer)

When Michael and I read about the Monterey Pop Festival, there wasn't much history behind such rock events. It seemed fairly easy to do. You rented the space and you had all these great rock groups come in and play. It wasn't a business venture for me, though it might well have been for Michael. He was more serious than I was about it. I was just having fun. I had no desire to be involved in the music industry. Miami was an oasis detached from what was happening in the 1960s. But we certainly read about what was going on in San Francisco as well as the music scene there.

The Miami Pop Festival was an attempt on our part to bring all of that cultural energy to Miami. It was very spontaneous and didn't really require a specific reason. The rain is what killed us, but we also had the problem of counterfeit tickets. Somebody had printed counterfeit tickets and that destroyed the gate. What's more, there was no covering over the flatbed trucks that were our stage. There was no protection from the elements. A big mistake was not having rain insurance. We didn't know about that. When it rained, we got burned.

A month after our two-day Miami concert was over, Michael and I put on a concert at the Miami Marine Stadium to try and recoup our earlier losses. We put on the Byrds, when they were at the height of their career, and Steppenwolf. That was the bill. It rained and we got burned again and couldn't pay them. Michael never seemed to have good luck with the weather. When it was all over, Michael packed up and went back to New York in late '68. He was broke. I still had a job at the Seaquarium. He left and took our Rolodex with him so he could put another concert together.

SKY RIVER ROCK FESTIVAL
AND LIGHTER THAN AIR FAIR
(August 31–September 2, 1968)

Mike Fisher
(Heart cofounder and band manager)

In April 1968, I was living in Seattle when I first heard about a free concert planned for three days in August. The event was going to be held in rural Sultan, Washington, about an hour northeast of the city. The *Helix*, Seattle's biweekly alternative newspaper, and the city's FM radio station, KRAB, were promoting something they called a Piano Drop on April 28 in Duval, near Sultan. The event was being held by a guy named Larry Van Over, whose farm would be used for the event. The promotion asked: "What does a piano sound like when dropped from a helicopter?" It was a great idea, since no one knew the answer, but everyone with time on their hands wanted to know.

I didn't go to the drop, but I heard that the promotion drew about 3,000 people, who saw the piano get released high above the field and shatter on impact. Then everyone who went got to hear Country Joe and the Fish perform. At the time, I had formed a band with my brother, Roger, called White Heart. I was twenty and Roger was eighteen. I thought a festival held up there in August with many bands over three days would be amazing, a retreat of sorts, for people our age.

By August, I read that a covered stage was going up. Then on August 31, the Sky River Rock Festival and Lighter Than Air Fair began and became one of the country's first multiday outdoor rock festivals. It was held on a large raspberry farm owned by Betty Nelson near the Skykomish River. Apparently, the festival got the second half of its name because Van Over wanted to give concertgoers rides on a hot-air balloon.

Tickets went on sale in July and posters were all over the place. I have no idea whether they booked many of the forty bands that were listed on the poster, but it looked cool and certainly was sufficient to attract everyone looking to get away for the Labor Day weekend. In keeping with the times, the psychedelic poster's centerpiece was an illustration of a frog smoking a joint.

131

I drove up there on the morning of the second day. My brother, Roger, and Mike Rainwater went up a day earlier. Mike was a friend and crew member in our band who let us rehearse in his basement. We all wanted to hear what name bands sounded like playing outdoors. I planned to camp out at the Sky River festival. It was the only way to hang out for the festival's three days.

When I arrived at the site, it was a crazy place. Cars were parked everywhere. I drove as close as I could to the grounds and found a spot. The gates had been trampled down. There was no security and no way to pay to get in. Hippies, then, loved their bands, bought their albums, and felt live music should be free, like some sort of bonus. I got out of my car and started wandering. Eventually, I bumped into Roger and Mike. The three of us milled around.

It was mind-boggling how well Santana could jam individually and then come together for the song. In addition to Santana, we saw Big Mama Thornton, James Cotton, Country Joe and the Fish, Dino Valenti, Byron Pope, the Peanut Butter Conspiracy, Alice Stuart Thomas, the Youngbloods, Quicksilver Messenger Service, It's a Beautiful Day, the New Lost City Ramblers, and local groups such as the Daily Flash, Juggernaut, and Easy Chair. There also were comedians who were little known then, such as Richard Pryor.

Everything was informal and the music was almost a religion. Everyone our age thought of it as something more than music, that it was good for your soul and made you a better person. It was a cause. Which is why when a couple of big-name bands agreed to play a festival back then, others followed in droves. No band wanted to miss out on playing for thousands of people. It was an amazing bond of love and oneness, of belonging to something new and a feeling that something wonderful was happening. This is what flower power was all about.

Roger Fisher
(Heart cofounder and lead guitarist)

The sun was out when we got there on the first day. Then the clouds closed in and, for the first two days, it poured. We were drenched.

132

An underground spring in the field where the audience was sitting bubbled up and turned the area into a marsh. People eventually gave up and rolled around in the mud. There even was a mud pit where people ran and slid. Others skinny-dipped in the river and there was a lot of sex and drugs everywhere you turned. As I recall, the sun came out on the last day, ironically around the time It's a Beautiful Day performed.

I recognized that all the surfaces of trees and leaves and pine needles bordering the field were reflecting the sound. That green wall created the most complex reverb I'd ever heard. Even though it poured, hardly anyone left. We stayed up all night and took some naps in Mike Rainwater's panel truck. The performers didn't get too wet. The stage had a roof to protect the band and all that electrical power and gear.

Most of the vendors sold hippie food, like brown rice with veggies and sandwich wraps that no one had seen before. In addition to health foods, there was Mexican and Asian food. It was beautiful to see so many cultures together. It felt like a global event. Nothing on that scale had happened before in the Seattle area or anywhere else. Sky River was our future—and our present. It reflected who were and who we were going to be. There weren't any hassles. Whatever sense of community we had was only strengthened by the music, the drugs, and the freedom to have sex. This is part of what tied a generation together.

ATLANTIC CITY POP FESTIVAL
(August 1–3, 1969)

Larry Magid
(promoter)

In 1969, I was looking for a rock festival venue with the Spivak brothers, who owned the Electric Factory ballroom in Philadelphia. We wanted a site outside the city that people could drive to. We found out that the Atlantic City Race Course in Hamilton Township had a dead period in the summer between race seasons. So we rented the track for

August 1, 2, and 3. I put together a show of twenty-nine acts, including Chicago Transit Authority, Janice Joplin, Booker T. & the MG's, Creedence Clearwater Revival, Jefferson Airplane, Dr. John, Joni Mitchell, Three Dog Night, and even Buddy Rich. All of them were different, but the sum of the parts was phenomenal.

We decided to put on the Atlantic City Pop Festival just weeks before Woodstock. When Woodstock was first advertised, it was only one day of folk and one day of rock. Just five acts were to perform each day. In Atlantic City, we put tickets on sale and advertised three days of music. We started selling tickets immediately at $6 per day or $15 for three days. Michael Lang and the guys who were promoting Woodstock noticed what we were doing and set out to book as many acts as possible. Had they put on just a two-day concert and not gotten crazy, they might have had time to set up properly by putting up gates and having people pay to get in. But then 400,000 people wouldn't have showed up.

We promoted our Atlantic City festival without much advertising. Word of mouth attracted 120,000 people over the three days, but we were in a controlled environment—a racetrack. One thing we knew how to do was collect money. We knew that people who came to our festival were probably going to drive up to Woodstock later that month. We found that festivals fed off each other. We held our acts to forty-five-minute performances each. The truth is most acts didn't have more than that in their repertoire anyway. Basically, they performed their latest album. Or they did their best stuff from two or three albums. People went to festivals for the feeling. We found that a lot of them went so they could go back home and tell everyone about the cool stuff they had done.

Going to festivals became a big social-status thing. It was a coming-of-age event between being a teenager and becoming an adult. People who went were changed. They were more grown-up when they left. They had a new appreciation of the music and they were part of this new culture that embraced nature, healthy food, and the virtues of rural life. They probably made new friends and felt part of a movement, not just someone who looked at images of hippies on the news.

WOODSTOCK
(August 15–18, 1969)

Michael Lang
(coproducer)

I decided to move to Woodstock in 1968 because it had a similar vibe as Florida's Coconut Grove—except for the cold weather. It, too, was an artist community that had attracted many musicians, including Bob Dylan and the Band. I started managing a band featuring a nascent Garland Jeffreys and began looking for a record deal. That's when I met Artie Kornfeld. He was vice president of A&R at Capitol Records and a successful songwriter. I had been a rock festival promoter. We began talking about holding a music festival in Woodstock.

Artie Kornfeld
(coproducer)

By 1967, I had written or cowritten more than eighty-five songs that reached the *Billboard* pop and R&B charts. Among them was a song inspired by the "flower power" movement emerging from San Francisco. It was a psychedelic hippie love song for the Cowsills—"The Rain, the Park & Other Things." It reached #2 and was a huge hit for the family pop group. That year, Charlie Koppelman introduced me to Alan Livingston, who had made a name for himself at Capitol Records with the Beatles and the Beach Boys. By then he was president of the label.

Livingston created a job for me in New York—Director of East Coast Contemporary Product. A fancy title for discovering and signing new rock bands. But it was a struggle. Many of the best new groups were already signed to Capitol and other labels. One day in late 1968, my secretary buzzed to say someone in reception wanted to see me. Most executives in the music business told their secretaries to give people who turned up unannounced the brush-off. I always viewed people who showed up unannounced as my next potential opportunity. When this guy came into my office, I liked him. He was managing a rock band called Train and handed me a demo reel. As I turned to put it on my tape player, the guy lit up a joint and handed it to me. The guy was Michael Lang.

135

We talked, I listened, and by the end of our meeting, Michael and I began talking about projects we wanted to do. Michael said he had produced the Miami Pop Festival in '68 and moved to Woodstock, New York. I told him about an idea I had for a Broadway musical called *The Concert*. He countered with an idea to put on a two-day rock festival up there using Capitol's funding. I thought it was a great idea, but Capitol wasn't going to invest in something like that. It was too risky. We talked about starting a recording studio near Woodstock.

Joel Rosenman
(cocreator and cofinancier)

There's a lot of myth surrounding the start of the Woodstock festival, including that Michael Lang and Artie Kornfeld responded to a classified ad that John Roberts and I placed. We did place an ad, but we were looking for entrepreneurs with wacky ideas we could use in a sitcom treatment we were developing. The truth is John and I had already financed two clients who were building a huge recording studio in Manhattan, and our lawyer thought Michael and Artie should speak to us about financing their studio idea. So at the end of January 1969, they came to our apartment to pitch us on their studio in the Woodstock woods.

John and I knew right away that Artie and Michael's idea didn't make sense. We knew it took dozens of clients, not just a handful, to keep a studio going 24/7, all year round. We were about to thank them for their time when I noticed a footnote in their proposal. It floated a ribbon-cutting party on the afternoon of the opening of their studio. The plan was to ask local celebrated musicians to attend so they could see the facility. I suggested we shelve their idea for a studio and, instead, put together a concert with the local talent.

For some reason they were vehemently opposed to the idea. It seemed too risky to them. Michael had lost money investing in the Miami Pop Festival the previous summer, and Artie wasn't looking for risk. They pushed again for the recording studio. John and I stuck to our guns about producing a festival. I can't remember who broke through the impasse, but it was probably John. He had a way of figuring out what would work for everybody.

The solution was that we would produce the festival and then with the profits we'd finance the building of the recording studio. We shook hands and drew up a partnership contract that I still have today: Woodstock Ventures LC. None of us had any real experience producing a major festival. So the four of us went to see the *Monterey Pop* documentary, which had been released in December 1968. Then we went to see it several more times.

Michael Lang

Joel Rosenman and John Roberts were going to handle the finance and ticketing for the festival. Artie was in charge of the promotion, and my task was to put on the concert—meaning book the bands, build the "city," assemble an incredible staff with my partners, and run the event. Woodstock was envisioned as celebrating the counterculture in all its art forms. We even planned art exhibits featuring sculpture and crafts by inner-city artists and Native American artists from New Mexico.

Artie Kornfeld

I left my job at Capitol. My new job in our Woodstock venture was to promote the festival. My marketing budget was tight, but I had composed enough hit records to know all the program directors and disc jockeys at major radio stations in top markets. Michael wanted to call the event the First Annual Aquarian Exposition. He came up with a psychedelic poster featuring Aquarius, the Water Bearer.

I said, "Michael, this is not what we talked about in my apartment. An Aquarian Exposition, whatever that means, is bullshit. First of all, it's not the age of Aquarius. Second, this isn't the first annual anything. You and I have a deal. We aren't doing another festival unless we agree on it together." We all finally agreed on the Woodstock Music & Art Fair.

Word of mouth drove music sales and concert attendance back then. My challenge was to let as many people as possible know about Woodstock. I picked my twenty key markets and then wrote copy for ads. Then I had each radio station program director customize the commercial for their market. That saved me a fortune, since they were doing half the work. We also added Jane Friedman of Wartoke Concern, a PR firm, and a few others to handle publicity.

137

I knew Woodstock needed to be a break in the action, not a furtherance of tensions and violence on TV. We had to inoculate the event before it even began. That's when I decided that all publicity, posters, and advertising had to make a big point that Woodstock was going to be "three days of peace and music" and in that order. We had to tell concertgoers what the event was going to be and what we viewed as priorities. We had to set expectations.

Money was tight, so I needed to be certain I was buying space in publications that would deliver the best results. I didn't think hippies in Greenwich Village and on communes were our target audience. They were a narrow slice of something larger. I thought we should be going after middle-class college kids. I needed to know whether I should put our money into underground publications like the *Village Voice* and *Ramparts* or the mainstream *New York Times* and *Los Angeles Times*.

I created a direct-marketing ad with a coupon that you could cut out. I placed the ad in the underground press and in the *New York Times* and *LA Times*. The coupon allowed you to mail in a check or money order to buy tickets for one day, two days, or three days. You also could check a box requesting more information about the festival. The publication that jumped off the chart was the *New York Times*. I was right. But something else happened. Not only was the response huge, but we also wound up selling about 100,000 three-day tickets at $18 apiece.

Joel Rosenman

We knew our concert had to be someplace in the country for the same reasons that the recording studio needed to be in the country. It had to be a retreat. We looked first in Woodstock for a venue but couldn't find a suitable place. The area was too well developed. Next we looked in Saugerties, New York, where Michael had found a guy who was "ready to sign." But it turned out the guy who owned the land had no interest in renting to us at any price.

Then we found a piece of raw land that was scheduled to be the site of an industrial park in Wallkill, New York. It was still somewhat bucolic, although not the paradise we had been envisioning. We applied to the zoning board for a permit for 50,000 people. While we waited for a response, we began building. We also started to blitz the media, the kind of media we had fifty years ago. We had radio, of course, and we had print media but not much else. We were racing the clock. August was creeping up on us.

Then on July 2, six weeks before opening day of the festival, the Wallkill deal fell apart. A coup at the town's zoning board resulted in the passing of a local ordinance prohibiting the gathering of more than 5,000 people. A month and a half before opening day and we had lost our site and all of the money and work that had gone into building it out. The next forty-eight hours were terrifying, interrupted by panic attacks.

Suddenly, a dairy farmer in Bethel, New York, Max Yasgur, offered us a cow pasture for the festival. We jumped at it. Artie and our public relations group got out the word that we were moving to a new location. That's when the poster was done. The pasture was a four-mile walk from White Lake, the closest community.

Artie Kornfeld

I called Arnold Skolnick, a graphic designer and ad director in New York. We met and I showed him the original Water Bearer poster. "What do you think?" I said. He said, "Not much." This was on a Thursday. I asked if he could get a new one done by Monday. "No problem," he said. I told him it was going to be a fair of music, arts, and crafts—three days of peace and music. Instead of designing a trippy Day-Glo poster that looked like everything else promoting acts at the Fillmore, Skolnick created the famous red poster with a plump white catbird sitting on the blue neck of a guitar. White Lake, New York, was used as the destination town. We loved the poster immediately.

Joel Rosenman

All that was left was to re-create in five weeks everything we had spent four months building in Wallkill. Some of the production-related shipments heading to Wallkill were redirected to Bethel. There also was continuous cash flow from ticket sales. If there was a shortfall, John would have covered that.

Michael Lang

I had gone to festivals around the country earlier that summer where attendees had rushed the gates because they thought music should be free. Tear gas was everywhere. The police claimed they had to restore order. But back then, there was an ever-widening gap between the counterculture and the cops, who looked for almost any excuse to beat them back.

Since the Woodstock posters and promotion were already out there, the name stuck. We planned Woodstock to ensure a peaceful, riot-free outcome. If you didn't have the money, we'd have free concert stages, free campgrounds, and free kitchens for you. Of course, the event turned out to be free for everyone who showed up. People thought this happened because we were overwhelmed by the sheer number of people pouring onto Max Yasgur's six-hundred-acre dairy farm in Bethel.

Actually, that wasn't true. We sold 186,000 tickets before the three-day event, so we knew what was coming. When people without tickets arrived, the first thing they did was go looking to buy them. The problem was we never got our ticket booths in place in time, so there was no place to buy them. So we just let everyone in. We had no choice at that point if we were going to hold to our vision for a peaceful crowd.

Artie Kornfeld

When I realized how many tickets we had sold, I called promoter Bill Graham and told him. He said, "You're kidding. Wow. But you'll never reach three hundred thousand." That's when Michael made a deal with Bill to have him help us pull in bands that were still unsigned.

Michael Lang

At the time, I wasn't known in the music business. To gain credibility, I booked three of the hottest groups: Creedence Clearwater Revival, Jefferson Airplane, and Canned Heat. I paid them what they asked and set a "favored nation" top price for top talent. Hector Morales, a booking agent, and I had become friends and he helped me through that whole process.

Building a "city" at the site for the expected 200,000 people was new as well. This had never been done before, so we made it up as we went along. For example, we had to figure out how many toilets we'd need. So early in July we sent staffers out to public places, such as baseball games and subways, to time people in the bathrooms. We also figured out how much garbage we'd have. We estimated how much the paper plates and cups would weigh to determine how many garbage bags we'd need. We also had to have food, water, sanitation, and medical facilities.

I stole a lot of people from Bill Graham's Fillmore East because he had staff with the most experience in the business. This included John Morris, who was seasoned in artist relations, Chip Monck for the lighting, Bill Hanley for sound, Chris Langhart for virtually anything, and Steve Cohen and a couple of dozen others for production and construction.

Artie and I also knew the festival had to be documented, as Monterey Pop had been by D. A. Pennebaker and my Miami Pop had been with home movies by drummer Mitch Mitchell and others and audio of Jimi Hendrix by Eddie Kramer, Jimi's sound engineer. We knew Woodstock was more than a music festival. We planned it that way. It was going to be a sociological experiment. Our film won an Oscar and would become one of the highest-grossing documentaries of all time. The involvement of Warner Bros. meant the festival would be documented on a whole different level that would bring Woodstock's three days of peace and music to the world.

We were coming out of that period where it looked like the whole hippie dream was about to die. Woodstock, for us, was a last-ditch effort to see if we could make this work. That's why we wanted to be in the country, out in nature. We were on our own, but we brought in great people. To ensure that the stage wasn't mobbed, we built a tall wooden wall that forced people to stay back a distance. If you got too close to the wall, you couldn't see anything onstage. We also created something of a platform between the wall and the stage for the documentary filmmakers to move around on free from distractions and the audience.

Artie Kornfeld

Without the film deal for a documentary that I cut with Fred Weintraub at Warner Bros., there wouldn't have been a legacy. Without film, Woodstock might have been just another forgotten '60s festival, only more

141

crowded. Without film, we would have been left with just still images and music to remind us about the three days—but no dramatic story, no documentation of bands' performances or how a half million young people remained peaceful and loving, despite the weather and cramped conditions.

Joel Rosenman

I got up to the festival site on Tuesday before the concert began on Friday. When I arrived, I had a meeting with the heads of the various construction groups in my trailer on Tuesday night. They presented me with a difficult choice. There was plenty of material and men, but what we didn't have was time. They asked, "Do you want the stage finished to the point where it's usable? Or do you want fences and ticket booths so you can make sure people who attend have bought tickets? There isn't enough time to give you both." In other words, "you can have a huge number of teenagers on site with nothing to hear, or you can have a financial disaster." It wasn't just my decision, so I decided to sleep on it and call John in the morning.

But when I woke up the next morning, I looked out of my trailer window and saw about 30,000 people there—two days before the festival was set to start. My decision was made for me. We weren't going to ask tens of thousands of kids to leave over the next two days so they could be readmitted as verified ticket holders. I told the construction crew to finish the stage. Those 30,000 kids also were evidence that this was going to be much bigger than we had imagined. The vibe we had tried to create in our promotion was clearly working. Kicking back was so appealing that people wanted to come early and turn a three-day weekend into five days.

The two days between Wednesday morning and the moment Richie Havens came out onstage to open the festival are sort of a blur. There was a lot to do. My first clear memory is being woken up really early on Friday morning by the New York State Police. They needed to drive me to where they thought the front end of a traffic jam was, a jam that now extended miles and miles from the festival in every direction. The reason I was dragged out to 17B by the police was to tell cars at the head of the line to turn around and leave. That was the police's plan for the traffic jam.

When I heard what the police wanted me to do, I refused. Not because I wanted a traffic jam but because I knew it would have been futile for me to try. I asked one of the officers what I was supposed to say to them. He said, "Fine, I'll tell them." Drivers would see the cops, roll down their window, and the cops would point at me and tell them: "See that guy? He's the festival organizer and he says you have to turn around." In addition to it being virtually impossible to turn around, nobody in that jam wanted to be among those who gave up after traveling so far. So they began to pull off the road and hike to Max's pasture.

Back at the festival, the pasture and hill were filling up. The stream of people flooding in seemed endless. Getting from one part of the festival to another quickly was nearly impossible. Even a motorcycle was too large to get through the crowd. You had to choose between looking cool on a Harley or actually getting to your destination on a motorized bicycle. Even then, for a good part of the journey, you could expect to be just walking your bike through the crowd because there wasn't enough open room to ride. It was an odd sensation—a huge, seamless carpet of a half million kids mixed with a personal trace of claustrophobia.

My biggest fear was that the infrastructure we had built at triple speed might collapse into the crowd with people on it. Or something bad would happen in degrees, like the food and water supply running out or portable toilets failing or some interruption in the music, leaving us with a half million kids with nothing to do. Or someone would suffer a health emergency in a place we couldn't easily reach.

Chris Stein
(Blondie cofounder, guitarist, and songwriter)

In the late spring and early summer of '69, there was a big buzz going on in New York about Woodstock. It was a huge deal. Print ads for Woodstock were running in underground newspapers. The festival was happening in August and the concert site was just a few hours north of the city. I had gone to San Francisco a couple of times in the summer of '67 and '68, so I was already plugged in to the hippie movement. Traveling to an outdoor rock festival and hooking up with people you didn't know was just part of the summer scene back then.

143

I was living in Brooklyn at the time. I heard about Woodstock early enough that I bought tickets through the mail. I had planned to go up with a friend but at the last minute he said, "Fuck it, I'm not going." So I decided to take a bus alone from the Port Authority, the big bus station in Manhattan. When I arrived in the terminal, it was super hot. While everyone was waiting in line for the bus to arrive, this girl got up on her boyfriend's shoulders and held a cigarette lighter under one of the sprinklers to cool us off. Water came raining down and the fire department came. They were really pissed off.

We finally got on the bus. It was Friday evening, and everybody was smoking pot like crazy. I can't remember whether we were dropped off in Bethel, New York, or we were stuck on the highway near the site and the driver let us all out. I recall it was a long walk to the site. When a bunch of us arrived, I asked the first people we ran into: "What do we do with our tickets?" They had no idea. It took forever to get close enough to hear.

I finally found a spot just after midnight. I didn't have a sleeping bag. I was just lying around pretty stoned. I mostly remember the second day, especially Canned Heat. They came on Saturday afternoon. They were one of the first hard rock bands. That was an elevating moment. Everybody went crazy. Then I ran into friends from Brooklyn. They had a van and campsite along one of the pathways. After that, I was all hooked up.

Artie Kornfeld

On the first night of the concert, the rain began at around midnight. That's when the miracle occurred. My "peace and music" copy for the posters, ads, and publicity had sold a massive audience on why they were there. Peace and self-control were the unspoken price of admission. Peace was something everyone was calling for in Vietnam and now the audience would have to embrace peace at Woodstock. By planting the seeds of peace months in advance, we ensured that cooperation, under-standing, and flower power would govern behavior.

When the wind picked up and the rain came down and everything became sloppy and uncertain, I looked out on that loud crowd trailing way off into the darkness and thought, "Peace and music, peace and music." I had faith that those words would stick, and they did. Was it a perfect event? Hardly. But it was a peaceful one and it showed the older generation that young people believed in the very thing they were calling for in Vietnam. It also showed young people all over the world that we had grown up, that we weren't our parents, and that we could make a statement through art while being peaceful and responsible. Which was the festival's purpose from the start.

Joel Rosenman

Then came the first crisis. I got a call late on Saturday from our chief electrician, Howard Pantel. He said the rain had turned the ground into mud and washed the covering off the cables supplying the huge flow of electricity demanded by all the audio and lighting onstage. This had been worrying him, but now he saw that all of the foot traffic over the exposed cables was wearing down the cables' insulation.

Pantel said we needed to shut down the power to the stage or risk electrocuting thousands of wet concertgoers. Shutting down the stage would be a big deal. The crowd was wet, hungry, tired, possibly on the edge of cranky. I didn't want to turn off the music. I asked Pantel if there were any alternatives. He said, "Maybe I could install a bypass around the crowd." I asked him how long it would take. He said less than an hour. Which is exactly what he did. So we solved the problem without losing a minute of music. Nobody else at the concert knew what had just happened.

I handled the situation as if I often made decisions like that. In truth, I felt like I had no right to make the call. If the work-around had failed and we'd had to shut down the stage, it might have been down for hours. It could have led to a riot. But I couldn't convene a committee to make the decision. My partners were either up to their necks solving their own near-crisis problems or grooving and in no condition to make such a decision. In the end it worked out.

After the cable crisis came a cash crunch. The managers of the Grateful Dead and the Who were smart. They could see the condition of our fences and ticket booths. Then they saw the crowd of half a million, factored in the rumors that the promoters were stretched thin financially, and did the math. They also knew we needed the Who and the Grateful Dead to go on as planned, since the audience expected them. They were paid about $10,000 combined, around $72,000 in 2021 dollars.

The managers told us they weren't going to accept our check as payment. "Cash only," they said. John Morris, our stage manager, and I had a brief discussion, during which he made it clear that we would have a very unhappy crowd on our hands if the Dead and the Who failed to go on. John Morris told the Dead's manager that I was getting him the cash and then talked them into performing on schedule Saturday night.

Eventually, I called Charlie Prince, our banker at the local branch of the Sullivan County National Bank. It was around midnight, and I woke him up. It took him a moment to understand what I was asking. He said, "I can't get cash for you. Everything is locked in the time vault when we closed for the weekend. Even I can't open that vault until Monday." I said, "Charlie, Monday is too late. Anything you can do?" He thought for a moment and said, "Wait a minute, actually I don't remember putting one of the teller's drawers in the time vault. There are cashier's checks in there." I asked how long it would take to get them and type the amounts in the checks. "Maybe too long. The roads are solid with cars from here to the bank."

I told him to go outside with a flashlight, that a helicopter would find him and pick him up. I told John Morris to send a helicopter for Charlie. We had several choppers on call ferrying acts to the site from their offsite accommodations. The helicopter John sent picked up Charlie and deposited him in the parking lot of the bank. Charlie called me to say he was inside and that the cashier's checks were indeed in the teller's drawer.

I headed off on my motorbike to the bank to pick up the checks from Charlie. The checks went in my pocket and I drove back to the concert grounds, threading my way through the crowd. On the screen, Janis was singing "Piece of My Heart," so it was probably between 2:30 and 3:00 a.m. She was lit up like a jewel in the dark. The Who was due to go on at 5:00 a.m. to perform most of *Tommy*.

Country Joe McDonald
(Country Joe and the Fish's lead singer and guitarist)

I performed at many smaller festivals prior to Woodstock. There seemed to be one every other month between Monterey and Woodstock. So for me, playing in front of a large crowd was nothing new. It was like going to work. Woodstock was just bigger and more expansive. But there were other things about Woodstock that were exciting. Having an all-access pass let me sit on the stage and watch the show and the audience. The rapport between the stage and the audience was very intimate and casual, like the Avalon. I walked through the audience and went around looking at stuff and nobody hassled me or anything. Everyone seemed very relaxed. It was like a giant family picnic.

Up on the stage, you had to turn your head all the way to the left and right to take it all in. What was incredible to me is that everyone out there was on the same page. People were calm and understanding, which is what most of the music was all about then, especially coming out of San Francisco. But I didn't look at the crowd and think, "Wow, now I can sell more records." Seeing so many people brought a certain sense of peace and love, that we were one. But we weren't out there hard selling peace and love from the stage. We weren't asked to talk about that from the stage. We weren't there to preach. People knew in advance that Woodstock was going to be different.

Mostly everyone who attended Woodstock was respectful. When you watch the *Woodstock* movie, you see older folks who lived in the Bethel area being interviewed and saying, "We love these kids. They're so nice." I mean, it was really unbelievable. Everyone was nice. I remember being onstage and looking out at the sea of faces. As I performed, some beef broke out between two guys. The crowd in that area opened in a circle to get away from the pending violence and to give the guys room to fight. They began waving their arms around and stuff, and then somebody handed one of them a joint. One of the guys took a puff, the other guy took a puff, they were handed beers, they hugged and sat back down in the audience. The people around them calmed the situation. And that was the worst thing I saw at Woodstock.

147

I went out and did ten songs and then came off. I asked Robin, my wife at the time, "Should I go back out and do the 'Fuck Cheer' and 'I-Feel-Like-I'm-Fixin'-to-Die Rag' or save it for the band later on?" She said, "Nobody's paying any attention to you. What difference does it make?" So I did it, and the audience responded. They even started singing with me. I was really surprised to see that. I thought, "Well, it's too late to stop now." And that's what happened. I came off the stage and felt I'd done a good job. They liked it. They liked my performance. And it was a success. I felt happy.

Chris Stein

I didn't see all of the artists who played on Saturday, but I did get to see Jimi Hendrix on Monday morning. He was amazing. There were a lot fewer people there by then. Hendrix came on after Sha Na Na. Many people who were there hated Sha Na Na, so they drove a lot of people away. It was the only time I ever saw Hendrix. As we were leaving, he was playing "The Star-Spangled Banner" behind us.

I had already been playing in a band with friends. We opened for the Velvet Underground in '67 in New York. That came about after a friend told me the band that was supposed to open for the Velvets at the Gymnasium canceled. So the band I was in, First Crow on the Moon, went to the Gymnasium and played instead. The Velvets followed and they were awesome. Woodstock was the same kind of fantasy only on a much bigger scale. What you saw—the scale and size of the audience—showed you what was possible if you could pull it together and stick with it. I remember thinking that concerts like this should be going on every weekend.

Henry Diltz
(Woodstock photographer)

The most amazing moment for me as a rock photographer happened at Woodstock. I was right onstage photographing Jimi Hendrix from about fifteen feet away. Toward the end, he played "The Star-Spangled Banner." To my mind, when I heard Hendrix start the song, I said to myself, "What's he playing that song for? That's the official government song." Here we were at Woodstock, with all those people out there, all in one place, united against the war in Vietnam, and we're listening to the national anthem. Then I realized Hendrix was reclaiming it for us. As he played, it became our song. Years later, Gerardo Velez, Hendrix's conga player at Woodstock, told me he roomed with Hendrix and that for weeks each morning before Woodstock, they'd reach into a box and pull out any vinyl album. Then they'd put it on and play to it.

Velez said Jimi had been rehearsing "The Star-Spangled Banner" for a couple of weeks. In the army, Hendrix had been in the 101st Airborne Division and had it in mind to play the national anthem. It wasn't spur of the moment. In his mind, he was saying, "This is our song, too, and this is how we hear it." Or by playing all of those machine-gun and bombing sounds on his guitar, he was saying, "Our generation is right, war is hell."

Joel Rosenman

On Sunday morning, Governor Rockefeller had wanted to send in 10,000 National Guard troops. Reports had reached him that Woodstock was quickly becoming a massively large and dangerous civil-disorder risk. The National Guard would be sent in case nearly a half million people became disorderly. In all fairness to the governor, it's his job to anticipate such things. But John Roberts and I were on the ground and saw that the mood was relaxed, not agitated. The National Guard would only raise tensions or even panic the audience. John took the governor's call. Among us, he had the most conservative, businesslike voice—an adult, authoritative sound. Whatever John said convinced the governor to stand down.

At the time, none of us considered Woodstock a historic, watershed moment. We were just relieved that the talented people working for us were solving sizable problems with creative solutions. We also were thrilled by the crowd's spirit, cooperation, and peaceful vibe. Immediately after the festival, Woodstock was widely criticized in the media as a financial and organizational disaster. I certainly wasn't going to argue with that one. It wasn't until months later—maybe when the movie and album came out in 1970—that it began to be romanticized and to be elevated to the status of minor miracle.

149

For the people who were at Woodstock, I'm sure many discovered they were no longer a fringe element of society with their tie-dye T-shirts, joints, and feelings about the establishment, wars, and capitalism. There was a vast wave there that shared the same values. Woodstock changed me as well. I spent time in that crowd, and even though I wasn't cut from the same cloth and didn't really share their culture, I came to feel we were all the same. I fell in love with my generation that weekend.

THE ALTAMONT FREE CONCERT
(December 6, 1969)

Michael Lang
   (organizer)

I first heard about the Altamont Free Concert three days before the event. It was put together at the last minute. I knew the Rolling Stones were on tour that summer in the States, but I didn't know they were involved in Altamont's free show. Then I got a call from the Grateful Dead's office asking if I would come out and help the promoters. They were having trouble with their site at Golden Gate Park in San Francisco. Permits hadn't been issued. So the promoters had to move to Altamont Raceway in Tracy, California, about an hour east of San Francisco.

A lot of my former crew was working on the Stones tour, so I said OK. But I didn't become aware of what it was about or what they were facing until I got there. In the past, the Hells Angels had done security for the Dead at some of their shows. Sam Cutler, the Stones' tour manager at the time, was English and must have had a different take on what they were about. I believe it was the Stones' organization that agreed to bring them in to handle security. When I watched the Hells Angels ride in that morning and park their motorcycles in front of the stage, I knew it was a formula for disaster. Their bikes were everything to them, and in a crowd of 100,000 or so pushing in on them, that wasn't a great idea.

Though people like to refer to Altamont as Woodstock West, I think it just was badly planned and very last-minute. They had to move to

Altamont the day before the scheduled start. There was no real preparation for anything. It was just all these stoned people jammed into a field with the Hells Angels defending the stage. Other than the Angels, there were no stage barriers to keep thousands of people from rushing the stage if they wanted to. The stage was only a few feet off the ground.

Albert Maysles
(*Gimme Shelter* documentary codirector)

The opportunity for my brother, David, and me to film the Rolling Stones in 1969 began in late November with a phone call from cinematographer Haskell Wexler. He was unable to realize his own project with the group, so Haskell urged us to visit the band's suite the next day at New York's Plaza Hotel. We called and set it up. When David and I arrived, Mick asked us to film them in concert. We weren't familiar with their music yet, so Mick invited us to join the group the next day at their Baltimore Civic Center concert. We went. I suppose he had seen *What's Happening! The Beatles in the U.S.A.*, our documentary of the Beatles' first visit to America in February 1964.

In Baltimore, we watched the Stones in awe. They had this tension and charismatic quality that I knew the camera would grasp immediately. I also knew this was going to be more than just a concert film and that we'd have to find a story. We insisted on creative control, and Mick agreed. We filmed the Stones in the weeks leading up to Altamont. I had my shoulder-mounted 16 mm camera and David captured sound on his tape recorder.

The Stones saw we took what we did seriously and that we were about capturing what unfolded—without trying to manage the truth. We were accepted almost immediately. I didn't want to be invisible with my camera. A fly on the wall wasn't going to work. That's contrary to what's natural. I'm obviously there. I wanted the interaction between the camera and our subject, and that's what we got.

From the start, *Gimme Shelter* wasn't going to be a concert film. We always started our documentaries with a hunch of what the story might be. Then we remained flexible so we could pick up on the best story when it emerged and follow it. We had only one goal with *Gimme Shelter*: no interviews, just observe with the cameras. You run into trouble when

151

you try to tell truths through interviews. Audiences don't need opinions as much as they need information.

Watching a documentary, the audience assumes you're just capturing what's happening anyway. That's what the viewer wants. They want to watch a story unfold and they don't like breaks in the action. But perspective, angles, and editing are all something.

Ethan Russell
(Rolling Stones' American tour photographer in 1969)

From November 7 to December 6, 1969, I traveled with the Rolling Stones as their photographer on their U.S. tour. The Altamont Free Concert wasn't even part of the official tour. It was added at the end, at the last minute. The Stones were constantly being asked by the media if they were going to do a free concert. The question was almost an obsession. It was as if the Stones were being taunted to see if they cared more about people or money.

Massive free concerts had become emblematic of the times. The Stones put off answering the question until near the end of the tour, when they relented and agreed to appear at a free concert being organized in California. The Stones were one of the only major touring rock bands that hadn't been at Woodstock two months earlier. There was this presumption that their November–December tour was going to be bigger and better than anything that preceded it. Everything back then was supposed to be bigger and better than the last big thing.

But unknown to most people, the Rolling Stones were broke. They had just spent $15,000 to $25,000 to produce their tour. If the tour didn't work out, they were going to be out of business. Palm Beach International Raceway in Florida was supposed to be the last stop on the tour before they flew back to Europe for a few more performances. Then the Northern California free concert was added. But the concert ultimately was held at Altamont Raceway in Tracy, California. It turned out to be nothing like Woodstock or anything else we encountered on the road. The clash of cultures that evening took me years to fully understand. Woodstock was largely a middle-class festival. Many of those kids were in college or had graduated. Altamont was much grittier.

Big Jay McNeely performing at Los Angeles's Olympic Auditorium in the fall of 1951. Bob Willoughby crawled onto the stage to photograph the saxophonist.

Owner Leo Mintz in front of his Cleveland, OH, record store in the early 1950s.

Jerry Leiber, left, and Mike Stoller in Los Angeles in about 1950.

DJ Alan Freed hosting an R&B record hop at a Cleveland ballroom in 1951.

Integrated audiences attending Alan Freed's rock 'n' roll shows at the Brooklyn Paramount Theatre could stay for continuous, all-day performances and a film.

In Chicago, from left, Leonard Chess, Phil Chess, and Leonard's son Marshall Chess in the 1960s.

After Chuck Berry's "Maybellene" became a #5 Billboard pop hit in 1955, he added his "duck walk" while performing. Overnight, the electric guitar replaced the saxophone in bands, launching rock 'n' roll.

Elvis Presley in Miami in August 1956. Two months later, he would appear at the Cotton Bowl in Dallas, marking rock 'n' roll's first stadium concert.

A female fan reacts to an Elvis Presley performance in 1957.

Wanda Jackson was the first female rockabilly artist to tour with Elvis Presley, in 1955.

Kay Wheeler, left, Elvis Presley's first fan-club president, with Barbara Hearn, his girlfriend at the time, in Dallas in 1956.

George Wein, right, launched the Newport Jazz Festival in 1954 with Elaine and Louis Lorillard. The multiday event in Newport, RI, became a blueprint for outdoor rock festivals of the 1960s.

Joan Baez at the March on Washington in Washington, D.C., on August 28, 1963.

Peter (right), Paul and Mary sing during a morning rehearsal at the Washington Monument before marching with the crowd to the Lincoln Memorial.

The Ronettes on stage with Joey Dee and the Starliters at New York's Peppermint Lounge in the early 1960s.

The Beach Boys perform in Sacramento, CA, in the early 1960s. The band, from left, included Al Jardine, Mike Love, Carl Wilson, Brian Wilson, and Dennis Wilson.

Bob Dylan at the Newport Folk Festival on July 25, 1965, when he played an electric set on a Fender Stratocaster.

Ringo, Paul, George, and John attempt to be heard over the screams of more than 55,000 fans at New York's Shea Stadium on August 15, 1965.

Guitarist Jimmy Page and Led Zeppelin at the Boston Tea Party in 1969.

Frank Barsalona in the New York office of his Premier Talent agency in 1978.

Don Law in his Boston Tea Party office in 1969.

A 1968 concert poster for Philadelphia's Electric Factory managed by Larry Magid.

Fans wait in line to enter the Fillmore East, which operated from 1968 to 1971.

Josh White's Joshua Light Show operated behind a rear screen at the Fillmore East, creating liquid color imagery with overhead projectors.

The Grateful Dead performing at the Human Be-In festival in San Francisco in January, 1967.

In June 1967, upward of 100,000 teens and college students began arriving in San Francisco, kicking off the Summer of Love.

Jimi Hendrix at the Monterey Pop Festival. Hendrix set fire to his guitar with lighter fluid after the Who trashed their instruments earlier.

Woodstock coproducer Michael Lang in his trailer at the festival site in August 1969.

Lighting designer Chip Monck assembling a spotlight rig at Woodstock in 1969.

Sound engineer Bill Hanley perched above Woodstock in 1969.

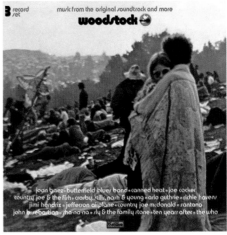

Music from Woodstock was released on a three-LP set in May 1970. The album and the Oscar-winning documentary, released two months earlier, celebrated the counterculture and turned the rock concert into a rite of passage.

Mick Jagger and the Rolling Stones at the Altamont Free Concert in December 1969. The concert was marred by disarray, beatings by the Hells Angels, and a stabbing near the stage.

The Beatles in January 1969 on the roof of London's Apple Corps being filmed to promote *Let It Be*, their last album.

Keith Richards disembarking from the Rolling Stones' private jet during the band's 1972 tour.

George Harrison, Bob Dylan, and Leon Russell perform at the Concert for Bangladesh at Madison Square Garden in August 1971.

Sly Stone with Jerry Martini, left, and Cynthia Robinson performing with the Family Stone at a Los Angeles benefit in the early 1970s.

The Allman Brothers Band in 1971 in Macon, GA. From left, Dickey Betts, Duane Allman, Gregg Allman, Jai Johanny Johanson, Berry Oakley, and Butch Trucks.

Ian Anderson of Jethro Tull performing in 1975.

Rock journalist Cameron Crowe, 17, in a hotel room while touring with Deep Purple in 1974.

Todd Rundgren in 1975.

Steve Miller at home in San Francisco in 1967.

Angus Young of AC/DC in 1979.

In 1969, shock-rock pioneer Alice Cooper opened shows by showering audiences with feathers by blasting a fire extinguisher into an open pillowcase. One night a live chicken was tossed onstage. The audience killed the bird and Cooper wound up with an enviable reputation.

The Grateful Dead's three-story, 28,000-watt Wall of Sound speaker rig in 1974 pushed many bands to upgrade their concert systems.

Bruce Springsteen and drummer Max Weinberg perform with the E Street Band in Atlanta in September 1978.

Pink Floyd's The Wall tour in 1980 and '81 was operatic in size and cinematic in scope. The most elaborate and theatrical rock tour to date, The Wall featured a range of special effects, including the stacking of white cardboard bricks during the show that came tumbling down at the end.

Summer Jam at Watkins Glen in July 1973 was attended by 600,000 fans, making it the largest outdoor rock concert to date.

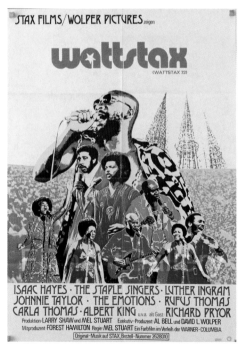

For California Jam, held in Ontario, CA, in April 1974, a stage system on rails was designed to tighten the time between acts.

Held at the Los Angeles Coliseum in August 1972, Wattstax was a one-day funk-rock concert that attracted more than 100,000 mostly Black fans and featured Stax recording artists.

After MTV launched on cable TV at midnight in August 1981, upcoming concert tours were announced each hour. The music channel's original VJs, clockwise from left, Nina Blackwood, Mark Goodman, J. J. Jackson, Martha Quinn, and Alan Hunter.

Grateful Dead fans wait on line for tickets in the summer of 1980 outside Radio City Music Hall. In the early days of electronic ticketing, fans routinely slept overnight at local outlets to buy seats.

John Oates and Daryl Hall performing at Live Aid in Philadelphia in July 1985.

Mick Jagger and Tina Turner perform "State of Shock" / "It's Only Rock 'n' Roll" at Live Aid in Philadelphia.

Live Aid producers Bob Geldof, left, and Harvey Goldsmith with the Who's Pete Townshend.

Drummer Phil Collins and his wife, Jill Tavelman, at London's Heathrow Airport. He had just performed at Live Aid at Wembley Stadium and was about to board the Concorde SST to New York and then on to Philadelphia to play Live Aid there.

When I arrived at Altamont on the afternoon of December 6, it was clear something was off. There was a general unease from the moment we stepped off the helicopter. Two helicopters flew us in. I came in on the second one with Bill Wyman and a couple of other people. The helicopters landed on the Altamont racetrack. When I hopped out, people were walking all across the field, and dogs and animals were wandering around. You could see there was no structure to how the concert was being staged or run. Mick had arrived in the first helicopter and was punched in the mouth by a ranting concertgoer. The mood was dark.

Earlier in the day, Keith had gone out to the site and found the scene mellow. That was the expectation everyone had. But by the time we got out there, the Grateful Dead had already bailed. They were supposed to go on before the Stones but they didn't like how things looked. The Stones were scheduled to go on at 5:00 p.m. They waited until early evening, since they didn't want to go on earlier, when the Hells Angels were menacing the audience and Jefferson Airplane.

To be fair, the promoters didn't have a venue until thirty-six hours before the concert. The initial venue for the free concert was Golden Gate Park. Sears Point Raceway in Sonoma was suggested, but the owners wanted a $100,000 escrow deposit. At the last minute, the owner of Altamont Raceway offered up his venue. The stage, lights, cables, and all the rest had to be moved within twenty-four hours.

Altamont was in Tracy, over an hour's drive to the east of San Francisco in the Central Valley. I grew up in San Francisco and I'd never even heard of the place. It was a completely different world from the city's Haight-Ashbury district. Moving the concert with so little time was driven by this belief that nothing could go wrong, that the organizers could make anything work. After all, it was music and we were taking over the world.

But a lot of people thought the scramble was a mistake and dreaded a disaster. Many thought the concert should be scrapped, including Bill Graham. The other thing was a new drug-culture mindset rising up then. In San Francisco, you had a "let's get high and listen to music" approach to drugs. Out in the far suburbs, where Altamont was, drug use was becoming more prevalent and reckless.

What's more, a lot of the Hells Angels who were brought in as security weren't from San Francisco. The Stones themselves had nothing to do with hiring the Hells Angels for security. I really do know that. The people who worked for the Stones handled that on a recommendation from the Dead's manager, Rock Scully. Also problematic was the stage, which only came up to your thigh. So people who were stoned were able to push up to the artists' knees, and some sat on the stage.

When I arrived at the racetrack, the crowd was already out of control. It felt horrible. My response was twofold, although largely unconscious. First, I didn't want anything the fuck to do with being there. I already had all the pictures I needed shooting the Stones at other stops on the tour. Second, I didn't have any real sense there was something going on in front of me that was different than earlier concerts or that I needed to cover.

Albert Maysles

The story we were looking for as documentarians emerged when the Hells Angels arrived on their motorcycles in the afternoon. The mood turned ugly pretty quickly. Our cameras were there when Marty Balin of Jefferson Airplane was beaten with pool cues and tensions climbed. We were there when the Dead decided not to play as a result.

When the Stones arrived by helicopter around 3:00 p.m., I walked with them to their trailer. Someone had to stomp down a low fence. Keith said, "Whoop, first act of violence." Talk about prescient. By the time the Stones went on, the Hells Angels were beating back people who were tripping and trying to climb on the stage. That guy Meredith Hunter was out of control and not happy about being roughed up by the Hells Angels initially.

When Hunter pulled the gun, he looked as though he was going to shoot Mick or someone onstage. A Hells Angel rushed forward and stabbed Meredith, killing him. Events unfolded too quickly. The group of cameramen we had filming there only had time to record what we saw. We shouldered 16 mm cameras that used film packs that lasted only ten minutes before they had to be changed. We didn't have the luxury of being afraid of what we were seeing. Fear requires time.

Ethan Russell

I should have caught what happened to Meredith Hunter. I was right there, on top of a truck, standing next to the cameraman who shot the footage for Albert Maysles's *Gimme Shelter* documentary. The stage was overloaded with people. It was terrifying, and Mick knew it. Bill Wyman later said to me: "The Rolling Stones have been scared maybe only two times. Altamont was one of them. Because you knew you could die. You knew. It was clear." I hated the event and wanted out. I took what pictures I did take. If I had been focused on what was happening, I would have had more images of the drama unfolding.

There were terrifying distractions. While the Stones were playing, holes would suddenly open up in the crowd in front of the stage as things became violent. People were pushing back to get clear of what was going on. Those holes occurred in response to things that were happening, without any warning. Up front, the crowd was cheek by jowl. I mean people were all pressed together so you couldn't move. I felt as if I was underwater, in some sort of nightmare I couldn't escape.

As the crowd pressed in, I felt like the oxygen was disappearing and it was becoming harder to breathe. You knew that beyond those rows of people you could see squeezed together up front were tens of thousands in the dark. Anything could go down.

To keep your cool, your mind automatically rationalizes the level of risk you're in. To make matters worse, the stage was in a field. There were no lights except the lights on the stage. You couldn't see anything out there in the pitch-black. If 50,000 people decided to stampede forward, it would happen fast and all at once. You'd never know what hit you.

Toward the end of the Stones' set, I got off the truck where I had been shooting and tried to get to the helicopter. Once you surrender to your fear, you have a single purpose—to get out. As I moved quickly to leave, I found myself blocked by a chain-link fence. It seemed impossible to climb. I managed to pull up the bottom and slither under. I found the helicopter and crawled in. There were two people already inside. I think it was certified to carry ten people plus the pilot.

By the time the Stones got on board fifteen minutes later, there were sixteen people in there. It was overloaded. Once the Stones boarded, nobody said a word. Everyone was in shock. I don't think they even looked at each other to exchange glances. I was on the floor. The helicopter blades started to turn but it couldn't take off vertically because of the weight. So the pilot had to taxi to take off. We just cleared the hill on our way to Livermore Municipal Airport, where cars were waiting to take us back to San Francisco.

The ride to Livermore was maybe ten minutes. Nobody said a thing. Once we landed, the Stones were gone. They were on their way back to San Francisco and then to Europe the next morning. Now I realize, of course, that the helicopter could have gone down in a heartbeat. I became a pilot years later, and the ride out of there that night with all that weight was so outside the envelope.

Everybody was responsible for the disaster at Altamont. Everybody. Mick was playing with "Sympathy for the Devil," but it was unintentional. He was doing that devil thing as a character. He put on a "costume" and played a role. After news of what happened at the concert circulated, the Stones were vilified as callous toughs who ignited a terrible thing to promote themselves. If Woodstock was about peace and music, the Stones were viewed as stirring the pot to generate drama and violence and bad-boy publicity they could later turn into profits. They still carry that stigma around with them. But this isn't true. I was there.

The Stones were just performing their tour act at a venue that was added at the last minute. The violent atmosphere was already thick when they arrived. They had no control over things and were at the mercy of the crowd. In many respects, they were prisoners of the situation. All you have to do is watch *Gimme Shelter*. Had the Stones cut their set short and left in a huff, there almost certainly would have been violence or a sudden massive rush by the audience, and we might not have been able to get out of there in one piece.

Albert Maysles

When *Gimme Shelter* came out, some critics said we were voyeurs who just watched the violence or exploited it for dramatic effect. There was no manipulation on our part, no encouraging anyone to do something or asking them to do something again. And there was no hidden message in the edit.

Our only point of view was to have no point of view. This unnerved a lot of critics. *Gimme Shelter* also altered perceptions of Mick Jagger and the Stones. The use of the Hells Angels for crowd control and the Stones' stage performance of "Sympathy for the Devil," "Under My Thumb," and "Street Fighting Man" during the beating scenes cast the group as sinister and callous. Which was totally unfair.

The Stones' song list was put together in advance. And the Stones clearly were horrified by what was taking place. They also feared that waves of stoned people were going to storm the stage. There were about 300,000 people in the stands and on the grassy hill overlooking the racetrack.

The Stones and the Grateful Dead took a lot of heat for bringing in the Hells Angels to serve as security. But you couldn't have a proper police force there. You would have needed a thousand officers. And everyone would have been arrested for drugs. I don't know if the crowd would have been more relaxed and in check if the Hells Angels weren't there. We could see class friction going on between the Hells Angels and the people in the front. They almost seemed to enjoy teaching the stoned kids a lesson.

To some extent, the Hells Angels were misunderstood. They really didn't know how to deal with what they were brought in to do. They were tough and knew how to look menacing, but they had no experience with crowd control and defusing dangerous situations. The problem was that the guy who was in charge of them wasn't there that day. He was sick or something. A younger, less experienced guy wound up in control of the others, and it turned out he couldn't manage them. Fortunately, I had my camera near Mick's trailer, where a lot of the freaky stuff was happening.

Mick was deeply touched by what happened that day. I think Charlie Watts was trying to make sense of the unfortunate circumstances, too. After we showed Mick the film, he had some strong reservations about it and didn't give me a release for six months. When he finally did, the

157

Stones had just one request: that none of the violence be shown separately, like for a promotion for the film. We understood what he meant and agreed.

We ended the film with the credits over people heading to their cars in the dark. It was very spacey. Charlotte Zwerin, our editor, wanted that left in. If the film had ended on Mick and then gone black, it would have said that Altamont was his fault, which wasn't the case.

Ethan Russell

Was Altamont the end of the 1960s? I don't think so. D-Day wasn't the end of World War II, but yeah, it was. Altamont wasn't the end of the '60s, but yeah, it was. It was the beginning of the end. When I asked the Stones' Mick Taylor if he thought Altamont was the end of the '60s, he thought for a minute and said, "Well, it was December, wasn't it?"

Mick Jagger's view and, to a certain extent, Keith Richards's view was that all of this turmoil in the United States wasn't the Stones' "war." They were just a band. That is the fundamental piece for them, and it's why they're still at it today. What Mick wants is for the audience to get up and dance and have a great time. He didn't want to be a movement's leader, except to the extent that it let him fill seats. Keith also didn't want anything more to do with it. The social turmoil was America's problem. And yet Altamont became the Stones' problem.

Woodstock was much more peaceful and much more wonderful, but there were problems there, too. They just weren't magnified. San Francisco was the heart of the national music, drug, and political culture. Woodstock, by contrast, was in Upstate New York. San Francisco and the region were out front, so it was the first to decay and show social cracks. I don't think you can overstate how quickly and dramatically mind-expanding drugs and transcendental aspirations became just plain shit-faced fucked up. Maybe Altamont wasn't the end of the '60s. Maybe it was the start of the '70s.

PART 3
THE 1970s

In 1970, the rock concert was in desperate need of an image over-
haul. Coverage of the violent events at Altamont by magazine journalists, photographers, and documentarians cast the free concert
in a shocking light. Outdoor free rock concerts had become dark
and unwieldy—attracting a runaway mix of hallucinogenic drugs,
thuggish elements, class hostility, violence, and bands onstage
projecting an aggressive image. What revived rock's reputation
and opened a new pathway to greater success was the rise of new
indoor sporting arenas, the proliferation of live albums promoting the appeal of these venues, and the expansion of mass-market
record-store chains that allowed rock to fragment into subcategories and find new audiences.

Rock album sales surged during the early 1970s largely because
young consumers acquired better stereo systems that included FM
radio bands. To meet the new demand for albums, department
stores boosted the size of their rock departments, and supermarket-
style discount record-store chains such as Tower and Sam Goody
expanded and dominated markets nationwide. By mid-decade, new
compact playback formats such as cassette tapes and 8-track cartridges joined vinyl in stores. The popularity of live albums early
in the decade was helped in part by the release of two Woodstock

soundtracks. They not only created a desire for rock concerts but also established the sporting arena as the best place to see them.

Greater floor space in record-store chains and department stores led to more product diversity. Bins needed to be filled, so record companies signed a broader number of distinctive artists and bands, widening the spectrum of rock styles in stores, on the radio, and in concert. Rock splintered into subcategories, and a new generation of journalists covering the music came up with names for the hybrids. Niche tastes developed as young consumers made choices based on what their friends were listening to, which concerts they attended, and which bands connected with their values. Gender, class, education, income, social causes, and even personal struggles, rather than collective generational issues such as peace and love, were now influencing rock choices in stores and on ticket lines. The result was a greater investment by record companies in album cover design and rock band imagery and promotion. The music of one-size-fits-all bands no longer had an emotional connection or appeal.

Chapter 11

IMAGE, MEDIA, AND BRANDING

In April 1970, Paul McCartney made the obvious official. Due to personal, business, and musical differences, McCartney announced, he was breaking with the Beatles. Which essentially meant the dissolution of the Fab Four. Five years after the Beatles' 1965 North American stadium tour laid the foundation for the modern rock concert, their divorce left a sizable cultural vacuum. Hard rock bands such as the Rolling Stones, Led Zeppelin, the Grateful Dead, and the Allman Brothers Band, to name a few, rushed to fill the void. In this regard, the 1970s began in January 1969, when the Beatles performed on the roof of Apple Records in London, running through songs for their upcoming final studio album, "Let It Be," for a TV documentary. When the TV project was scrapped, the documentary became a feature film that came out in May 1970, less than two months after the release of the popular "Woodstock" documentary and weeks after McCartney publicly called it quits. Rock and the rock concert began a period of reinvention as the Beatles slipped away.

Ethan Russell
(Beatles photographer in January 1969)

One day in 1968, after I left the States to live in London, rock journalist Jonathan Cott, a friend of my roommate, came to visit. He saw my photography at our flat, and before he left, he asked if I wanted to photograph his next interview subject. Jonathan was an American living in London and writing for *Rolling Stone* magazine. When I asked who his subject was, Jonathan said Mick Jagger. That's how I became involved with rock. After photographing Mick, which I had assumed was a one-shot opportunity, Jonathan called and got me John Lennon. John and I got on. In December 1968, after Neil Aspinall, the head of Apple Corps, saw my images, I asked if I could photograph the Beatles at Twickenham Studios. They were there rehearsing the music for what would become their *Let It Be* album.

Neil said absolutely not. A documentary was being filmed of them rehearsing and recording. I'd be in the way. Fortunately, the entire crew shooting *Let It Be* was the same crew that shot *The Rolling Stones Rock and Roll Circus* in 1968, including director Michael Lindsay-Hogg. I got along with them and knew I wouldn't be a bother. So I just drove down to Twickenham, about a half hour southwest of London. At Twickenham, I stood in the shadows, far from everyone else. Suddenly, I felt the presence of someone behind me. I wheeled around and there was Neil. He said he'd let me shoot for three days.

When I went to Apple to show Neil what I had taken, I put together a slideshow. Neil was there with Beatles' publicist Derek Taylor, the Beatles' personal assistant Peter Brown, George Harrison, John Lennon, and Paul McCartney. They liked what they saw. Someone suggested they do a book of images from the rehearsal. And so I photographed them for thirty days in January 1969 rehearsing and recording at Twickenham and at Apple Studios in London. Out of all of this came the images that became the cover of *Let It Be*.

On January 30, the last day of the Apple shoot, we all moved to the rooftop of Apple Corps. Lindsay-Hogg wanted to film the Beatles doing a spectacular event to promote the *Let It Be* documentary, which wound up being released in May 1970. What Michael had in the can was about the making of the album, which was great. But he wanted a bit of showbiz sizzle. I don't know whose idea it was to have them perform up there. The idea was probably the only thing they could all agree on.

The Beatles weren't on the same page by then. They were at odds with each other and starting to come apart and go their separate ways. The roof was a rather tame idea, actually. As I recall, Michael wanted to shoot them at the pyramids in Egypt. John also thought it might be fun. But each one of them had an idea the others shot down. The rooftop idea was the path of least resistance. It was just upstairs. And even that almost didn't happen.

At the time I was given the assignment, I didn't have a sense of their squabbles, but I sensed something was up when George walked out and they shut down for a week. As far as I could tell, George didn't seem to like being directed endlessly about how and what he had to do to make this thing work. He got fed up. So there was stress.

On January 21, when they moved from Twickenham to Apple, George returned. The roof footage shot on January 30 was to give the movie an ending. It was a private performance, even though they knew they'd be heard playing up and down Savile Row below. I don't think they paid much attention to it. You couldn't see them from the street, so psychologically they were invisible and protected from the threat of lingering Beatlemania. What I found impressive was how these guys could pull it together given all of the emotional baggage. They basically performed the songs straight through.

Everybody there was starstruck, including the policemen who came up to get them to turn it down. They were still the Beatles. I was starstruck. They had it all—the impossible talent, the lean looks, the money, and the extraordinary fame. They walked on water and were larger-than-life. That's why it was so hard to comprehend why they weren't getting along with each other and why they seemed to be tossing it all away. Everyone wanted to be one of the Beatles. But actually being a Beatle was a different matter, of course, with the stress, egos, family issues, business things, creative pressures, music deadlines, and so on. It was a lot of emotional work and there was never a break.

Strictly speaking, the rooftop filming wasn't a concert for those who were up there that day or for those on the street below. It was for those who would see the *Let It Be* film when it was released. Interestingly, the Beatles were playing live outdoors and for free at a time when free outdoor concerts were still the rage. The fact that there wasn't an audience made it more intriguing. So what wasn't a concert became a concert because people assumed it was or wanted to believe it was.

163

What I remember most about that day on the roof is throwing my leg halfway over the guard railing and leaning back. You see this in the film. We were five stories up, and there I was trying to get a wide-angle shot by backing up. If that guardrail had given way or shifted, I would have been down on the street sprawled on the sidewalk. It was a tough day for me as a photographer. I didn't have a motor drive that could have taken ten photos per second. I also didn't have an assistant to hand me cameras reloaded with film. I was alone. So I was racing around trying to get the best shots I could.

I didn't shoot a ton because I had only four rolls of color and black-and-white film. None of us knew the Beatles would never perform live together again or that Paul would announce the group's official breakup in April of 1970, long after they had split up.

My favorite photo from that day is the one I shot from a distance on the roof of a building next door. In the image, I was shooting them from behind. In the picture, they seem small in relation to the backdrop and expanse of old London rooftops. When you see the Beatles in the middle of the centuries-old city performing, they seem smaller and less looming. They were singing and playing for no one in particular surrounded by historic buildings that had been there forever. In that instant, they seemed less forever than their surroundings.

The Beatles' exit opened the market to a greater number of bands vying to become rock's top moneymakers. More bands and concerts meant more news, giving rise to new approaches to cover rock. The New Journalism of the late 1960s had created magazine writers who were more novelistic. Articles were more likely to express the writer's perspective beyond just the facts. Better rock journalists of the early 1970s covered bands and the music with this new writing style in mind. Prior to the New Journalism, most media covering bands were fan magazines such as "Teen Beat," "Flip," and "16." Cover headlines were gossipy and geared mostly to girls—"My Life with the Monkees," "Sonny and Cher's Twins," and "Swingin' With the Doors." The music and artists' personalities were largely ignored. The emergence of the rock album in the mid-1960s and the rise of the counterculture inspired Paul Williams to found "Crawdaddy" magazine in 1966. In '67, Jann Wenner and Ralph J. Gleason launched "Rolling Stone" magazine. Its stated mission was to cover not only rock but also "the things and attitudes that music embraces." The magazine would become a lifestyle publication. In 1969, "Creem" and "Circus" magazines arrived. The more fans learned about bands, musicians, and concerts through in-depth features and candid photos, the more popular rock and rock concerts became. One of the finest and youngest of the new rock journalists was Cameron Crowe.

Cameron Crowe
(*Rolling Stone* magazine contributing editor and writer)

I grew up in San Diego, skipped a few grades in school, and was always much younger than the other kids in my classes. My rapid advancement left me isolated, so I turned to music. Since I enjoyed writing, I began contributing rock album reviews at age thirteen to local underground newspapers and national music magazines such as *Creem* and *Circus*. After I graduated from high school in 1973 at age fifteen, I became a contributing editor at *Rolling Stone*.

By then, owner and editor Jann Wenner had been publishing and editing the magazine for six years. He had become even more driven to cover rock and the culture surrounding it with sophistication and attitude. Until *Rolling Stone* appeared, rock fans had little information about favorite bands except photos on album covers and, if they were lucky, some liner notes. Editorially, Jann set a high standard with his 1970 interview of John Lennon. That was the magazine's first lengthy interview where a rock artist went down deep in his replies to an interviewer's questions. Going forward, Jann was willing to let an interview run long or to break it into parts over several issues if it was revealing.

Internally, Jann's Lennon interview created a grid for other *Rolling Stone* writers. If you were going to write a *Rolling Stone* cover story, you had to bring something forward that wasn't known about the artist and get to the heart of what made him or her tick. From a kid's standpoint back then, when you read these articles, the music and band took on new meaning and you wound up with a greater understanding of them. The

165

willingness to wait in long lines for concert tickets was partly motivated by what kids learned about artists in magazine articles. The personal is always the universal.

Covering hard rock musicians and bands in the early '70s was like writing about outsiders. More established music writers wanted to cover top rock-folk artists and bands that were big then. Hard rock wasn't fully accepted yet, so there was plenty of easy access to them, and rock musicians were willing to talk and open up. Rock journalism was in its infancy, and no one from major media publications was pushing to interview musicians yet. I was fifteen, so most publicists and bands wanted to give me a break. I suppose they also saw me as someone who could help them gain exposure and attention.

At first, tours by rock bands weren't widely advertised. Ads in the underground press and mentions on FM stations were only about concerts coming in the next bunch of weeks. Hard rock was still below the radar. Unless you had a friend who worked in the box office of a rock concert venue or you knew someone who worked with a rock promoter, you had no idea who was going out on tour and coming to town months in advance.

I remember being at the San Diego Sports Arena in 1972. There was this wonderful company called Concert Associates. The guy who ran it was Larry Vallon. He was the first guy to let me backstage to do an interview, with a band called Wild Turkey. They were an offshoot band from Jethro Tull, featuring their former bassist, Glenn Cornick. Larry had this sonorous voice. In between acts during a concert, Larry would announce the bands playing in the coming weeks and months. If it was July, he might rattle off who was coming to the venue each week for the rest of the summer. Then, at the end, he'd add, "And December twelfth, Led Zeppelin." Obviously, the venue had just booked the band. The place would explode. No one knew that Zeppelin was going to perform until that moment. Larry's announcement was always a big dramatic thing.

The first time I went on the road for *Rolling Stone* was with the Allman Brothers Band, in '73. They were on the rise and let me into their "club." They knew I was serious because I had this huge notebook full of handwritten questions. I'd sit down and pull out my tape recorder and then the notebook. Their eyes would widen. They'd see pages and pages of meticulously detailed questions and their reaction often came in two parts: "Holy shit," and "Finally, somebody who knows our music."

What blew my mind most about rock musicians was the community that surrounded them. I didn't have a lot of friends when I was in school and I was smaller than everybody else. But in the rock world, they accepted me. Not solely because I could write a good story but because I also could talk music with them. The roadies were so good to me, providing access and insights. I also loved that they kind of looked like the musicians they were working for. On a Stevie Nicks tour, the women looked like Stevie. On a Neil Young tour, a lot of Pendleton shirts. I was happy to be in the club and I used the opportunity to ask tough questions.

There was some crazy stuff in between shows. Joe Walsh was famously a guy who could rev up a chainsaw in the hotel hallway. Maybe he was high, maybe just crazy, maybe all of it or none of it. It was showmanship on Joe's part. I've never met a musician who decided to be a rock star so he could get sex and drugs. In most cases, they heard a song that changed their lives, and they couldn't say no and they couldn't do anything else for a living. There just happened to be sex and drugs everywhere, but I don't think those things were first on the list of stuff to do or they wouldn't have been so happy to talk to me.

I considered some of the rock musicians I interviewed as role models because I didn't have a brother. Glenn Frey of the Eagles was one of my first interviews. He had little rules for how to conduct yourself on a date, for example. I soaked it up. As for female rockers such as Bonnie Raitt or Ann and Nancy Wilson from Heart, I grew up with women. So when I had to interview or tour with women, I always got along with them well. I don't think I was playing a role. No matter who it was, I was a kid in a candy store. Until the door shut on me, I was going to ask as many questions as I could.

Early on, my mother had her doubts. She said, "This isn't a career, this will never be a career for you. You're just going to be making managers rich. That's why they're being nice to you. We moved across the street from the University of San Diego, the best law school in San Diego, so you could go to law school. Now you're asking me to drive you to an Allman Brothers concert? Who are the Allman Brothers? What are they going to do for you when you're washed up at eighteen?" I didn't let my mother get me down. I just kept writing, and she became my best editor. She read my stuff and said, "That's pretty good." Or when I struggled, she had solutions and knew how to move paragraphs around. My mother didn't have newspaper or magazine experience. She was an English teacher and a reader and philosopher. If my copy went long, it was because I was so geeked out on the music that I just wanted to know all that stuff. It was really important to know, and it's still important to know.

I avoided the trap many writers fell into then—writing a glowing piece on a musician they admired. I didn't think consciously about avoiding that pitfall. It came naturally in response to editors who constantly warned me off this. On a Led Zeppelin profile, my editor said that if I was going to write about Zeppelin, I'd better take Robert Plant to task about those flowery lyrics. So I prepared to ask him about the lyrics but I also planned on asking him everything a fan would ask. I always imagined I was reporting from a front-row seat. If I had done a decent job, my piece was informative. I did get knocked for some stuff. I did a couple of pieces where I felt I needed to show some teeth. In retrospect, I was probably too tough. One was on a band I didn't really love. I didn't hate them, but I didn't love them. I felt as though it was a waste of a couple of days. So I decided to be snarky, but in the end, I wasn't proud of it.

A concert that stands out is the Who at the San Diego Sports Arena in 1972. The concert was almost a séance. I didn't have a general seating ticket. I had a ticket for up in the stands. When I saw that the guards weren't being real sharp about keeping people off the main floor, I wandered down and floated around. When the lights went down and everybody screamed, I rushed onto the main floor to find a seat. But suddenly, the audience surged forward and I got caught in the crowd and was pressed against the barrier at the front. I couldn't breathe.

The Who came out and Pete Townshend was wearing a crown and his white jumpsuit. He said, "Hello, San Diego, what a pleasure to play your trash can." The arena's design looked like one. They launched into a series of big Who songs. At one point, there was so much pressure moving forward, I thought I was going to get crushed or trampled. Suddenly, I kind of wound up under the human traffic and was spit out by the side of the stage. There was no way back onto the main floor after that. It was chaotic and somehow freeing at the same time, kind of like the Who's music. There also was a great view from that spot. I felt like I belonged there, with other people who felt like me.

The other big concert for me was going on tour with Neil Young in '76. Every night was different, and the set list always changed. Neil wasn't happy during a performance unless he went to that emotional place. I remember somebody asked him once, "How do you know when you're going to play 'Cowgirl in the Sand?'" He said, "When the man at the back of the arena tells me to." That's what made this holy to me and not just entertainment.

The notion that rock tours were a mobile world of groupies and excess always felt inflated by the outside world and the entertaining stereotype of decadent rock stardom. Many of those who partied hard worked harder, in my view. The tours were long and grueling, but the time spent onstage was always sacrosanct. And while there were certainly plenty of female platform-heeled "band aids," as they were known, there were plenty of women roadies and DJs and publicists who had a lot to contribute to the music and the performances. They were passionate and a significant part of the community that made the music so personal.

For example, Betsy Heimann worked with Neil Young as a wardrobe person and film assistant. She later worked in Hollywood as a costume designer on the movies *Reservoir Dogs* and *Pulp Fiction*. Later we worked together on my films, *Jerry Maguire* and *Almost Famous*. That feeling of closeness and community and the power of what happens in the dark when the lights go down and the show begins is with me to this day. It's more than entertainment. It was and still is everything.

To attract media attention, bands in the 1970s needed an image and a brand. Both defined who the band was and why they were special. Part of that image was established and fed by journalists and photographers. But the other part was handled by band managers, label marketers, and art directors who controlled the look of album covers and use of graphics. Rock band branding dates back to the Beatles' drop-T logo on Ringo's bass drum in 1963. The Who's target logo with upward-pointing arrow came next in 1964, followed by the Doors' geometric typeface in 1967, created by Elektra Records' art department. But these were mere labels. In the early '70s, a hit single or album was no longer enough for a rock band to stand out. To book lengthy tours and sell out venues over multiple days, bands needed a personality, a story to tell, and a mystique. Two arena rock bands that pulled this off in different ways at the dawn of the decade were Chicago and the Rolling Stones.

Nick Fasciano
(graphic artist and designer of Chicago's first nine studio albums)

Back in the late 1960s, I did a lot of work for Columbia Records. John Berg, Columbia's art director, frequently gave me freelance album cover assignments when hand-lettering solutions were needed. One day in 1969, he called me at home on Long Island and told me that Columbia had just recorded a new rock band with horns called the Chicago Transit Authority. They needed a graphic treatment on the album cover. We brainstormed and landed on using lettering that looked as if it was on a sign at an old Chicago rapid transit station. I drew a couple of roughs, John picked one, and I hand-lettered and painted the final directly onto a piece of old barn wood I'd been cutting up.

After the album came out, the city's transit authority objected to us using its name without permission. So for the next album, in 1970, Columbia cut the band's name short to just Chicago. John decided we wouldn't use anything on the cover except the word "Chicago." There was no conscious decision on my part to make the scripted Chicago lettering look like the Coca-Cola, Ford, or Chicago White Sox logo.

Subconsciously, we were using lettering to create a personality for a band that wasn't pictured on the front cover. Back then, most groups were on their covers to create a connection with record buyers or those listening to the albums. I'm not sure if the corporate decision was made because there wasn't time to gather all seven of them for a photo shoot or if the label didn't want to bother spending the money on a shoot because the band's future was still uncertain. Most likely, John wanted something out of the box to reintroduce the band as Chicago. During our conversation, he wanted the *Chicago II* album in 1970 to look strong, as though the lettering and cover were made of brushed aluminum. John wanted to make a bold, creative statement.

When the double album came out, it was a huge hit and was nominated for three Grammys, including for best cover. John figured, why mess with success. Going forward, covers would simply feature "Chicago"—using the same size logo with the same lettering in the same position. The only element that would change was how the name playfully appeared. John's thinking was that fans of the group would look forward to each album just to see the cool way the word "Chicago" was treated. Through the use of lettering, we'd give Chicago a clever, playful image. There was always a heaviness and strength to the lettering, offset by a lightness to the execution. Which is what the group was about—confident, sophisticated musicians playing catchy hit songs. I remember at one point founding member and songwriter Robert Lamm saying to me: "We are the logo."

This image carried over to their concerts. Even though they weren't on the cover, audiences had a feel for their personalities through the out-there, playful quality of their covers. There was an unspoken message in the design. Even though the band wasn't on the cover, you knew just by seeing the logo what you could expect once you tore through the plastic shrink-wrap and put the album on. The Chicago logo was a bold, soulful statement. That was always the goal.

Marshall Chess
(president of Rolling Stones Records from 1970 to 1977)
The sudden death of my father, Leonard Chess, in October 1969 was difficult enough. He was only fifty-two when he had a heart attack at the wheel of his car. The second shock was that he never signed his estate plans. Even though he'd had several heart attacks, he was superstitious.

Several months earlier, he and his brother, Phil, sold Chess Records to General Recorded Tape (GRT), a maker of reel-to-reel tapes, 8-track cartridges, and cassette tapes. Tape was becoming really big then as inexpensive players entered the market from Japan and allowed people to listen to music with convenience in their cars and at home. GRT needed music content and they had a lot of cash.

They bought Chess mostly for stock. I got restricted stock at $17 a share, but I couldn't sell it for a set period. When I finally could sell, I got $1.78 per share. Now, when I look back, it's all part of the trip. The new owners thought I was too young to run the business. They got rid of my uncle and all the old-timers. While attorneys were settling my father's estate, I decided to quit Chess. The new owners didn't understand that recording in Chicago was key to what we were about. I left in the spring of 1970.

One day the phone rang. It was Bob Krasnow, who co-owned Blue Thumb Records. Bob said he'd heard that the Rolling Stones wanted to get rid of their manager and that their label deals in the U.S. and U.K. with London Records and Decca were expiring. They wanted to start their own record company. Bob gave me Mick's home number. When I called Mick, he answered. I told him my dad had died, that Chess had been sold, and that I quit after the new owner took over. I said, "I heard you wanted to start something new." He invited me over to London to talk.

Two weeks later, in the summer of '70, I flew to London. Two days after I arrived, Mick called and asked me to come over to his place. He lived on Cheyne Walk, a high-end street in the Chelsea section, right on the river. I went over and rang the bell. Upstairs, we were alone in his living room. It was a whole other world of oriental rugs and paintings. He also had a long table with a ton of vinyl LPs out of their jackets, the way I kept them. I sat on his couch and we talked about what we could do together.

At some point, he put on Clifton Chenier's "Black Snake Blues" and started to dance back and forth in front of me. That's how we had our conversation. He said they had a rehearsal that night and that I should come to the rehearsal space and meet the guys. He said, "Why don't you go down to Keith's place and talk to him. He's a block away." He called up Keith and told him I was coming. I left and rang Keith's doorbell. I was let in and went upstairs. Keith and Gram Parsons were at a piano painted in psychedelic colors, writing songs.

I was a little nervous, since I was trying to get a new life started. I really wanted this to happen. That night I went to the rehearsal hall in East London. They were great. I told them I might be starting a label and that I had to hear back about their offer to start a Stones label in a couple of weeks.

On the fourteenth day, I got a Western Union telegram in Chicago from the Stones: "Let's make a deal. Come to London." So I did and met Prince Rupert Loewenstein, their business adviser. We signed papers. The Stones wanted to be on Atlantic. I knew cofounders Ahmet Ertegun and his brother, Nesuhi, who had been at my bar mitzvah. So I cut a distribution deal with Atlantic and set up Rolling Stones Records as a subsidiary. I was president. Ahmet said to me: "Just get me an album every eighteen months."

Sticky Fingers was going to be the first studio album on Rolling Stones Records. We had yet to come up with a design for the new label. We had all kinds of ideas. At this point, the Stones were in Rotterdam performing. So I flew to Amsterdam and rented a car. On the way, I had to gas up and pulled into a Shell station. In the United States, Shell stations had a yellow shell with a red border and red lettering. Not in Europe. All you saw was the yellow shell with a red border, no lettering. The image was so strong it didn't have to say "Shell."

That night, I said to the guys: "Let's try to develop a logo that's recognizable without typeface." That was my contribution. One of the guys in the band knew John Pasche, an art student in London. For some reason it became a tongue and lips, and we had many versions. Meanwhile, designer Craig Braun in L.A. was waiting for the final version so he could move forward with *Sticky Fingers*.

Craig Braun
(designer of the Rolling Stones' album *Sticky Fingers*)

When Marshall Chess first told me about the Stones' *Sticky Fingers* album project in early 1970, I asked him to let me design it. He told me

173

that Mick wanted to use an idea Andy Warhol had given him for the cover—a pair of jeans with a real zipper. For custom packaging like that, I was the industry's go-to guy. At that time, my company specialized in going outside the realm of traditional covers.

For *Sticky Fingers*, I comped up a half dozen different album package designs in addition to three zipper concepts. Meanwhile, I received a Polaroid from Warhol with his idea. I comped up all of the ideas and presented them to Marshall in mid-1970. All were really good. One was a triptych of Villa Nellcôte, a chateau Keith Richards owned in Nice, France. Another comp was in the style of Bambú rolling papers. It played into the Stones' rebellious image.

Marshall loved the Bambú mockup, but the design wasn't quite right. I wound up giving it to producer Lou Adler for Cheech and Chong's second album, *Big Bambú*, in '72. I also comped up Andy's zipper idea. My original concept was to have the cover unfold in three panels to display a full-length pair of jeans, from belt to cuffs, like a poster. Marshall and Nesuhi Ertegun at Atlantic looked over all of the comps. Marshall said they wanted to develop Andy's idea.

I kept working on the zipper cover and refined it through 1970. Fortunately, the music was being recorded at a range of studios, so we had time. The person in the jeans wasn't Mick or Andy or actor Joe Dallesandro. It was Corey Tippin, one of the hangers-on at Warhol's Factory. The concept we had was to make people think it was Mick. Ultimately, the zipper cover was approved by Mick and Marshall.

I asked Marshall when the logo art would be done. I told him I needed the logo—or at least a sketch so I had some idea of what it looked like. I wanted it for the inner sleeve and the spine and cover. Marshall said he had a stamp made using a black-and-white sketch that John Pasche had done. Marshall was using it when sending out notes to disc jockeys and stuff like that. Marshall sent me this small silhouette smudge of lips and a tongue.

Now we're into early 1971 and I was under pressure to deliver the artwork for approval to meet our deadlines. They wanted to release the album simultaneously in Europe and America in April to avoid the risk of bootlegging. I called in my studio manager and told him to blow up the image we had to twelve inches, top to bottom. Since I didn't have a due date for John Pasche's final image, I decided to move forward and design the logo based on what we had, and have my team make refinements. I was influenced by the stamp they sent and the lips and tongue of a woman airbrushed by Alan Aldridge in his book *The Beatles Illustrated Lyrics* in 1969. For the song "Day Tripper," Aldridge had featured a woman with large lips licking an ice pop.

After about six different logo design iterations, we had one I liked. Then we put the mechanicals together. The mechanicals are a blueprint of the finished product. You paste up all the graphics on the art board so the client can see what it will look like. The logo I art-directed is the logo you see everywhere today. In the perception of young people buying rock records then, the logo had a "fuck you" attitude. It was unisex and was meant to match the image of the Stones as bad boys. It also implied that it was Mick's mouth and tongue. The logo boiled down what the Stones were all about in one brandable graphic, the way corporations used symbols and typeface. All you had to see was the logo to know it was the Stones. Marshall insisted it should be only an image, without type.

After the mechanical art was pasted up, I didn't tell Marshall that I couldn't wait, so I went forward with my logo version. I sent an account executive on a plane with the final mechanicals to London. I told Marshall that the guy would be in the Stones' office in the morning. Marshall said he and Mick would arrive at the office late morning. I told the account executive not to leave the album artwork there and not to say anything about the logo. I said he should just put it in front of them and get them to approve it. The logo looked fine to them, and they both signed off on it. My account executive brought the artwork back to New York and we put the final art into production and made the color separations so I could start printing.

The Stones had enormous branding success with the logo at concerts. Starting in 1972, an image of the lips logo became part of the Stones' set design on tour. The logo also appeared on the side of the

Stones' chartered jet for their '72 American tour. It appeared on Mick Jagger's jumpsuit and on a sequined white tank top worn by Mick Taylor onstage during the tour. From then on, the lips logo became the dominant graphic whenever the Stones toured worldwide. When the *Sticky Fingers* album was first released in late April 1971, I remember saying: "One day, the Stones logo might be as familiar as Playboy's." For the record, it dwarfed the bunny.

Chapter 12

ARENAS, STADIUMS, AND TOURS

While arena and stadium rock tours seemed glamorous to audiences and group-
ies, the business of rock became grueling, lonely, and tedious in the early 1970s.
The pressure to perform, travel long distances between venues, wait in hotels
between shows to avoid fans, write songs, and record was cyclical and unrelent-
ing. One of the first arena rock concerts was held at Madison Square Garden
on November 2, 1968, nine months after the new sports arena opened. Deep
Purple opened for Cream on their farewell tour. But most arenas around the
country weren't as quick to embrace rock. Many arena owners feared that
rowdy concertgoers would damage the facility or that drug overdoses would
expose them to liability and tarnish the reputation of home teams that played
there. By the mid-1970s, however, arena resistance to rock began to ease. By
then, many professional sports venues were competing with affordable color
TV sets, and arenas with losing teams were in a bind as their fan bases shrank.
Much to arena owners' surprise, rock audiences turned out to be less rowdy
than expected and easier to manage.

Don Law
(Boston rock concert promoter)
In the early 1970s, the head of the Boston Garden hated rock, even
though concerts would ease the Garden's problem of having an empty
hall on the nights teams were on the road. What changed his mind

was the development of "peer-group security." After I started Don Law Productions in 1971, we decided it probably wasn't a good idea to put the police in front of the stage. The cultural clash between hippies and the police was combustible.

We decided that the police should be at the back of the hall and at the entrance. In their place, we put our people in plain clothes at the front of the stage, so there was a less highly charged cultural clash. These people looked like the people in the audience. I hired a group of guys who went to Harvard and established a red-shirt security team. They were big and burly, but when confronted, they were smart enough not to punch back. Instead, they defused situations with psychology and reason. It was the opposite of having the Hells Angels come in as security. That was an important transition because we had to convince the police that we could keep order and that audiences wouldn't destroy the building. Everyone wised up to this.

Larry Magid
(Philadelphia rock concert promoter)

After I started Electric Factory Concerts in the early 1970s, we began holding concerts at Philadelphia's Academy of Music, which seated 2,900 people. In 1975, we became the exclusive promoter of rock concerts at the Philadelphia Spectrum. This was no easy task, but fortunately we had the law on our side—or at least on rock's side.

The venue's original owner had gone into bankruptcy. The owner of the Philadelphia Flyers hockey team was presented with a very attractive deal by the bankruptcy judge to acquire the venue with little money down as long as we, the bookers, guaranteed twelve concerts a year. Concerts meant revenue.

The Flyers were early to get in there, followed by the Philadelphia 76ers basketball team. The teams didn't draw a lot of people then, so the Spectrum was looking for events to fill its roughly 17,000 seats and the financial void while teams were out of town. The Spectrum had been holding rock concerts since 1968, but we were able to dominate as bookers.

Kids from the suburbs began coming to the Spectrum's concerts. Some of them even wore long wigs so they'd fit in. When they returned home to more conservative neighborhoods and schools, the wigs came off. Suburban kids made us popular. You couldn't exist then in my business without a suburban presence. Philadelphia's community of concertgoing kids was only around 2,000 and not nearly enough to sustain the business week after week. So we had to look for other ways to sell tickets. We found out early that people came to shows no matter who was on the bill.

As the popularity of going to concerts grew in Philadelphia, people from three different states came in from 60 to 120 miles away. As a kid, all you needed was one friend with a driver's license. You also had fans leapfrogging cities—seeing the same show in multiple venues by driving a couple of hours and staying over at friends' apartments or with college friends in their dorms. Walking through the Spectrum's parking lot, I saw cars with out-of-state license plates.

I also saw that kids from different areas had different ways of dressing. But they all fundamentally looked the same—long hair, jeans, aviator glasses, Frye boots, and so on. Most had ties to Philadelphia or were drawn to the city's nightlife. I saw that early. Going to arena concerts was fast becoming a thing, a place to be among those who looked like you, shared the same values, had parents who were bugging them, and smoked the same weed.

In 1975, we also bought Philadelphia's Tower Theater, which had 3,100 seats. The Tower was a nice size and, because it was outside of Philadelphia, there wasn't any sales tax. There also was ample free parking. Soon after we bought the Tower, the acts we booked were getting bigger: Genesis, David Bowie, and Bruce Springsteen.

Jerry Mickelson
(Chicago rock concert promoter)
Most rock acts started their careers playing small clubs in Chicago like the Quiet Knight. That's where Bob Marley, Jimmy Buffett, Bruce Springsteen, and others first performed. Once acts grew in popularity, major promoters would snag them for 3,000-seat theaters and then larger arenas. To gain entry to the Chicago market, my partner in Jam Productions, Arny Granat, and I decided to build relationships with acts early in their careers so we would remain their promoters on their way up.

In early March of '72, we broke through with an agent at American Talent International after Triangle Productions and Howard Stein passed on a show. The agent sold us a show in Saint Paul, Minnesota, with Savoy Brown as the headliner, Fleetwood Mac as the middle act, and Long John Baldry as the opener. This was before any of those bands had hits. Just before we put tickets on sale, Savoy Brown had a huge hit called "Tell Mama," and Fleetwood Mac had just come out with their *Bare Trees* album. Our very first arena show sold out all 10,000 tickets.

At first, Jam wasn't able to produce major shows in Chicago. The competition was too stiff. So we branched out to get headliner shows at major venues in secondary markets. We booked concerts in Minneapolis–Saint Paul; Columbus and Dayton, Ohio; Indianapolis; and other smaller cities throughout the Midwest. In the process, we created something of a farm team. We started out booking bands in small venues and growing with them until they were big enough to fill arenas.

For example, we booked Van Halen as an opening act on many shows. We did the same with Journey in approximately twenty cities. Also with Def Leppard, Todd Rundgren, and Black Sabbath. That's what our model was based on. Build a relationship and then book them into fifteen or twenty cities. We grew with the performers we booked. They relied on us and we relied on them, and it worked. Instead of bands not being able to tour until they had a Top 40 hit, they could tour if their new album gained traction on FM stations. Throughout the 1970s, we produced shows in arenas in the Chicago region. By the late 1970s, we started to book stadium shows.

While regional promoters continued to develop strategies for cornering the concert market, rock and the sports arena earned a new level of respect after two concerts for Bangladesh were held at Madison Square Garden on August 1, 1971. Organized by George Harrison, the concerts aided East Pakistan refugees and raised an estimated $12 million. The resulting three-album box set, "Concert for Bangladesh," was a major critical and financial success, topping the charts in multiple countries and winning a Grammy. The live album further established the arena as a viable concert venue, and the concerts became a model for future charitable events, including the Festival of Hope (1972) at

*New York's Roosevelt Raceway, No Nukes (1979) at Madison Square Garden,
and Live Aid (1985) at JFK Stadium in Philadelphia and Wembley Stadium in
London. In addition, the Concert for Bangladesh helped repair the reputation
of rock stars damaged by the events at Altamont nearly two years earlier. For
the remainder of his career, Harrison would be thought of by fans as selfless
and altruistic. And he was.*

Henry Diltz
(Concert for Bangladesh photographer)

For me, as a photographer, the Concert for Bangladesh in 1971 was
similar to Monterey Pop in June '67, the Miami Pop Festival in December
'68, and Woodstock in August '69. I focused on the small picture—what
I saw onstage through my camera's viewfinder, not the music or the
historical significance of the event. Many of the artists at the Bangladesh
concert, including George Harrison, Bob Dylan, and Leon Russell, were
in critical transitional periods of their creative careers. Harrison, in particular, was finding his own way after the Beatles broke up. After his trip
to India in 1968, he felt strongly enough about the culture and people in
Bangladesh that he coproduced with Ravi Shankar two concerts to raise
money to help the refugee crisis going on over there.

I attended both concerts for Bangladesh at Madison Square Garden
on Sunday, August 1—one at 2:30 p.m. and another at 8:00 p.m. I wasn't
on assignment for a publication or shooting for any of the artists. I wound
up there by accident. Chip Monck, who was handling the concert's lighting, thought it would be good for me to take pictures and document it.
Bangladesh had been ravaged, first by a deadly cyclone that struck in
November 1970 and then by a genocidal war for independence with
West Pakistan in '71. The refugee crisis reached epic proportions, with
millions displaced without food or water. From what we saw and read
in the news, it was a horrible humanitarian crisis.

In 1970, I had spent four months in England living with guitarist
Stephen Stills at his Brookfield manor in Elstead. At some point that
October, he said to everyone there: "Come on, we're going to Amsterdam
today." He wanted to see Chip, who was doing the lights for a Rolling
Stones concert there. Stephen had an upcoming Madison Square Garden

181

concert on July 30, 1971. It was going to be his first solo performance at a major arena. He wanted to ask Chip to be his stage manager and lighting guy. So we went to Amsterdam and met the Stones backstage.

Stephen asked Chip if he'd do his concert, and Chip agreed. At Stephen's July concert at Madison Square Garden, Chip said to me backstage: "Henry, we're having a huge concert here on Sunday to raise money for Bangladesh. George Harrison, Bob Dylan, Leon Russell, and others are going to perform. You should be here, too." I said I'd love to but I didn't personally know any of the artists on the bill, so I wasn't sure how to go about getting a photo pass. Chip said, "Come early on Sunday and I'll give you an all-access crew pass."

When I arrived backstage that Sunday, Chip had me stash my camera bag under the lighting console onstage. He wanted me to blend in, like a member of the crew. Even though Chip's main console was way out in the audience, he had a smaller one in the wing. I put my camera bag under his control board. I had two Nikon Fs—one for black-and-white and the other for color—plus my lenses, a light meter, and stuff like that. I put on the crew pass and walked around like one of the workers, taking it all in. Out in the audience, I saw Allen Klein, George Harrison's manager. He was sitting a few rows back from the stage. He looked imperial, holding onto his cane. In the row behind him were two goons dressed like chauffeurs. Suddenly Klein pointed his cane at someone and said, "Who's that guy? Get him out of here." Obviously, I had to be careful not to touch my cameras until I had to. I didn't want to get kicked out by Klein and his cane.

When the afternoon concert began, I was with Chip in the wing near his soundboard and my camera bag. The concert opened with Ravi Shankar and his group. Then during intermission, a film was shown documenting the misery of East Pakistani refugees. It was heartbreaking. After, Harrison came out with Eric Clapton and Jesse Ed Davis on guitars. Leon Russell was on piano, Billy Preston was on organ, Klaus Voormann was on bass, and Ringo Starr and Jim Keltner were on drums. There also were horns and members of Badfinger, a group Harrison was producing at Apple.

After a lengthy set, Harrison introduced Bob Dylan, who came out, and they played a set. Up until then, I hadn't taken out my cameras. Probably because I didn't want to get booted, I was too struck by what I was hearing and seeing, and because I knew there was an evening concert later. But when I saw Dylan and Harrison together, it was time. The first pictures I took were with my telephoto lens. After lifting the camera to my eye, I waited until I saw the thing that was most interesting to me and then pressed the shutter button. I got Dylan in profile, with Harrison staring at him and playing. It's still my favorite image from the concert.

During the second show, I was more comfortable and no longer feared Klein. I went out front and took a straight-on shot of Harrison at the microphone in his white suit. I had never really seen Harrison alone onstage before. There was a certain intensity about George, a fierce seriousness. The uncertainty following the Beatles breakup a year earlier may have been part of it. There also was fatigue. The work that went into setting up the concert and calling around to ask friends to perform must have been exhausting and stressful. And then there was the concert's purpose and the humanitarian crisis in Bangladesh that hung over the event. All of this was part of George's expression.

At the time, I didn't have a historical sense of the concert. It was the first time that all-star rock musicians were coming together to perform for a charitable cause on such a large scale in an arena. I was wrapped up in my scene. I was in there under false pretenses with a crew pass, so I was just trying to avoid being exposed and bounced. To me, this was just part of a long series of significant rock events I had photographed. But it also was the first concert that showed rock stars cared about the world they sang about. They were ambitious, they were driven, but they also had deep souls and big hearts. Bangladesh was a full-blown fundraiser.

The rock band that first exploited the arena format and stagecraft in the early 1970s and became identified with sizable indoor performing before moving on to stadiums was the Rolling Stones. Mick Jagger's strutting onstage and taunting singing style backed by the Stones' half-lit, solemn faces and British helmet hair styles were rock-noir perfection. Though their two-month 1972 American

183

tour was plagued with crowd violence and arrests as well as fan and police injuries, the band was the first to grasp the importance of granting access to celebrity journalists and novelists and photographers and filmmakers, such as Peter Whitehead ("Charlie Is My Darling"), Jean-Luc Godard ("Sympathy for the Devil"), Rollin Binzer ("Ladies and Gentlemen: The Rolling Stones"), and Robert Frank ("Cocksucker Blues"). They also created a formula for simultaneously empowering and enticing male and female fans, largely through stagecraft that spoke to different groups, all while avoiding another Altamont. This push and pull created nervous energy both onstage and in the seats.

Marshall Chess
(president of Rolling Stones Records from 1970 to 1977)

Mick Jagger and Keith Richards were the Rolling Stones' coleaders, even though at times they weren't on speaking terms. They were partners in songwriting. Mick took touring very seriously. He went on diets before tours because it was so strenuous, physically. For the '72 tour, we began by finding a place for the Stones to rehearse for two to three weeks before the tour started. The band would get together every day with their assistants. Peter Rudge, their manager, would shuttle back and forth between them.

The Stones would start rehearsing in the afternoons and go all night. They'd jam and slowly go through their material, working out a set. Once the set list of songs was established, that's what they performed for the entire tour. It was like an act, but it had to be crafted. Each day, they'd play and play and eventually, two or three nights before the first concert, they'd narrow down the list and rehearse the set through. Then they'd make a few final moves and the set would be locked. These guys worked hard.

Then came the first concert. That's when the crafting really started. On nights following the first and second gigs and after the first week, we'd all get together and tweak the show to make it better and better. Some gigs had an encore, others didn't, and the Stones typically left as soon as the concert was over. They took polishing and perfecting seriously. It's what set them apart. They worked harder than most other bands, and it showed. But it wasn't just the music.

Six weeks before the first concert, Mick would spend a lot of time with Chip Monck, who was doing production—lighting and sound. Chip was big on detail, on knowing every little thing. They'd review details about how songs would be performed and how each member of the band should be lit, including what colors, when a color would change, what kinds of speakers and mix, and so on. Mick and Keith were very much in control. They knew what they wanted after years of doing it and they were in charge. Then we'd discuss their decisions.

Chip Monck
(lighting director for the Rolling Stones in the 1970s)

Whether it was lighting Monterey Pop in 1967, Woodstock and Altamont in 1969, or the Rolling Stones in the 1970s, the only thing that made my craft different was the specific use of follow spots, what I call my paintbrushes. When a band like the Stones has a principal artist like Mick Jagger and a secondary principal like Keith Richards backed by supporting players, there are levels of importance for lighting each member on songs, depending on their actions at any given moment onstage.

Each song has a color to it, and there's a lighting choreography that takes place throughout the song that must be worked out in detail before a performance with the artists. My lighting choices are based on my interpretations of what the lyric line and melodic line need. The importance of the follow spots rests with their size; the intensity, being the brightness of the light; and the color used, which may be one or two frames to get a color that is mildly less than that of the one used on the principal.

Color illustrates and enhances a song's thematic elements expressed by the lyrics and melody. Color's purpose is to make the audience feel more deeply about what they're hearing. For example, I used a goldish hue when lighting "Satisfaction" because, psychologically, the song is about someone who is unsatisfied and they're looking for a pot of gold. It's an unconscious thing. So I lit Mick a light orange-amber, which is in the gold register. Mick Taylor and Keith are fighting each other for their principal grasp, so they may be lit with a deeper shade of orange-amber along with Charlie Watts. The rest of the band might be different shades of lavender. The goal is to take the principal and bring him out of the pool.

If I did my job correctly, the audience felt fulfilled. The audience came to hear the Stones, having heard an album or being a fan. In their seats, they were seeing it. But the electrifying thrill of seeing stars like the Stones onstage wore off quickly without lighting. As performers, they needed to be lit properly to intensify the mood of what you were hearing. I'm not telling you anything the Stones don't know. It's why they wanted me there. All I was trying to do is substantiate an audience's interest and the cost of their tickets.

I like to think I pioneered the art of making something onstage more emotional and enthralling so the audience felt that the music they heard at home was even bigger and more dimensional. Since the invention of electricity, lighting has been functional and dramatic. For me, it also is a way to push the audience's psychological buttons and make the experience more rewarding. That didn't exist at rock concerts previously.

Marshall Chess

In the hotel, everything the Stones needed was in the room or could be brought in. Typically, they didn't go out. There was too much risk and money on the line. Most of the time, the Stones and everyone else just sat around in the common suite during the day, like in a college dorm or a reception area. Usually it was very quiet. People were reading the paper or just talking. After a show, they were so drained, there was nothing left. It's like a meditative state of quiet and reflection. It's a relaxed vibe. I was shocked. I never knew how they felt between shows until I experienced those blocks of time firsthand.

Before a concert in the '70s, Mick didn't really say too much. Like all performers, great ones and average ones alike, he had nervous tension about getting out there. I hung out with Keith more than anyone. He was the most relaxed. Mick Taylor in the beginning was intense. Like many artists, he had a touch of stage fright. It takes a lot out of you to get onstage in front of so many people and play well, to put your emotions out front and be on your game night after night. In some cases, you hate the wait and want to get out there immediately. All that nervous energy is bottled up inside of you ready to explode.

Playing indoors or outdoors didn't really matter to the Stones. Arenas were safer in many ways than festivals had been, but there were many arenas that were shit. Outdoors placed you on a stage that was up and away from a mass audience, but stadiums were weakest in terms of sound. If you asked the Stones, they would have rather played smaller venues. The magic is totally different indoors. Now, outdoor concerts have evolved and crowds look at concerts differently. They watch the Stones on big screens and the digital systems are much better and easier to tweak and control. No matter where you're sitting or standing, you feel as if you've had an intimate concert experience.

After the chaos of Altamont and the rise of arenas, the Stones were happy having that kind of controlled environment. But they were comfortable wherever they played. My first concert experience with the Stones in the United States was after Altamont and during their American tour in '72. By then they had learned their lesson and there was better professional security. But crowds could still get out of hand. You'd see all kinds of stuff at a concert. Everyone was excited, many of the people there were high, and it was the Stones.

As the 1970s evolved, the touring bar was raised considerably. There were more venues, more nights in the same place, and greater tensions. To a fan, touring looks exciting, and it was in many respects. But a fan who has tickets to see a concert is there for a couple of hours and then goes home to talk about it. For the Stones, they're doing this for weeks on end or longer, with the stress of travel, uneven sleeping hours, hassles, loneliness, and everything else. And by then, they were so big and easily recognized on the street that they became captives of hotel suites.

While I was in charge, they were #1 on the album charts in the United States and in many other countries around the world. That included *Get Yer Ya-Ya's Out!*, *Sticky Fingers*, *Exile on Main St.*, *Goats Head Soup*, *It's Only Rock 'n' Roll*, and *Black and Blue*. When I left in '77, *Some Girls* was being made. By then, I was ready to change chapters. The Stones didn't rely on outside people or bands to craft their thing on albums or in concert. They were very on top of their own image and performance. Little by little on the road in the 1970s, they morphed into the roles they had been playing onstage and in the press—British bad boys.

The Stones weren't the only band with high standards and growing pains. Other major rock bands in the early 1970s found themselves vaulting from ballrooms and theaters to arenas almost overnight. The ability to draw huge arena crowds was almost always the result of a hit album and the ability to jam on songs. Long solos were a selling point. Among the musically skilled bands that could pull this off were Jethro Tull, Sly and the Family Stone, Todd Rundgren's Utopia, the Steve Miller Band, and Thin Lizzy. But all struggled to adjust to louder arena sound, a much larger stage, and blinding lights.

Ian Anderson
(Jethro Tull founder, songwriter, lead vocalist, flutist, and guitarist)

At the start of our arena experience, Jethro Tull, unlike a lot of bands, didn't pack the stage with more and more speakers and amps. That always seemed to be unproductive as a musician, as a record producer, and as someone with an ever-adjusting eye for technology. At arenas, it was far better to have a great PA system and not to make too much noise onstage. Let the PA do the work and keep your amplification to a minimum.

That's because the quality of sound tended to be erratic, especially at arenas. Guitar amps were like a searchlight beam of high-energy audio reaching out into the audience and deafening people. But not everyone out there was touched. We found that people who were three or four feet on either side of that sound beam experienced the audio level dropping off by many decibels. So you had some people who were being blasted out of their seats by a guitar or vocal while others were neglected.

But what we did onstage had to change a bit at arenas. There was more stage to fill, and the arena audience expected theatrics of some sort. Alice Cooper, in a very obvious way, understood and pioneered this. With our *Thick as a Brick* album tour in '72, we started doing things with stage props and people coming on the stage. They were weird, surreal little elements in the show that were fun and amateurish. That was the era in which all of this grew up in terms of going from the rather shambolic rock band wandering casually onstage and then spending ten minutes tuning up. We wanted to make the stage more dramatic and exciting. You couldn't just stand there and play. The audience needed visual engagement and stimulation.

Which only made sense. I was out there preoccupied with remembering the set list, all the notes, all the lyrics and putting everything in the right order. I also had to control the physicality of my performance, because I'm jumping around and doing stuff that I do while singing and playing the flute. It was a pretty aerobic and demanding thing. So like a tournament tennis player, I constantly had to monitor my performance and what I was doing physically. The key was not to overdo it, to keep something in reserve. You're totally absorbed in all that stuff, trying to get the job done.

Large-venue concerts could be nasty. In October 1971, we were due to play the Red Rocks Amphitheatre, an open-air venue built into the craggy landscape about ten miles west of Denver with nearly 10,000 seats. When we got there, the police wouldn't let us go up the hill to the venue to perform because there were too many people and the crowd was getting rowdy. The police told us the show was canceled. I said if we weren't allowed up there, it would get a whole lot worse. They still wouldn't let us up.

So we ran the police roadblock and headed up the hill, followed by police cars. I jumped out and went straight onto the stage. Through the PA, I pleaded with the audience to calm down and pleaded with the police to stop lobbing tear gas into the crowd. We actually went on and played. We had to leave the stage a couple of times because of the gas, but we did actually get through the show and calmed a situation that could have been dreadful had we not done that. It was very apparent that we had to try and be the peacekeeper, to try and keep calm and exercise what authority we could in that regard.

As a performer, I was very active onstage. I became very full of the music, and the music took me over. But all that jumping around took its toll on my ankles, knees, and wrists. I had a lot of stage injuries. I damaged both knees progressively over the years because I was wearing either shoes or boots that had very hard solid soles and heels, like cowboy boots. Just the jarring of my stomping and jumping caused me progressively a lot of knee problems, which I still have to this day.

189

In addition to the pounding, arena stages were quite dangerous in the dark. There were places where panels came undone and other places where you bumped into things and tripped over other things. Injuries were inevitable when you played night after night after night. What I would do is try and learn the stage's geography during sound check in the afternoon, when the venue was brightly lit. I'd learn where the trouble spots were. During our performance, I'd be blinded by spotlights, which made me feel as if I was in the dark. Even things as simple as getting on and off the stage were dangerous. You didn't want to head the wrong way and then step off an eight-foot-high stage into oblivion.

I'd pace out everything and get sidelines and directions in my head so I could do it in the dark. During the sound check, I'd walk the stage to determine the solid, safe areas and limit my activity during the show to those zones. I also would try and play whatever songs we were due to play that night. I'd take my position onstage and look around. I'd also review with the lighting director where I should be during songs to make sure the lights were focused where they had to be and it was a safe area. It's probably like the way race car drivers walk the track to see where the problems are and what should be avoided.

With success came more work. In the mid-'70s, we began transporting our own stages so they were the same each night we performed. There were certain risers and bits and bobs on the stage that were more or less familiar. By the late 1970s, we had two crews and two trucks, leapfrogging —one arriving at the venue and the other going on to the next one. And there were two nine-foot Steinway grand pianos leapfrogging the same way. So while you were playing one show, the other crew in the other truck were setting up the next place. The drag is it was double the cost. The only way we could afford that is by selling a ton of tickets to an awful lot of people. Which meant more arenas. It was a vicious cycle. This necessity made me yearn even more for the simplicity of theaters and for a small crew.

We didn't have hangers-on with us. Everyone was part of a tight-knit group of people working together. There's something invigorating about that. By the late '70s, we began introducing theaters back into the mix. But during all of this in the '70s, as concerts were held in larger and larger places, the music business became ugly. Arenas were more profit-able, so they became a bigger deal, like a sporting event rather than a concert. Trying to manage an audience high on drugs and booze or just the rowdy atmosphere of the place was a challenge. Audiences could be loud and demanding, which I found threatening and uncomfortable. As we became bigger, I felt embarrassed by the attention and the hype that surrounded any successful band. It became increasingly difficult to live up to that mass demand.

The concert business became more organized in this climate and became increasingly ruthless, anonymous, and uncaring. Promoters were a big, important part of the scene, but of course, they had to adjust and change, too. Like us, many of them in the '70s had started off as ama-teurs and had to figure out how to make it all work. They were finding their feet. They had to figure out how to do things efficiently and cost-effectively. Once things started to become a process, the earthiness and human quality got squeezed.

As the concert process developed, touring became increasingly gruel-ing. You traveled, you waited, you played many of the same songs each night in different cities. Some musicians were happy only when they were onstage exposing their emotions. Offstage, they felt either lonely or disturbed, or they felt desperate. They couldn't let it go. They had to have people around them, like the entourage Jimi Hendrix had around him toward the end of his life. Artists like that couldn't bear to be alone.

I was always happy in my own company. The same was true of our guitarist, Martin Barre, when we were superstars, as it were. We would go back to our hotel rooms and read Agatha Christie novels or watch *The Dick Cavett Show* on TV or something. Completely the opposite of what you would imagine, because we actually enjoyed the privacy of being alone and doing something we enjoyed, no matter how uncool it might have seemed for a rock star. I looked forward to playing in New York because I could go to a favorite delicatessen on Eighth Avenue that had enormous sandwiches.

Martin and I would get strawberry milkshakes and enormous roast beef sandwiches. They were so thick you literally couldn't get your hands around them. We'd live off those for about three weeks.

It was a life completely opposite of what you'd expect of a rocker. After a concert, I loved getting back to my hotel room. I'd do my own laundry, hang up all of my soaking wet clothes, get naked, lie on the bed with a cold beer, and watch Dick Cavett on TV. What a perfect postconcert pastime.

Jerry Martini
(Sly and the Family Stone cofounder and saxophonist)

One of the first big venues that Sly and the Family Stone played was the Oakland–Alameda County Coliseum Arena in Oakland, California, in March 1967. It opened a year earlier and was home to hockey and basketball teams. We first played there just months after Sly and I formed Sly and the Family Stone in '66. I can't remember how many people showed up that night, but the arena had around 15,000 seats.

I had known Sly since the late 1950s. We played together in the Bay Area. He tried three times to put together a band in the early 1960s, but each time it didn't work out. The problem wasn't Sly. He was driven and took music seriously. He'd rehearse six hours a day. He gave up initially because the musicians he recruited didn't show up or they turned up late or they were messed up when they did.

Cynthia Robinson
(Sly and the Family Stone cofounder, trumpeter, and vocalist)

When our first album came out, Epic didn't do much for it. They didn't promote us or anything. Epic was a throwaway label then, so the album wasn't supposed to make any money. CBS Records talked to Sly about writing music that was more danceable. Sly could write those all day long. So he wrote "Dance to the Music," and it took off. The title is sort of funny. CBS asked for something people could dance to. So Sly came back with "Dance to the Music," almost tongue-in-cheek, like: "Here's the song you asked for about telling listeners to dance to the music." He didn't want me to sing the words. He wanted me to shout, "Get up and dance to the music." That's why I'm screaming. It had greater impact. The music was commercial, but it was serious. Sly knew only one way. Suddenly the throwaway label had a hot act.

Jerry Martini

The first time we played New York's Apollo Theater, in July 1969, I got booed. The Black audience up there wasn't used to seeing a white face onstage. We used to get introduced and come out one at a time. I went right after trumpeter Cynthia Robinson. Well, I came out and people started booing me. It freaked me out. Then Sly came out and stopped the concert. We hadn't really started yet. He went up to the mic and said, "You know what? It ain't about what color you are in this band. In the Family Stone, I don't care if you're Black or you're white. If you can play, you have a chance to be in this band. Play, Jerry." After I got through freaking out, I closed my eyes and played some blues without accompaniment. Then a girl in the audience yelled out, "Send that boy out here." The guys in the audience started laughing. Sly counted off the band and we started playing.

That August, we were at Woodstock. After Woodstock, we started being booked into arenas. Sly was very much into audience control from the stage. He had eyes that could look through you, even onstage. By that time, he was so popular and charismatic, he could start a riot or stop one. One night, when we played Madison Square Garden in the early 1970s, people kept getting rowdy. The cops came in, and it looked like they were getting ready to beat people over the head. Sly stopped the concert and he said to the audience: "Look, do you want the cops to say you guys can't control yourselves?" The audience yelled back: "No!" Sly said, "Can y'all control yourselves?" Sly pointed at the biggest guys he could see from the stage and appointed them sergeants at arms. He told them to control their areas and keep people from moving forward. They could stand up, but moving toward the stage was a threat.

He did stuff like that back then and audiences responded. At the Garden, they calmed down and didn't get out of hand or try to rush the stage. He warned them by saying, "If you don't control yourselves, they'll control you." To those sergeants at arms, he said, "If people around you get out of hand, tell them to cut it out." It wasn't like an order or anything, just obvious. But the big guys he picked felt empowered and they took responsibility. Then he turned to the cops, who were ready to come in and kick ass. He looked at them and said, "I know you do a good job and everything, but if you could do me a favor and stand down, right now, I promise there won't be anybody running up on the stage and nobody will get out of hand." And the cops backed off. At the next concert where all of that happened again, the cops backed off and we saw them all dancing to the music.

Cynthia Robinson

After we went into arenas and were pulling in crowds, other artists and bands envied that we could be ourselves without giving up our feel. Guys like James Brown, Rufus Thomas, George Clinton, Stevie Wonder, Kool and the Gang, and others. They figured out what we were doing and did it. We could go long and really open up at concerts like at the Fillmore because we practiced for hours. When we reached a level of perfection, the guys often added another rhythm thing and we'd have to rework the horn parts. We constantly changed the groove because we could.

Jerry Martini

As the number of arena concerts we played picked up, we no longer had $20 speakers and $10 sound people. We had better gear and professionals setting us up. We didn't have to do nothing except be ourselves, which was Sly's dream to begin with. Arenas meant more money, and more money meant better clothes, better people working for us, and bigger stages. For us, 20,000 people at arenas loving what we were doing and singing along was an adrenaline rush.

When we performed, I liked to find somebody in the audience I could lock eyes with. That gave me energy and motivation. I looked for people who weren't digging Sly. Every concert had a certain number of people who loved horns and watched me and Cynthia. Just regular people, all ages, all genders. Playing the saxophone in arenas back then was tough from an acoustic standpoint. You didn't have wireless mics yet. You had to get close to your standing mic and play your ass off. Same with Cynthia. You had to put everything into it to be heard.

When we started playing arenas, we had more room to put on a show so we set up wider. Our music also became louder in those large venues. It's one of the reasons why I'm partially deaf now. Roadies used to compete with how many amplifiers they could stack on that damn stage behind us. We had to stand in front of those things and get hammered. You'd be tormented by the sound. By the mid-'70s, Sly turned me loose. I was able to blow some real solos. Up until then, we just played our parts and it didn't matter. I'd get stoned and play my horn parts and put on a happy face. But I liked being able to blow and expand.

Cynthia Robinson

All the songs we were doing were different. They made a political statement, either about racial justice or just kindness. When we got up onstage at arenas to play them, they sounded easy to the audience, almost childlike. Songs like "Hot Fun in the Summertime" and "Everyday People." But they were all different and very sophisticated. Everyone in the band had to pay close attention to the rhythm section and Sly. He often cut something off and went right into something else, which came from his disc jockey experience. You had to be ready for that. The band sounded improvisational, but we were highly choreographed and rehearsed. Meanwhile, with all those people screaming and our sound system cranked up, we'd try to hear him above it all. You played with the dread that at any minute, he might shout, drop his hand, and go into something else. So you watched him out of the corner of your eye. You definitely didn't want to get caught hanging.

Todd Rundgren
(Utopia founder, singer-songwriter, instrumentalist, and producer)

Early in my tour days, in 1972, when my band opened for Alice Cooper at a number of his gigs, we played small 7,000-seat arenas like the Knoxville Civic Coliseum in Knoxville, Tennessee, and the Orlando Sports Stadium, an indoor arena in Orlando, Florida. At the time, these midsize sporting arenas were mostly in the South and could handle college sports teams and students. We didn't have a whole lot of special effects at the time. Alice was chopping his head off and hanging himself and stuff like that. Our thing was we essentially could play forever.

In the early '70s, I had a different existence than most other musicians. While I fronted a band, I also had a thriving production career. Inevitably, I was going to end up in the studio producing someone. But in those days, I was as likely to play new material live before we recorded it as I was to write and record other artists in the studio. So yeah, we got a lot out of the live experience. As a matter of fact, playing was one of those things we would sometimes get lost in.

Our shows sometimes ran three and a half hours. That's because everybody in the band would solo on every song. So we'd go into another zone. Audiences back then loved that. Remember, the audience was in another zone, too. It was fairly commonplace for at least half the audience to be on some mind-altering something or other. It was the unseen aspect that went into every show in those days. What kind of chemicals was the audience swimming around in.

In 1974 and beyond, when I performed, I liked to interact with people in the first row. But I was always on guard not to get yanked into the seats. I'd stand in a slight crouch, a defensive position, so I could pull back. Reaching out to audiences was a symbol of comradery. I think when you grow up feeling generally unaccepted as I did, you feel like a troubled, isolated loner. When the troubled loner reaches out to connect, it is a pleasant surprise when complete strangers suddenly accept what you're doing. I was eternally grateful for that, I guess, because I spent so much of my youth failing at everything, having terrible grades, not being able to play sports, and losing a high school girlfriend I cared about.

My audiences were somewhat different. They fully expected my music to change and songs to sound different from our albums. They expected to be challenged and they took a certain amount of pride in their ability to endure it and ultimately to understand it. But it was all based on the assumption that my flamboyance and eccentricity wasn't being done to manipulate them. I was doing it from my heart. I can't help doing what I do. The process was something so insular and so about where my head was at, that there was never any question of me pandering to my audience.

In the '70s, and it's still true today, I don't know how to pander. I only know how to make music about what I'm thinking.

Chris Stein
(Blondie cofounder, songwriter, and guitarist)

By the late 1970s, a lot of people found the term "punk" no longer palatable. Punk had started out as stripped-down, radical art music. But along the way, the word became code for "scary" and "outsider." The word struggled to translate beyond those who were already fans and showing up at clubs. The rage, the ripped clothes, and the "society's loser" image had become all too common among punk bands. The form itself was becoming tired and had run its course. Some bands that started out as punk evolved, integrating pop, reggae, disco, and other forms into their music. Music writers, clubs, and record labels began seeking a new term to describe these eclectic, breakaway artists that was a little hipper and sounded like money. The term they came up with was "new wave."

Debbie Harry and I weren't plotting to change music terminology. We just did stuff we liked. Whatever Blondie was doing to evolve wasn't motivated by a scheme to record hits. When we started out in 1973 and '74, we played New York's CBGB every weekend for seven months in a row at one point. The audience was pretty calm. The first time we toured in the U.K., in 1977, we went over in support of Television. Everybody in the audience was physically nuts, jumping all over the place. It was really exciting because New York was still in this sort of beatnik, coffeehouse mode, where they just kind of sat there and snapped their fingers. So when we saw everyone flinging themselves around in the U.K., it was super exciting. It didn't get crazy, physically, in New York until a little later, after the first wave of punk passed.

Early on, we played big halls with one amp. But shit was so primitive back then. The first time we went to Australia in 1977, John Denver was there and it was such a huge deal. Every time we tried to rent a piece of equipment, the answer was: "Oh, John Denver has it." It was like there were only three amplifiers and all of them were on John's truck. We did most of our performing in large theaters. Debbie and I did an arena tour with David Bowie and Iggy Pop for Iggy's *The Idiot* in '77. It was different from our tours with some of our peer bands, when things got competitive. During the tour, Bowie told Debbie how to work the stage in three sections—left, right, and center. They really just wanted the whole show to be as smooth and friendly as possible.

With Bowie and Iggy, we always got sound checks and that kind of thing. The aesthetic of rock 'n' roll eventually became performing at these huge venues. I felt that when we played giant venues here or abroad, audiences became a one-hive mind. You looked out and it was a swarm. In smaller places, everybody was separate, and you could see people as individuals. When you saw 20,000 people in a space, it was like this big organic mass. It was like one giant person.

Steve Miller
(Steve Miller Band founder, singer-songwriter, and lead guitarist)

In the early '70s, when the logistics and tech at arena concert performances hadn't been worked out yet, you performed on the edge. You knew that at any turn, something awful could happen with your sound system or the cables in the U.S. or abroad. In the '70s, we were in Holland on a European tour. All our shows were sold out. We were playing the Royal Concert Hall in Amsterdam. To reach the stage, you entered by walking down descending stairs that ran from a balcony behind the stage.

When the audience first saw us, they started cheering and rushed the stage. Onstage, we had two technicians: one guy who worked on the stage and one guy who ran the sound and lights. When we arrived at our spots, the stage guy was still plugging stuff in. I gave him a look. He said he wasn't ready yet. I said we were starting the show. Of course, the PA started giving off full-tilt feedback that lasted for ten minutes. It was the worst thing. The sound guy finally crawled through the audience and got to the board and shut it down. We went on with the show.

The next night we went to London to play two sold-out shows at the Rainbow Theatre. We had a Hammond B3 organ and we wanted to use our amps, which were wired for American 110-decibel power. So we had rented all these power converters and done a lot of special electrical patching. The first show went well. But at the start of the second show, the B3 organ burned up and it smelled really bad. The whole theater had the smell. We kept the concert going as a trio. Then more electric stuff broke down, which led to a roadie coming out to fuss around with stuff on the floor. Finally, I asked him to stop fussing at my feet and bring me an acoustic guitar. I sat down and played and sang. Then the PA broke down. There was dead silence in the hall. Some guy in the audience burped.

As the '70s rolled on and the business became better organized, you could go to a sound company and tell them you wanted a beautiful-sounding system and that you planned to use it for the next two years. They'd customize a system for you and lease it to you. They'd provide the trucks to transport it to your tour venues and guys to set it up once it arrived. You could even help design it.

If it wasn't for all these innovative businesses and guys who could execute quickly on the road, the rock concert might have peaked, or bands would have had to leave arenas and just play regionally and perform only at a small number of venues. I always referred to my guys as scurvy pirates. They set everything up, they tore it down, they lived in buses, and they drove all summer long to different venues. The road crews, the equipment designers, the lighting people, the lighting trusses—all of these things were advancing at the same speed we were.

I also could relate to these guys. This was labor and craft—backbreaking work plus engineering smarts in terms of assembly and wiring and ensuring that things erected didn't screw up or come tumbling down on you. Some performers never even thought about their crews. Not me. I've had the same truck drivers now for thirty years. I love these guys. I can't rock and roll without my crew.

Scott Gorham
(American lead guitarist for Thin Lizzy)

Everyone who performs dreads rejection. Before you go on, a million questions are flying through your head, and many of them are negative, what-if thoughts. They shouldn't be there. I remember what helped me when we came out onstage. Thin Lizzy bassist and leader Phil Lynott just stood out there like it was his house. He grabbed the audience by

199

their scruff and dragged them along with him. Looking over at him being so positive and strong, I fed off his entry and learned that part of it.

After our sixth album, *Jailbreak*, was released in March 1976 and our singles—"The Boys Are Back in Town" and "Jailbreak"—became hits in the U. S., Thin Lizzy played concert arenas in the States as an opener for Aerosmith and REO Speedwagon. Phil taught me so much about interacting with a large audience. He taught me not to show fear. Playing a pub or ballroom is one thing. When you come out and you're facing 20,000 kids, you nearly shit yourself the first bunch of times. It's hard not to.

When a crowd is that large and loud, you feel them analyzing and judging every little thing you do. It kind of paralyzes you at first. Then you start worrying you're going to forget how a song goes or the lyrics. Rock stars perform for an audience; they don't just play their instrument. You need to relax and get yourself into a zone. Phil taught me to have confidence. If you show that, the audience will go wherever you take them. It's a learned experience. You have to learn it, reason with it, and look cool and collected. Over time, you learn to be natural up there, as if you're in your garage or living room.

Chapter 13

Sight and Sound

Midway through the 1970s, a band's look and sound system became increasingly important to the concert experience. Bands that played arenas needed ways to hold existing fans, win over new ones, and stand out to attract attention. For many, fashion and volume were fast ways to bring the album experience to life. Both also came to define a band's image. As glam bands proved, the more outrageous the costumes and makeup onstage, the bigger the buzz after among fans. The same was true of speaker systems. As venues grew in size, audio and visual needed to be spectacular. At times, experiments backfired.

Bill Legend
(drummer for T. Rex)

By nature, Marc Bolan, the lead singer and guitarist of T. Rex, was an instigator and an innovator. He was petite and part of a pretty-boy group emerging in the early '70s. He knew he attracted both sexes and played off of that. He took on the glam look, but behind all of the visuals, the music was pure rock. The feminized look that his female friend introduced him to on London's King's Road appealed to women in the audience, but the rock we played connected with guys. Bassist Steve Currie and I never got into the glam look. We just wore normal clothing with a bit of style that was comfortable to play in.

Todd Rundgren
(Utopia founder, singer-songwriter, instrumentalist, and producer)

I first became conscious of rock fashion when I saw the Beatles in matching suits and ties in the '60s. All of the bands dressed that way back then, but the Beatles always gave their look a twist. Their Chelsea boots were a cool touch, and their suit pants were always tailored tight. But they were consciously fashion-forward, even within the suit-and-tie thing: like with those Pierre Cardin collarless jackets in '63 or the sort of military-style ones they wore while performing at Shea Stadium in 1965. When I began wearing androgynous outfits for my concerts in the early '70s, I was aware of rock fashion and its importance for standing out. Looking exotic onstage was part of my persona. It expressed my music and vulnerability.

Seeing the Who perform in the late 1960s was a big influence on my decision to take style risks. Their level of fashion consciousness went beyond the tailored black suit and tie and the satin psychedelic costumes of the Beatles for their *Sgt. Pepper* album. Guitarist Pete Townshend of the Who wore these lacy, pre-Victorian and French royal court kinds of things. He also wore op art and mod outfits or a jacket made completely from a Union Jack. Things like that. Then Pete began wearing a white jumpsuit onstage, and lead singer Roger Daltrey wore open shirts and buckskin jackets with lots of fringe. That was the first time I saw a band where everybody was making his own fashion statement. The Who broke through the conformity to a fashion style that expressed something personal.

I suppose early on, rock groups dressing alike in suits and ties was a reflection of the times and who held the power back in the early '60s—buttoned-up record company executives. By the late '60s, the power shifted to the artists. Standing out became more important than fitting in, and the arena stage was more than just a space to sing and play instruments. It was a platform for performance, and performance meant theater, role-playing, and costumes. At first, I thought I had to go shopping at mod London stores. But by Woodstock, San Francisco and the hippie thrift-store scene had replaced London's King's Road as a fashion ideal. Suddenly, men wore their hair long and clothes were earthier and unisex. The response from London in 1972 was glittery androgyny, which appealed to me as it did to a number of rock musicians at that moment in time.

But I wasn't making these fashion choices. I was just open to them. What I wore on my face, in my hair, and on my body was chosen and designed for me by Nikki Nichols, a costume designer and makeup artist who traveled with me all the time. I first met Nikki in 1971 on the set of Rob Skelton's short experimental film *Intersection 1972*. You can see the film on YouTube. It was shot in Los Angeles and ran about eighteen minutes. Nikki put me in a weird silver jumpsuit open to the waist with a rhinestone jacket, silver streaks in my hair, turquoise eye makeup, lip rouge, and stuff like that.

The first time I met Nikki, he had it in his head to stick rhinestones at the base of my neck and down the center of my exposed chest and across the tops of my hands for the film. But he ran out of eyelash glue in the middle of pasting them on and couldn't find anything else that worked. He went down to the office in the studio where we were filming and came back with some sort of superglue and finished the job. Fortunately, the ones he put on my neck and head were still held in place with eyelash glue. But the ones on my chest and stomach were superglued, and they didn't come off after the session was done. In fact, I had to fly back to New York and they were still stuck on me. Eventually, a water blister formed under the glue and they came off. Now I have little round scars where the rhinestones were glued.

I hired Nikki right after that. He was my housekeeper for a while. He lived in our house, he cooked, and he made costumes and toured with us. I'd just let him come up with stuff, like the rhinestone-covered jumpsuit and the peacock outfit I wore on *The Midnight Special* in 1973, among others. I rarely had suggestions for Nikki. He was so full of ideas. Nikki traveled with a sewing machine. If we were doing something like a TV show, he'd go all out. Like the whole thing with the feathers on my face for *The Midnight Special*.

I just sat down in his chair, and he said, "I've got an idea for this." He finished the costume just before I went on and started taping "Hello It's Me." When I saw the costume, I thought it was pretty wild. It was just me being willing to go along with Nikki's idea and to be shockingly theatrical. I believed that concerts weren't solely musical events but fashion events as well. It was all about the outrage and the statement.

In 1973 and '74, I fronted Todd Rundgren's Utopia. As new, bigger arenas opened, everyone was adding bigger and bigger effects because the horizon for the audience was farther off in the distance. In other words, in the early '70s, audiences extended half a football field into the back of an auditorium. What could you do on an instrument that would touch them given how far away they were? Not much. That's when you started getting out the freaking pillars of fire, confetti cannons, smoke machines, and lights that reached to the far ends of the venue.

The band had a super high concept for our first tour, for which we dressed like aliens from outer space. We wanted to do something hyper-theatrical, something that everyone would remember and be talking about for years. The Sales brothers in my band knew a lot of people because they were in show business. They approached fashion designer Norma Kamali, who designed these black spandex jumpsuits for us with silver glitter wings on them and platform boots with transparent tops that went all the way up to our hips. We came out in these outfits wearing welding helmets that were painted white.

Norma Kamali
(pioneering fashion designer)

Rock style was about what you loved personally and felt comfortable in. In most cases, rockers weren't outfitted by stylists or girlfriends. Girlfriends may have tagged along or taken them to the stores they discovered on King's Road, but these guys knew what looked smart and put together their own signature looks.

In 1969, I opened my basement boutique in Manhattan on East Fifty-Third Street. There was a really fantastic girl, Jeanine, who was running my New York store. We worked very close together. She was amazing and talented and she had red hair and was a real character.

And I guess I was like the dark-haired version of that. And she and I would just sell like crazy. One day in 1972, the New York Dolls came in and dressed in the clothes I sold to women. Jeanine was perfect for them, her personality. She just said, "Here, try this, try this, try this." They really styled themselves. It wasn't like we were dressing them. They just came in and we made it easy for them to pick stuff without telling them who was supposed to wear what. There were no rules. They wore the clothes they bought at my boutique on the cover of *New York Dolls*, their first album, in 1973.

By the early '70s, half my customers were men. We actually started to try and figure out the ratio. At the end of each day, we'd look at all the sales slips and separate them. It was 50 percent men and 50 percent women. It wasn't that the clothes fit them better or that they were Lycra and stretchy, though that was part of it. It also wasn't about dressing in drag. It was more about the attitude of the clothes, especially for guys who were part of the emerging downtown New York scene or played in bands. I have no idea why rockers came in for clothes. I didn't ask. I also never reached out to stars to ask them to wear my clothes or gave celebrities clothes with hopes they'd be photographed wearing them. There's something that I do that connects with them. I have no idea what it is. When Sly Stone came in back in the '70s, he liked my feather jackets in bright colors. Robert Plant wore my shirts. I didn't design them for him specifically. He just wore them. And Keith Richards bought stuff of mine, too.

In fact, I didn't design for guys. So I think it was just great when that happened. I think it was just about what I do and what they want that seemed to connect. It's a meeting of attitudes. Even though I'm in fashion and they're in music, rockers identified something about me and my designs that were on their wavelength. A lot about the '70s was counter to the restrictiveness of the 1950s and even the '60s, when I had to wear a garter belt and a girdle and stockings and felt horrible.

Then all of a sudden, it was just like being released from captivity and I no longer had to hold my breasts up. What a relief. And to just wear my hair any way I wanted to and not to have to have my shoes match my handbag, all of that. I could let go and be me. When fashion freed up and no longer was confining, it led to the most open, spirited, creative time. That's why guitar music could be so expressive and energizing with enormous skill. Some bands could get away with a few hits if they didn't have much talent, and there were so many of those bands. They recorded great songs, but the groups didn't last very long. On the other hand, the really talented musicians had longevity. They were timeless.

Marc Bolan of T. Rex played with a female persona onstage, but the energy level and the music with the guitar were so masculine. It's fascinating and so appealing. Or look at Joan Jett. I used to sell her clothes. She's tough, tough, tough but so vulnerable. The blending of masculine and feminine traits was so exciting. And it was authentic and expressive. Once artists started adding stylists and a village of people who made choices for them, it all became a little slick and contrived. Todd Rundgren also let himself channel his feminine side. I have so much respect for him. He was and is such a brilliant musician and songwriter. The spirit of somebody like that, you have to be really smart. Mick Jagger is very smart. All of these rockers at that creative level are super smart. They're thinking artists.

Steve Miller

Performing was about effects. For our *Fly Like an Eagle* tour in 1977, we had gone from footlights and Super Trouper spotlights on earlier tours to rear-projection screens, a massive overhead lighting rig, and an onstage green laser light show. We'd focus mirrors over the audience and create these laser sculptures by bouncing the light around with reflections. It was risky. That laser could put a hole in the moon.

The machine was on the stage behind the drummer and needed sixty gallons of water a minute to keep cool. It produced a green beam an inch and a half thick. Our laser operator was a genius from Hawaii. He helped put the system together, but he was always picking up girls in the crowd and letting them run the lasers. We used to carry a huge mirror ball and we'd shoot the laser into the mirror ball, which would shoot multiple beams into the audience. We're lucky we didn't burn people's skin or blind them.

In the early 1970s, we brought a laser show into Atlanta's Omni Coliseum, which was brand-new at the time. It was this beautiful new giant arena that had 17,000 seats. I had put together a laser effect where I had the laser beam split into thirty-two beams above me, which then put a cone of light around me. I had a foot pedal set up where I could activate the cone and have the beams rotating around me. I could break up the beams by running my arms through the lights, which was a very exciting, dynamic thing to see. But the laser arrived at the last minute and we didn't get a chance to actually practice it before the first Omni show. At least it was better than lighter fluid.

To enhance the laser light, we needed a lot of mist created by dry ice. We had a dry ice machine and a pump with a two-hundred-foot-long, twelve-inch-diameter hose that looked like a giant elephant trunk. It ran from backstage to the foot of my mic. At the Omni, roadies turned the dry ice machine on during our sound check at 3:00 p.m. but forgot to turn it off. So the machine and pump were on all afternoon. Later that night, with the machine running the entire time, we got to the big moment in the show when I hit the pedal that turned on the laser and started it spinning. The mist from the dry ice was supposed to billow around my feet.

But the hose suddenly broke from the hours of mounting pressure, and mist starting spilling all over the place. There was so much dry-ice mist blowing from an out-of-control hose that I couldn't see anything, got vertigo, and I was afraid I was going to freeze my lungs. Finally, somebody from the crew got up there and grabbed the hose and tied it down. At arenas, everything had to get bigger. The risks were bigger, too.

John Meyer
(Meyer Sound Laboratories cofounder and CEO)

The Dead's soundman was Owsley Stanley, who was known then as Bear. He was constantly experimenting with speakers and amps. When I first met him, he wanted differential microphones—two AKG mics taped together so lead vocalist Bob Weir could sing into them. By doing this, one mic would cancel the noise of the other and produce clearer sound. In 1974, the Dead was using its three-story, 28,800-watt Wall of Sound bank of speakers that Bear had designed through trial and error. But Bear wasn't happy with it. He came to me at McCune Audio and said, "We're not making it to the balcony."

Apparently, he'd sit in different parts of a theater to hear how the Dead sounded and then add hundreds of speakers to project the sound from each instrument and vocalist. He wanted to reach all parts of a theater, but the balcony was a challenge. While the Wall of Sound had its limitations and wasn't necessarily efficient, it looked very, very impressive—and cool counted if you were a band hoping to put people in seats at concerts.

We talked about how to get the Dead's music up that high. Bear had been stacking speakers on top of speakers and attaching them to a scaffold system behind the band, which created that Wall of Sound. But sonically, the solution wasn't to stack the speakers up higher to reach the balcony. That was impractical. Even coming close wouldn't solve the problem. When you stack speakers in a flat plain, sound just projects straight out, like a beam of light. Instead, I suggested they build a curved cluster of speakers that looked like an early space satellite from the front. By designing the cluster in an arc, the sound would disperse like that curve and reach the balcony. Bear had my design built and it worked.

In 1977, the Dead reached out again. While their system had been great for a few thousand people in 1974 and '75, it fell short at stadiums and major arenas. They also were being assaulted by the sound, since all of those speakers were behind them. They came to me and said, "Our system is killing us. We're being mowed down." I told them about new linear monitor speakers I had designed. They were small and powerful and let you listen to yourself while performing.

My wife, Helen, and I started Meyer Sound Laboratories in 1979. I was already connected to Frank Zappa, the Dead, and other bands, so word spread fast and we were busy as soon as we opened for business. We did a lot of trial and error with bands. They'd try something I designed. If it wasn't good, we'd send them something else. I didn't hang out with bands. When you do, you become part of their family, and I wanted to maintain some distance.

Helen Meyer
(Meyer Sound Laboratories cofounder)

Meyer Sound had five thousand square feet in San Leandro, California, near the Oakland airport. We started with two employees and then by the end of '79 we had four people. And then six. Business grew quickly. The bands we worked with really cared about how they sounded and they were willing to try new things, because they wanted to create a fantastic experience for their fans.

We worked with a company called Hard Truckers that also built our cabinets. We stuffed the cabinets with speakers and built the racks for the amplifiers and control electronics in our small shop in San Leandro between 1979 and 1983. We pioneered the idea of control electronics, and these units were part of the amplifier rack. The control electronics protected the speakers, equalized them, and kept the system running smoothly. We used other manufacturers' amplifiers.

John Meyer

Frank Zappa wanted a sound system to play arenas. We had just designed our MSL-3 cabinet speakers, and they were perfect for Zappa because you could use multiple units for bigger or smaller venues. Frank listened to it and wanted more sparkle in the highs. Instead of changing the speaker, I built a bank of tweeters to add on. With a huge amount of power, we could push the sound coming out of the tweeters into the venue. He was very happy with the result.

Soon more bands wanted a setup that sounded great. The Dead wanted their system to be everything the band wanted and everything the audience wanted. I always wanted to make sure musicians were happy. That was the key to the whole thing. Ultimately, it's the content that matters.

Steve Miller

Because my name was the band's brand, I had to be on top of every detail. I had to be up on existing and new technology and figure out ways to make it all sound and look better. I also had to know about the latest stage and recording technology and be familiar with album cover design. I learned to design my stages and sets. I liked being involved in everything. I had creative control over as much of the experience as possible. I was always the guy who said, "It's too loud. It doesn't sound good enough," while everyone else was saying, "What's wrong with you, man? Turn it up!"

The arena allowed us to work on a bigger canvas, especially the audio. It was hard in the beginning because it took a long time before we could design our own sound system and take it out on the road. A lot of times we'd get to places and the existing sound system would be outdated and sound terrible. Or the promoter employed a bad sound company. That was normal. "Fly Like an Eagle" was the hit that changed all of that for us. Suddenly, I could afford two trucks on tour to transport a sound system and lighting rig. I finally could say that our concerts were about good sound, not noise.

As more bands shifted to arenas in the '70s, an entire subindustry grew up to meet the demands. These niche businesses included sound companies, production companies, lighting directors, makers of light fixtures, light show and prop specialists, pyrotechnicians, and so on. The growing number of companies in this niche led to another stratum of businesses that designed and fabricated the cables, the amps, the speakers, and the rigging that supported all the other stuff. Those businesses were followed by yet another subindustry that could move all of it, make it compact to reduce size and weight, and put stuff on wheels.

In addition to the music, in addition to what songs you were going to play that night, you also had to be aware of when the effects would start, how they worked, and the dangers to avoid. There were like a hundred things performers had to think about. I had a lot of sound effects, including electronic music like Stockhausen on a tape recorder on the floor. I had colored leader tape between the different sound effects. A foot pedal let me fast-forward, rewind, play my electronic effects, and stop them on demand midperformance. I would be playing and running this tape with my foot and then pop it in and turn on the electronics and play to that for a while. All with my foot. It was crazy the stuff we tried to do.

Mike Fisher
(Heart band manager, cofounder, and coproducer)

Heart was pretty picky about sound. I built our sound systems from the time we started the Army in the late 1960s up until we became Heart playing as an opening act in the early 1970s. We couldn't wait to bring our own customized system with us on the road. But we couldn't in the beginning. We weren't big enough. As an opening act, we were expected to use the systems provided by the headlining acts. These systems often suited the headliner but not necessarily us. Along the way, I met this brilliant guy who had novel ideas about sound. As Heart began to headline, we figured out how to build this sound system big enough to do coliseum shows. Our system was a departure from the way they were being done.

In 1977, at one of our first concerts as a headliner, Foreigner was our opening act. We liked their first hit on the radio, "Feels Like the First Time," and we were excited to hear them. Our sound system was trucked to the venue and set up. We did the first show and it was kind of weird. The system didn't really sound the way I wanted it to. It was an all-cone speaker system with no compression drivers, and it used dome tweeters. Each box had four ten-inch speakers, sixteen five-inch speakers, and sixteen dome tweeters. These boxes were all in vertical arrays so the wavelengths would be ideal. But the system was inefficient. When Foreigner played, they were really, really loud. Too loud, making it impossible to get a decent mix.

The next night, there was something wrong with the electronic crossover—the essence of the sound system. It was built by hand by the guy I was partners with in our sound-system venture. We couldn't get it to work. The city we were in was a union town where they were strict with what you could do. That was slowing things down. I wasn't even allowed to carry my cassette recorder from the front of the house up to the stage. I had to have a union guy carry it for me. Meanwhile we were soldering away trying to get this thing to work. In those days, you

211

couldn't buy one of these things, so we had to reschedule the show. We sent the system back to Seattle and used someone else's.

When we opened for Jefferson Starship later in the tour, I encountered a groundbreaking audio system by FM Productions, a company owned by San Francisco concert promoter Bill Graham that provided production services to bands. Graham was just as picky as we were about good sound. At the time, Bill Graham was promoting Day on the Green at the Oakland–Alameda County Coliseum Arena in Oakland, California. Day on the Green was a series of huge outdoor shows, with 55,000 people every weekend. So FM had extraordinary ideas for sound and they had a chance to try lots of things, to experiment, and to work out the kinks. They didn't hire ordinary tech guys to set up this gear. They drew from a community of intensely focused and dedicated audio enthusiasts, many with advanced degrees.

Once we started headlining in 1977 and '78, we used FM Productions. It was more efficient. The concert system FM used was designed by an amazing group of audio pioneers including John Meyer. The FM system Heart used was super sophisticated and refined and had accurate sound reproduction for the time.

Robert "Toe-Cutter" Burton
(rock band roadie)

The first concert I ever saw was Heart playing at my high school dance in Seattle. My friend Bob knew about Heart from a gig the band had played at a hotel club. His dad was a bartender at the hotel, and Bob snuck in a few times when Heart was playing. I loved Heart so much. Eventually, I got to meet Steve Fossen, Heart's bass player. I was seventeen and underage. So Steve let me carry his guitar into the club where they were playing. He'd tell the people at the door: "He's with us." I would get in this way almost every night. I kept on going as much as I could.

One of their road guys was all stressed out and pissed off about the money and the work. He planned to quit. John Hannah, the band's keyboard player at the time, said to the other Heart musicians, "Hey, Rob wants to work with us. What do you think?" I had been helping to unload and load their gear and set up the stage. I also was helping Mike Fisher set up the sound gear. One day, Mike took me aside and talked to me. A couple days later, Mike said, "Yeah, you can work for us. Everybody likes you." That's how I began working as a roadie for Heart.

At the time in 1974, Heart was just starting out playing local Seattle clubs. To learn what I needed to know, I flew by the seat of my pants. It was scary. I'd never soldered microphone cords or connector cords for boxes or monitor speakers in my life. I didn't even know what was inside the speakers' shielding. I'd take the sheath off and see three wires in there. I figured it out by looking at wires attached correctly on other speakers and copying them. Luckily everything worked out. Nobody taught you how to do the job. You just figured it out in your head.

In my favor was that I didn't have to be shown what to do every night. I put the monitors in place and Mike would run patching cords from monitor to monitor for sisters Ann and Nancy Wilson and Mike's brother Roger, the lead guitarist. I'd see how it was done and make mental notes. The next night, I knew instinctively how it was supposed to look.

Early on, we didn't have a proper electronic guitar tuner. So it was done with John Hannah and his synthesizer or his Hammond B3 organ. John would give me a note and I'd tune to his organ. In the early days, I learned to tension tune. Especially if a string had snapped and the rest of the strings were in tune. I'd feel the tension of the strings—E, A, and D and G—and figure out how tight the new string should be. I got it so close that Roger was amazed. I didn't have a workstation for guitars, so I had to get good at changing and tuning strings on the fly.

One night in '77, in Calgary or Toronto, Roger broke a high E string on his guitar while playing "Magic Man." So I grabbed a string from the case and onstage, while he was playing, I threaded the string through the back of his guitar up the neck and into the tuning peg. I put it on and tuned it while Roger was playing in front of several thousand people. Randy Bachman, from Bachman-Turner Overdrive, was onstage playing with Roger. Randy looks at Roger and says, "Who the hell is that guy? That's amazing."

213

Probably the biggest crisis I had was fixing monitor speakers while Ann Wilson was singing and moving around onstage. I was a distraction, so it was hard. Typically, the band would stretch out the song for a few minutes while I was scrambling around to attach a working microphone cable to her mic and then patch in. Singers routinely abused the cable. They constantly pulled on the mic cable, so the connector at the base of the cable would separate or break.

I started putting tape on Ann's microphone. I'd have to use an X-Acto knife to cut the old tape off and retape it. During the band's club days, we were so short on cords and had zero left over for microphones in an emergency. Sometimes Ann would be waiting for her microphone to be handed back, so the pressure was on me to get the job done.

Lead guitarist Roger Fisher liked to be all over the stage. In the early days, his curled cord might get caught up with Ann's mic cord or Nancy's curled guitar cord. I had to untangle the spaghetti fast. They'd circle each other and suddenly there would be a rat's nest of cord in front of the drum riser on center stage. I had to figure out who to move first, who had to turn around to detach, and so on. The straight cord was a big help for Roger, who loved to get up on the speakers to play. Every night, he'd say, "Find me a way to get up there. I want to get on top of this box," or "Get me a ladder or some chairs." He would climb up the back of the speakers and then stand as far up as he could get.

What irritated me sometimes were guests backstage before a show. If they were in your way, they'd slow you down, especially if they were tripping on LSD. In other cases, we'd have to deal with union stuff. We'd get to a venue, and I'd like to load the stage fast. I was picking up two and three guitars to get my work done. I'd get shit from our road managers. "Slow down, we're going to get a fine. See those guys over there? Tell them what you need and where to put your equipment. Otherwise, we're going to get a fine. Don't work. Don't pick up anything because they're glaring at you. Stop working."

I had to learn to drive a five-ton truck on the road. I didn't have a truck license. I didn't know what the third pedal was for. And I'd never driven a stick. Here I am plowing across Canada in a blizzard to get to the next venue. During this tour, we opened for ZZ Top. In the blizzard, two of their semis ended up in a ditch in a total whiteout. Only one truck with equipment showed up at 10:30 the night of the concert in Winnipeg. Only a hundred people were left in the audience. ZZ Top came out onstage and said, "One of our trucks finally showed up. Do you want the show to go on or not?" The hundred people there screamed, "Yeah, we want to see the show." So the audience helped unload the truck backstage and the roadies set up all the band gear and whatever sound equipment showed up. Heart did three songs and ZZ Top did about six and that was it.

Chuck Leavell
(Allman Brothers Band pianist)

Studying jazz piano players and performances, I noticed there were certain ones who would get really deep and avant-garde. They muted the strings of the piano with their left hand to create a plucking effect and played with their right on the keys. Well, I started incorporating that into long instrumentals with the Allman Brothers Band, like on "In Memory of Elizabeth Reed" and "High Falls."

Twiggs Lyndon, my roadie at the time, saw what I was doing and said, "Man, you can't use both hands if you're doing that. Let me make you something." So he invented and built a piano mute, which had this hydraulic pedal on the floor that shot the fluid through a tube up to this apparatus that muted the strings of the piano. It was fantastic. The muting created a very different sound, to experiment, to do something out of the ordinary, something unusual. And it always got the attention of the audience. What is he doing? What is that? Where is that sound coming from?

The only drawback to flashy stage costumes and more sophisticated sound was that they were static. Once you saw the outfits and heard the music, the thrill was gone. To keep audiences animated, movement onstage was critical. But activity on such a large platform came with risks. Early on, rock guitarists and bassists struggled. Crossing the stage meant dragging a long tail of coiled

215

wire attached to instruments, increasing the possibility of frayed jacks, injury following entanglement, and electrical shock. The solution was a device called the Schaffer-Vega diversity system. Invented in 1975, it allowed guitarists to play wirelessly. Created by Ken Schaffer, it revolutionized the rock concert by freeing musicians such as Angus Young of AC/DC and Keith Richards of the Rolling Stones to be more mobile and expressive and allowed bands like Pink Floyd to perform on different levels onstage.

Ken Schaffer
(Schaffer-Vega diversity system inventor)

In 1975, I was living with Lynne Volkman, who at the time was one of the first female rock tour managers. She handled tours for the Rolling Stones, the Who, Lynyrd Skynyrd, Cat Stevens, James Taylor, Linda Ronstadt, and many others. You know how tour managers used to fly their girlfriends out to join them at concerts on the weekends? Flip it around. On the Rolling Stones Tour of the Americas '75, Lynne sent for me some weekends. I had a great view of that tour.

At arenas where they performed, I noticed the Stones did something unusual. They sold seats behind the stage. This was one of the first instances of a band doing this. And they filled every seat, even though many of them faced the back of their amp stack. To play to fans seated behind the stage, Mick Jagger used a wireless handheld microphone. He'd move around with the mic a few times during each set and do half a song for the fans in the back. And every night, the wireless mic he was using crapped out.

I saw three main problems. First, every time Jagger used the wireless, the sound was awful. Second, as often as not, the signal would fade and drop out whenever he moved six feet or more in any direction. That's because the VHF frequencies used by the mic experienced gaps in coverage. Third, the system's receiver picked up other users of the frequency, like dispatchers for cops and car services.

Even the best wireless system in those days was intended for church pastors at modest sound levels. I knew I could build a better radio microphone than that. Back at my New York apartment, I started designing one that conquered those three obstacles. Before I showed anyone what

I had come up with, I realized I was building just a better mousetrap. A better wireless microphone was a minor invention. Instead, I realized I had an opportunity to do something really big that no one had done before—create a wireless electric guitar. It really was mostly the same device but packaged in a different form. Instead of being built into a hand mic, the transmitter would be housed in a small pack that would go on the strap of the guitar.

The first person to see the guitar demonstrated was a member of Kiss. He came up to my apartment in Manhattan one night in 1975. I lived in the penthouse and had a big terrace. After I played the wireless guitar for him outside, we came back into my apartment and I asked him what he thought. He wasn't that impressed. I assumed his mind would light up with staging possibilities, but he just didn't get it. The following week, I met with Jeff Lynne and Bev Bevan of Electric Light Orchestra. They went bananas. They became the first arena-size band to ever go wireless. For ELO, I made four units by hand. They took a month to build. In one rack were all four units.

By then, in early 1976, I was going back and forth to California looking for a company to manufacture the system. I found Cetec Vega. They made unimaginative but very good, solidly constructed wireless equipment. They had production lines and sourcing and all that junk. I decided to use them. We called the unit the Schaffer-Vega diversity system. I delivered ELO's systems to them in the U.K., where they were rehearsing in an aircraft hangar outside of London. Because they were the first band using my stuff, I stayed with them throughout their weeklong rehearsals. I'd be in a sleeping bag in the middle of the aircraft hangar listening to: "It's a livin' thing. It's a terrible thing to lose. It's a givin' thing. What a terrible thing to lose."

About six months later, in December 1976, I was back home in New York when my phone rang. It was the Kiss band member calling from Lakeland, Florida, at 11:00 p.m. He wanted to know if I was still making "those radio things." I told him I was. As it turned out, Ace Frehley, Kiss's lead guitarist, had an accident earlier that night at the Lakeland Civic Center. Their stage was built from metal pipes to form platforms on two or three levels. During a solo, Ace had grabbed onto one of the metal pipes to steady himself at the same time the ground on his guitar cord went bad. He was nearly killed. He was thrown off the stage and had to be revived by doctors. The band ordered around a dozen units at about $4,000 each.

AC/DC's Angus Young was one of the first to really exploit the wireless unit. He'd get on the shoulders of lead vocalist Bon Scott, who'd run out into the audience with Angus wailing away. A guitarist like Angus also could be more physically expressive without worrying about tripping over the wire or getting it wrapped around someone else onstage. The unit's clean, powerful sound also was a big deal. In the 1970s, I outfitted maybe two hundred bands, which freed players to move around. That's the reason everyone wanted it. But once they used it, many found that it did something incredible to their sound. If you used it on a bass guitar, it was as if the sound waves were coming out from the cabinets, hugging you and pulling you into them.

Angus Young
(AC/DC cofounder, lead guitarist, and songwriter)

I was eighteen when my brother Malcolm and I started AC/DC in Burwood, Australia, in 1973. Our family had moved from Glasgow, Scotland, in 1963, after my parents had had enough of the cold winters. Australia looked like paradise in ads. When Mal and I were starting the band, our older sister, Margaret, went to Mal and said she had a great idea for me. She said he should get me into my school suit.

When I was younger and going to state school, I had to wear a uniform—a jacket, shorts, and a cap. She thought I was so cute at home, me sitting there in a uniform, with a big guitar, playing away in my room. Mal liked the idea, mostly because the audience would relate, since many of them had to dress that way, too, in school. It also made me look quite young. Convincing me to get into my school suit fell to Margaret and our older brother George.

At first, I was a bit resistant. I didn't want to look like a freak or something. But then I gave in and said I'd give it a try. The first time I wore the outfit at a gig, I was really nervous. I got onstage and was a bit shaken wearing it. I felt vulnerable, like a target. So I figured I'd better

218

keep moving. You always get the odd heckler at local gigs and I didn't want to get dinged by a missile. The crowd loved it. After the gig, Mal said the uniform was really something. "Just keep doing that," he said.

But I couldn't really run around abstractly onstage. I remembered that one of my little nephews, when he was young, would break into a Chuck Berry duckwalk when he'd hear rock. So I imitated my nephew's version of Chuck's thing. This also cranked up audiences, since it was a tribute to rock's early days. In my school suit, doing my nephew's duckwalk, I'd want to disappear. I was always a daydreamer, drifting off someplace in my head. I soon became known for my trance-like appearance while performing. That, too, gripped the audience.

Chapter 14

CONCERT MAXIMUS

As rock concerts grew in popularity in the early 1970s, football stadiums and racetracks with strong fencing and tightly controlled entrance gates became viable venues. Outdoor free rock festivals had all but disappeared in the years immediately following Altamont, but the crowds for live rock and rock-related hybrids continued to grow. In part, the expanding size of concert audiences was due to the influx of a new demographic—the younger brothers and sisters of those who had attended concerts in the 1960s. Too young to tag along then, they were coming of age in the '70s. In other cases, supersized concerts were a strategy by record companies such as Stax to feature their label's artists in one show. But there was a third phenomenon: groups such as the Grateful Dead and the Allman Brothers Band developed a cultlike following of fans who attended entire tours, not just individual concerts. The rock concert had become a lifestyle.

Bob Weir
(Grateful Dead cofounder, guitarist, and lead singer)

The hardest thing about the way we toured was getting up in the morning. We were young and full of fun, and we didn't go to bed real early. We were on the road a lot and our "celebrations" probably made touring more difficult than it had to be. But that was the name of the game for us. It's how we made our living.

Our touring schedule was relentless, even in the beginning. We'd play a gig, stay up late, and then fly to our next gig on a commercial flight first thing in the morning. Most of the time, our equipment was trucked overnight to the next destination. Once we landed, we often went straight to our venue for a sound check. Later, we'd play a three-hour gig and go back to where we were staying. Often times there was a little so-called celebration there. We'd sleep for an hour or so and head to the airport. It was an endless cycle.

In the band's early days, Robert Hunter occasionally traveled with us on the road. He was a great guitarist, but he wasn't a playing member of the band. He was a friend and our lyricist. He had ears. He would write lyrics and hand us the sheets. We'd work on the music and vocal harmonies. Then we'd jam on the songs for audiences until we had it just right. Even still, we'd never play a song the same way twice onstage. It wasn't who we were, and our fans wouldn't have wanted it that way.

Amir Bar-Lev
(director of *Long Strange Trip*, the Grateful Dead documentary)

If you were a fan of the Grateful Dead, you were spoiled. Performances by other rock bands were preplanned and felt polished, in some ways like theater, not music. There was this sense with the Dead that a rock concert was an improvisational journey to be taken by the audience and the band together, as a collective entity. I think this came from the Acid Tests—the radically egalitarian psychedelic parties held by Ken Kesey in San Francisco starting in 1965.

The Acid Tests introduced the idea that even in psychedelics' extremely vulnerable headspace, you could be on the dance floor with strangers. One could easily argue that having to do that much socializing and intermingling with other people is a terrible idea on LSD. But at the Acid Tests, participants found that magic happened on acid that could never occur lying alone on a couch with eyeshades on. The Dead was born out of this discovery.

One thing that older Deadheads were always saying to me during the making of my *Long Strange Trip* documentary was: "Don't forget, we always saw the Dead as a dance band." Over time, psychedelic rock, with its long, virtuosic, mystical explorations, took on an almost progressive rock role in the public's imagination. But in that moment, in the late '60s and '70s, the Dead was playing music primarily for dancing hours on end.

As they became increasingly popular, having that kind of intimate connection with their audience became more and more challenging. Sound became an obsession that drove them to spend all of their money building the world's greatest concert system and, ultimately, bankrupted them. Virtually everything about the Dead was unusual and unique. The studio versions of their songs were just a blueprint for something much bigger. A Dead song was considered a living, dynamic, and fungible thing to be constantly reinterpreted and colored by the environment in which it was performed. There were no set lists. They'd just start a song, play it, and then decide in the brief moments between songs what they'd play next. In the Dead's hands, live music was a protean thing that wanted to grow and evolve.

From the start, the Dead didn't understand why people wanted to tape every one of their concerts. But their outlook was: if someone is doing something you don't understand, rather than excluding it, you welcome it and see if it has any value. In *Long Strange Trip*, we gravitated toward the idea that this all goes back to Jerry Garcia, as a six-year-old, deciding to make a friend of the Frankenstein monster he was repulsed by at the movies.

That way of looking at life carried forward into Jerry's and the Dead's relationship with the Hells Angels, the tapers, the hordes of neophyte fans like myself who arrived in the 1980s—virtually everyone who came into the band's orbit. You were absorbed, not looked down upon. The band's way of thinking was: "We may not entirely understand what you're about, but hey, get in here and help shape what this thing is going to be." That's why the Grateful Dead was America's band, because it's radically pluralistic.

Bill Walton
(former NBA basketball center and self-described Deadhead)

I first heard the Dead in 1967, when I was fifteen. I had an AM/FM transistor radio and heard them on San Diego's KPRI-FM. The station's

DJ, Gabriel Wisdom, played their music and talked about the band. In
'67, the music and his commentary were a response to the madness of the
Vietnam War, racism, and hatred. That world produced what emerged
in San Francisco as our Summer of Love.

I was a very shy person as a young boy. I was extremely self-conscious,
and I was plagued with a severe stuttering problem. I couldn't say hello
or talk to anybody without stammering, stumbling, or spitting. So I
tended to stay to myself. But at the Dead concerts, I felt the way I did
on the basketball court. Expression, freedom, and independence were
encouraged. Nobody told you no at a Dead show. Instead, the spirit was
to celebrate the wonders of life and nature. I fell in love with the band,
the music, and the whole scene the very first time I went.

Up front, where I always tried to be, I could feel the creativity,
the imagination, and the free form that I loved with sports. The music
wasn't structured. It was teamwork. The Dead didn't seem to have an
official leader. It was: Who wants to be in charge? The outcome rested
on personalities, the egos, the drive, and how members of the band
were feeling that day. That's how basketball teams work. The Dead
never seemed to be in a race to finish. Their attitude was: we're here,
we're ready to go, and there's no place else we'd rather be other than
here playing for you. They didn't hold back, and they were eager to
see where the music took them.

The pressure and stress on the Dead to deliver a peak performance
on command inspires how they play, how they interpret the music, and
how we feel it. Shows are a giant reflection of how we're living and
what's going on in our minds and souls. In basketball, there's constant
pressure to bring a fresh game each time. It was the same back then for
the Grateful Dead. I knew immediately that it was all one.

The band being on tour night after night wasn't much different than
being part of or following a basketball team and attending games. It's the
same game and yet completely different every night. It's always about the
players involved, how they feel that night, and how they're interacting
with teammates and the opposing team. The basketball by itself does
nothing. The guitars, the bass, the drums, the keyboards, the equipment,
the tools by themselves do nothing. How the artists use everything as an

extension of their minds results in a completely different concert experi-ence each time. How the crowd responds to the music has an impact on the Dead's direction. The audience changes things.

As a Deadhead, I've experienced the anticipation, the excitement, and the knowledge that something is probably going to happen that I'd never seen before. And then how exhilarating all of that is. Eventually, you realize that all of the Dead concerts you've seen are really one long song with pauses between the shows. The music lifts you up and takes you and guides you, it deposits you, it places you, and then at the end, when they finally stop for the night, you say to yourself: I'm with those guys spiritually. Where are they going from here?

I don't rank, rate, or compare concerts. I just try to enjoy them. I used to care what they played and where they played. I'd show up with a handwritten list of all the songs I wanted to hear. I would go backstage and talk to the guys about why they didn't play a specific song or a particular riff. Over the decades, I've changed. I no longer care what they play. What I do care about is that they continue to play and how they play. There's no one concert that's best. That's the beauty of the Dead and of life. You've got to listen to it all. And live it. I have a ton of their music. Now, instead of choosing songs I want or think I should hear, I just leave it to the iTunes shuffle. It's amazing. The shuffle knows.

Elizabeth Marvel
(film and TV actress and self-described Deadhead)

My girlfriend, Rosie, took me to my first Grateful Dead concert in California in the early 1980s. I was fourteen and had just started high school. I had two older brothers, so I was familiar with the Dead's *American Beauty* album. At the Dead concert, I was an instant convert. The music put me in a meditative state and, afterward, I fully immersed myself in the Dead's music and the surrounding scene at concerts. That summer I began following the band on their western tour by bumming rides from people I met there. I was a child living like an adult. The follow-ing summer I went east to see shows. After I left school at age sixteen,

I bought my first car, a cherry-red 1969 Karmann Ghia, and drove up and down the coast of California going to Dead shows. That's when I joined the caravan.

Why follow the band? Two things happened to me simultaneously. First, I was very young and had to look after myself while traveling independently. Second, I lived on a psychedelic plain so I identified with the Dead and the Deadheads. They gave me a sense of family and they looked after me, making sure I had food and had a place to sleep. I never felt alone. Once I joined the so-called circus, I felt a part of it.

When I first started going to concerts, I just tagged along. Then I began to think about how to get into these shows for free. I also had to figure out how to get in with the people who were safe and smart and cool and creative. I started making simple clothes with brightly colored material. I'd sell or trade them for food and tickets. I didn't have a group of school friends, so I was at the mercy of many different people. On the West Coast, I found myself part of a massive crew of people moving from concert to concert. I suppose for many Deadheads, there was no going home, either because they didn't want to or because home didn't really exist. Then I'd see the same people year after year, but I wouldn't stay in touch with them between tours.

At concerts, I was a spinner—people who twirled around and around as the Dead performed. I was indoctrinated by a couple of young women who were older than me. I was on such a hallucinatory plain, it was otherworldly. It was quite a cosmic experience. There would be an area set aside for spinners on the left, if you're facing the stage. The tapers— people who showed up with equipment to tape shows—were in the middle. There were sections. Spinners were a very considerate group of people. Everyone got their space.

Many rock bands that attracted a huge concert following in the 1970s and beyond had a dramatic survival story. This was true of the Allman Brothers Band. Guitarist Duane Allman died in a motorcycle accident in October '71, and bassist Berry Oakley died the same way in November '72. Fans who had purchased the Allman Brothers Band's first live album in the summer of

1971, "At Fillmore East," felt their loss. The gatefold inside the band's fourth studio album, "Brothers and Sisters," released in August 1973, featured band members and their extended families in a communal group shot. Fans felt a special kinship.

Chuck Leavell
(Allman Brothers Band pianist from 1972 to 1976)

After Duane Allman died in 1971, five members of the band went out on the road to complete concert obligations. When they returned to Macon, Ga., they were physically and mentally drained and decided to take a short break. In the summer of 1972, Gregg Allman began working on his first solo album, *Laid Back*. I got called to rehearse with him. Everything went great.

Rehearsing and recording songs for the album helped Gregg heal from the loss of his brother. As the recording progressed, we began these after-hours jam sessions at Capricorn Records. All the guys in the Allman Brothers Band came down—Gregg, Dickey Betts, Butch Trucks, Jai Johanny Johanson, and Berry Oakley. We would just pick a key and go. It was great. This went on for a few weeks. It gave everybody a little bit of direction and maybe a little piece of hope for the future. Within two or three weeks after those jam sessions, I got a call to come to the office of Phil Walden, the label's cofounder. I wondered if I had done something wrong. When I arrived, all of the guys were there and pleasantries were exchanged. Then, the other shoe dropped. They said things were feeling pretty good, how would I feel about joining the band? I did a couple of dates with the Allman Brothers Band in '72, in between the recording.

In November, Berry died in a motorcycle crash. The loss was devastating, especially coming so soon after Duane's. We finished recording *Brothers and Sisters* in late '72 and did a select number of concert dates. Both *Brothers and Sisters* and Gregg's *Laid Back* came out in 1973. We were becoming hugely popular and embarked on a combination of arena and stadium tours. It was a big leap moving from theaters to huge venues. I think maybe more so for me than the rest of the band, since they had already played arenas after the success of the *At Fillmore East* album and *Eat a Peach*.

Playing sports venues was an adjustment. At arenas, the Allman Brothers tended to fill them up to capacity. To look out and see 20,000 people instead of 5,000 or 7,500 was a big boost and exhilarating. We felt like we were reaching more people with our music, and that was a good thing. Despite the lack of intimacy, there was a lot of excitement. We were becoming a bigger deal and connecting with audiences. It was a thrilling time.

Thanks to the Allman Brothers Band, Southern rock took off. It was a unique sound that emerged from a combination of influences, including country, rock 'n' roll, jazz to a degree, and the blues, which was the biggest part of it. Even when we put all of that into the pot and stirred it up, the music still emerged with a distinct Southern flavor. People from every region of the country saw themselves in the band on the cover of *At Fillmore East* and were united. This shattered the notion of what someone from the South looked like and how that person behaved.

People forget that long hair, in those years, was a highly inflammatory political statement. It sent a message that you opposed the Vietnam War, that you were a hippie with hippie values, and that you had no problem looking like a woman. No matter where you were from, we all were subject to being harassed for having long hair. As the music rapidly became more and more popular and more rock musicians had long hair, that attitude evaporated.

Honestly, I think the band's long hair and other factors helped create a brotherhood. Even though there were only two Allman brothers, all of us in the band were brothers in this thing. And it started out that way before I was ever with them and it continued during the time I was there. Even the title of the record that we did, *Brothers and Sisters*, reflected that feeling. We were in this together. We all want a better world. We all want to make great music and have people be happy.

One of the highest-attended stadium concerts in the U.S. in the early 1970s was Wattstax, a music festival held at the Los Angeles Coliseum on August

20, 1972. All of the groups that performed there were signed to the Stax label, which at the time had shifted to a funk-rock format. Though a free concert series called the Harlem Cultural Festival held over six Sundays at a Harlem park in the summer of 1969 attracted a total of more than 300,000 to hear soul, funk, and gospel artists perform, Wattstax became the largest one-day gathering of Black concertgoers at a stadium, with 112,000 attending. The Coliseum's owners fully expected the promoter, Al Bell, to fail at attracting a sizable crowd, so they asked for their money up front. Bell surprised them.

Al Bell
(Wattstax promoter and Stax Records' co-owner)

In 1965, I came to the attention of Jim Stewart, the co-owner of Stax Records in Memphis. By then, I had been a successful DJ in Little Rock, Arkansas, and in Washington, D.C. I also had been booking concerts in Maryland. One day, Jim called me and said, "Al, we're ninety thousand dollars in the hole. I need you to come to work for us in Memphis as Stax's vice president of promotion." His sister and co-owner, Estelle Axton, and Jim agreed that if I was successful, they'd give me an equity stake in the company. I took the job. The promise of an equity position was an incentive.

Two years later, disaster struck. Stax's top-earning superstar, Otis Redding, died in an airplane crash in December '67. Then in '68, Atlantic merged with Warner and Elektra. I didn't know and neither did Jim that if Atlantic merged or was sold, Atlantic would have the rights to our entire back catalog. That meant we wouldn't reap the benefit of sales of singles and albums already released, only new material we recorded going forward. The industry declared us dead. Jim and Estelle named me executive vice president, and I now had to figure out how to remake Stax. This meant rebuilding a new catalog without Otis. Then Estelle left and sold her shares to me, which made me co-owner.

To build our new catalog as fast as possible, I began signing acts such as the Staple Singers, the Emotions, and Isaac Hayes. I also recorded new material with existing artists, including Rufus Thomas, William Bell, Shirley Brown, Johnnie Taylor, and others. I told Jim we needed to announce to the industry that we were going to release twenty-eight new albums that year. The industry laughed, viewing the claim as overly ambitious. But we released twenty-seven of them and sold more than $3 million in product during our first national sales meeting. In the mix was Hayes's *Hot Buttered Soul* and the Staples' *Be Altitude: Respect Yourself*, both of which were game changers.

By 1971, I had gotten to the point where I needed to penetrate the Southern California market. I opened an office there, Stax West, with Forrest Hamilton managing it. One day he called me and told me about the Watts Summer Festival. Restaurants and businesses came out and sold food on the street and showed off their wares. People in the neighborhood strolled the booths and trucks, and there were all kinds of cultural events. Forrest told me the festival needed help. I knew we could take a couple of Stax acts into a nice venue out there, but Stax artists weren't well known in Black communities in Southern California.

Forrest and I liked the idea of doing something. It would bring attention to the Watts Summer Festival and raise Stax's visibility. But even more, Stax would stand for something and the concert could go national. We soon realized we wanted to do something gigantic that hadn't been done before. We knew about Woodstock, but we thought of it as a hippie gathering. We weren't inspired by anything other than trying to help out the Watts Summer Festival, raising spirits, and gaining exposure. We knew how to put on a major event.

When Forrest mentioned the L.A. Coliseum, the first thing I asked about was the capacity. He said it could hold 90,000. I said, "Great! Let's put together the entire roster of Stax artists and figure out a way to fill it up." The Coliseum was in sync with the scope of what we wanted to achieve. So we went to the Coliseum's owners and sat with management—all white guys—to talk to them about us and Stax. Other than Isaac Hayes and the "Theme from Shaft," they didn't know anything about us.

They said, "You're talking about renting the Los Angeles Coliseum. Do you know how large this place is?" I said, "Yeah, we want to rent it because we think we can pack it." One of the guys told us how much it would cost. He asked if I could write them a check for the full amount. I said we could, but there was a condition: I didn't want any Los Angeles police as security. I said that would just generate friction. The Coliseum guy said, "No problem, write a check." At that point, you could see he believed we weren't going to be able to put a hundred people in there. He figured it was easy money.

Instead of the LAPD, he said we could use our own security. His thinking was for us to give him the money and then go lose our way. They were trying to close a deal they thought would benefit them, whether all the seats were filled or not. All the other stuff didn't matter. The concert date they gave us was August 20, 1972. I suppose from their perspective, our proposition was ridiculous based on what they knew about filling 90,000 seats. I wrote the check for something like $10,000 or $15,000 [$63,000 or $94,000 in 2021 dollars]. Whatever it was, we had to pay the fee in full. Six weeks later we had a contract. They put in writing that there would be no LAPD as security.

So now we had the stadium and the date, and we had a roster of artists. But we needed a name. The Stax team threw around names. We knew we were going to promote both Stax and Watts. Then we agreed the community was more important, so Watts had to be first. Besides, people in the region would certainly know Watts before Stax. We came up with Wattstax. Once the name was set, we had to plan the logistics, and we faced the massive challenge of getting the word out and putting people in seats. Ticketing and pricing were going to be important.

The first thing I did was come up with the ticket price, prior to even looking at the sum total of the dollar amount we were spending. We decided to charge $1 per person for admission. From my radio days, I knew that when you put on a promotion where you wanted to attract a lot of people and get a lot of talk going on in the community, you charged $1. To build an audience, we focused on KGFJ-AM, the one radio station that played Black records. It was early '72 and the concert wasn't until August, which gave us time. We had Wattstax posters printed to put up on the Sunset Strip, and we printed doorknob notices.

We also wanted a movie crew. *Monterey Pop* had documented the Monterey Pop Festival, and *Woodstock* captured what went on at their festival. *Woodstock* was massively successful when it came out in 1970. In addition to documenting Wattstax, we wanted America to see what this concert was about. We wanted the movie to be like a mirror, so Black Americans could see themselves enjoying Black culture at a concert put on by a Black record label. For white audiences, the movie would be a peephole where they could get a picture of us as a community.

I asked David Wolper, a major TV and film producer with a specialty in documentaries, to underwrite it. But he didn't want to deal with something like that. He didn't think it would work. We talked about it several times and I couldn't convince him. Finally I told him I'd finance it myself. He said if I did that, he would produce the film. I then asked him to find me the best director. He suggested Mel Stuart, who had just directed *Willy Wonka and the Chocolate Factory*. Stuart agreed to do it and teamed with Larry Shaw as codirector.

We wound up selling 112,000 seats. We had 90,000 tickets to sell, but when the Coliseum gatekeeper mentioned they had held events in the past with more people, we moved things around and put in 20,000 additional seats. We added a balcony and reorganized the field. I know the count because the gatekeeper told me that 112,000 people had come through the gates.

The concert started around 3:00 p.m. and ended around midnight. There were no incidents. We had our own security. We had around forty guys and no guns, none of that. The head of security was actor-composer Melvin Van Peebles. Melvin walked around talking to all of the guys in security. It was literally a family affair. That's why when you watch the film, you see all of those different ages in there. You see grandchildren, you see children, you see parents and grandparents. You see Ruby Dee, you see Ossie Davis. And you see Crips and Bloods gang members sitting side by side—and they were at war with each other at that time.

Wally Heider Studios was one of the best outdoor recording operations in L.A. They taped the concert with multitrack recorders. As a result, I had enough material for two live albums. They both went gold, and I made back my investment on the recording and wound up with additional funds, part of which went toward donations to the Watts Summer Festival and Black social and civil rights organizations, starting with the NAACP.

After Wattstax, the Watts community was proud of us. Our records started to be played on Black and white stations, and we became a mass-market label with many of our artists, including the Staple Singers, Mel and Tim, Johnnie Taylor, and others. So mission accomplished. Wattstax intimidated a lot of people and disrupted a lot of things. I didn't realize it then, but I understand it now.

On July 28, 1973, the largest outdoor rock concert until that point took place at Watkins Glen International, a Grand Prix racetrack about an hour west of Ithaca, New York. Known officially as the Summer Jam at Watkins Glen, the Saturday concert was copromoted by Jim Koplik and Shelly Finkel. It attracted an estimated 600,000 fans, who came to see just three bands—the Grateful Dead, the Band, and the Allman Brothers Band. The one-day event proved that the demand for live outdoor rock concerts was stronger than many had thought, largely due to a demographic shift. Based on video and photographs from the concert, instead of hippies in bohemian thrift-shop garb like those who had attended Woodstock, Watkins Glen was more of a suburban interpretation of San Francisco. In videos and photographs, many of the male attendees can be seen shirtless and in jeans, while many of the women wore jeans, gray T-shirts or halters, and ponytails emerging from below red or blue headkerchiefs. The outdoor rock concert now included the younger brothers and sisters of Woodstock attendees.

Jim Koplik
(Summer Jam at Watkins Glen coproducer)

Even though the problems at Woodstock and Altamont were still fresh in people's minds, I still wanted to put on an outdoor rock concert in 1973. I was twenty-two and stupid, which was a good thing. My partner, Shelly Finkel, was twenty-eight and a risk-taker. We didn't have a whole lot of money to lose, and we had two acts we were close with—the Grateful Dead and the Allman Brothers Band. We felt tickets to such an event would sell very well.

The biggest issue we faced was complying with the newly passed state and local mass-gatherings laws enacted after Woodstock. You had to provide a toilet for every thousand people attending, you had to have a certain amount of space, you had to have water, a certain number of police, fire equipment, blah, blah, blah. They became known as the Woodstock laws. Smart promoters would have seen those hurdles as daunting. I wasn't at Woodstock or Altamont, so part of what my partner and I were doing was making up for what we had missed.

The idea for the Watkins Glen Summer Jam in '73 was Shelly's. We approached the community of Watkins Glen because we were New Yorkers and felt holding the concert in New York State was being local and loyal. We chose Watkins Glen because the Grand Prix racetrack at Watkins Glen International was nearby. We thought the track was perfect. They were used to crowds of 100,000. The roads could handle the traffic and so could the facilities. The track owner wasn't going to freak out when 100,000 people showed up. The concert was going to be held outside on a grass parking lot. So we had to secure portable toilets, drinkable water, and things like that.

First we had to get permission from New York State. We had to follow the new mass-gatherings code. Officials came to the site a week before the show and literally counted how many toilets we had. We were a little short at 920 instead of 1,000, but they let us slide. We were way short on water, though, so we had to do an emergency run at a time before bottled water. We set up big jerry jugs of water that people would use to fill up cups.

We assumed most of the people who showed up would be hippies who cared about the common person. I trusted that hippies would be kind and act like hippies, which they did. Meaning they wouldn't down the whole jug or take it back to their own area. Instead, they'd pour the water into a cup, walk away with the cup, and say to the person behind them, "Hey, man, you're next. Have some water." They had a communal attitude, and that was key to what eventually made the concert so successful. I give credit to the crowd.

233

Basically, Shelly and I took the Woodstock concept and narrowed it down to what we thought would be successful. We moved it from three days to one and dropped the audience capacity down to 100,000 to 150,000 people. That would be easier to control. I give a lot of the credit for our success at Watkins Glen to Bill Graham and his FM Productions. He built the stage and backstage area and, while the Dead, we had the best sound system in the business. They put everything together. We got lucky. We were working with the right people.

Shelly and I decided on the bands. We knew we wanted the Dead and the Allmans. We just needed a third act. We spoke to Leon Russell about doing it. Leon was all in, but then the Dead's Jerry Garcia didn't want him for some reason. Instead, Jerry wanted the Band. He said he felt that Upstate New York was the Band's home and that it was only appropriate that the Band be on the bill. We didn't want more than three acts on the show, so Shelly had to call Leon and disinvite him. We paid him half what he would have gotten had he performed. This was before we even put tickets on sale.

We used only three acts because we scheduled the show to start at noon and wanted it over by 11:00 p.m. That was eleven hours. The Dead were famous for three-hour shows, the Allmans were famous for two-to-three-hour shows, and we felt the Band would play a two-hour show. So right there was eight of the eleven hours. Then there were stage changeovers that took time back then to swap out gear.

We needed a good hour in between bands to make the changes. Putting another act on would only water down the musical experience and not necessarily guarantee greater audience satisfaction. The Dead was the great hippie band by 1973, with their long sets and jams. We got lucky with the Allman Brothers, because when we booked them, they weren't quite as big as they'd soon become. They had put out *Eat a Peach* in early '72 and were due to release *Brothers and Sisters* in August '73. They played songs from the new album as well as earlier material. And the Band was the Band.

On Friday, a day before the event, Jaimoe of the Allmans came up to me and said they just wanted to do a sound check for thirty minutes but couldn't. The Dead was on the third hour of their sound check. There was real competition between the two bands. When the Allmans finally did their sound check, they played for two hours just to show their stuff. Then came the Band, which did around an hour. That was just the sound check. I remember asking Shelly if we could go home and pretend we just had the concert.

After I went to sleep in my trailer that night, I woke at dawn, looked out at the field, and saw we had lost the gates. More than 200,000 people were there. At the time, I could see about 200,000, but we had no idea who was sitting behind them. It turned out that the overflow of people arriving the evening before had parked along the road into the site. Thousands of others were parking on the New York State Thruway along both sides. Then they walked ten or fifteen miles to the site. They were all young, adventurous kids. They were following in the footsteps of those who had been at Woodstock in '69.

As I watched more people arrive at the event, they seemed to be the younger brothers and sisters of those who were at Woodstock. The younger siblings weren't old enough to go to Bethel, New York, but now here they were, four years older and ready to do what their siblings and those in the *Woodstock* movie had done—or at least try. In truth, Woodstock was painful for many people who were there, because it was poorly organized, they ran out of water, and the rain and mud were miserable. But the movie didn't make it seem so painful.

Bill Graham worked our staging and was a consummate professional. Although it rained when the Band went on after the Dead, it didn't matter. They could go back on immediately after it stopped because we had a good roof and the stage was dry. Bill did a good job building the stage. Then the Allman Brothers closed the show. There was really no time element. We did get the show over by around midnight, as we had planned, despite the rain.

The beauty of working with Bill was that we were able to use the Dead's sound system. It was the first time anybody had ever used a delay system. Every hundred yards into the audience, they had set up a whole new set of speakers on scaffolding. It ended up that they covered most of the audience with that, and you heard notes as they were played, not a second later. We set up for 200,000, because ticket sales ended up being around 150,000. Even though 600,000 showed up, not that many sitting in the back cared about the quality of the sound. There was no complaining about the sound or anything else, because people weren't there for days. They went home that night after the concert.

We wanted to do a movie of the concert. We knew the *Woodstock* documentary had made the promoters money, not the festival. But the Dead wouldn't allow us to film. They just outright said no. We asked if we could at least put out an album. They refused that as well. We were terribly disappointed. It would have provided us and them with a lot more revenue, but they didn't want us involved in it. Then without us knowing it, the Allmans and the Dead recorded their sets on their own. They've released parts of it.

Watkins Glen wasn't the cultural event that Woodstock or Altamont was. If anything, it became a model for the corporate rock festivals that followed, like California Jam at Ontario Motor Speedway the following year. We were more concerned about making money than advancing a cause. We weren't the hippies that Michael Lang was. Shelly and I were businessmen.

At the end of the day, we made $500,000, which was really quite a lot back in 1973. That's about $3 million in 2021 dollars. What Watkins Glen did was show the industry that supersized outdoor concerts were possible from a safety and financial perspective. I'm not talking about the 14,000 to 20,000 crowds but the 50,000 to 100,000 shows. California Jam two years later was big, made more money, and had corporate involvement. Watkins Glen led directly to the outdoor stadium business. Ours was the last big field concert—and the largest.

Sepp Donahower
(California Jam coproducer)

In 1970, I formed a Los Angeles–based concert promotion company with friends Gary Perkins and Robert Bogdanovich. We called it Pacific Presentations and focused initially on secondary markets like Santa

Barbara, Fresno, Sacramento, and San Bernardino. We linked up with American Talent International, a new talent agency, and booked as many dates as possible with their clients—Rod Stewart and the Faces, Savoy Brown, Deep Purple, and others.

Gary and I both had our MBAs from USC, we had street smarts, and we knew the ropes. We quickly became a national concert force. The demand for live rock was growing rapidly and we expanded. Frank Barsalona and Barbara Skydel at Premier Talent, one of the country's most powerful talent agencies and bookers, also favored us in many markets.

In 1973, promoters Lenny Stogel and Don Branker, attorney and producer Sandy Feldman, and ABC executives approached us to work with them on a rock festival called California Jam. They planned to stage it in California, and it would be produced by ABC Entertainment for television broadcast. ABC had a show called *In Concert* that had launched in 1972 and done well. Bands played live onstage and the show was broadcast live simultaneously on TV and FM radio. They wanted to stage a daylong multiband concert and air it the same way but on a grand scale.

Gary and I were hired to negotiate and book the Ontario Motor Speedway venue, sign all the talent, and oversee the festival's advertising and marketing. We were paid a flat fee of $75,000 ($400,000 in 2021 dollars) and all expenses. Not bad for guys in their twenties. We also received a credit line on all advertising and publicity. Everyone decided that Gary and I would do the deal with Ontario Motor Speedway. ABC knew that if they went out there to book the track, they'd have to pay top dollar. It was a wise and well-planned hustle.

When Gary and I arrived at the speedway, the manager was arrogant. In the past, he had been approached by a number of young promoters who wanted to book the site but then couldn't pull off a festival or concert. When we told the manager what we wanted to do, he cut us off and said he'd need all of the money up front—$50,000—to hold a date. So we wrote him a check on the spot for the full amount and had him issue contracts.

He didn't know that ABC Entertainment was involved. He just figured we were two green kids following in the footsteps of others who came before us. Gary and I booked Black Sabbath; Deep Purple; Emerson, Lake & Palmer; Rare Earth; the Eagles; Seals and Crofts; Earth, Wind & Fire; and Black Oak Arkansas.

They didn't want bands like the Grateful Dead or the Allman Brothers. ABC wanted mainstream acts for their national TV show. In those days, the big crowds in Southern California were being pulled in by Black Sabbath, Deep Purple, and ELP. Never underestimate the strength of metal, especially in the mid-'70s. Everybody wanted to do the show. We negotiated the deals, which wasn't easy. The artists were giving up all their rights to audio and video in perpetuity, which means forever. So we paid top dollar for the time, and the bands and their management knew the exposure would accelerate their careers.

In February 1974, we launched a print, radio, and TV ad campaign promoting the twelve-hour concert on April 6. There had not been a major festival on the West Coast in some time, as festivals had so many issues with poor planning and violence. After Altamont, states were afraid of them. We sold close to 200,000 tickets at $10 a head, bringing in a gross of close to $2 million. Woodstock and Watkins Glen had more people, but we had more paying fans. We had the highest paid attendance for a single concert or event at that point.

Just as important, we had a contained environment. You couldn't get in without a ticket. The speedway was fenced and access roads were controlled. Tickets were sold at the venue and at Ticketron outlets. We also had all the record stores, head shops, and a network of ticket outlets all over Southern California that were very effective at selling tickets. We decided to hold the concert in April because that's when spring break fell that year. But it wasn't just spring break. It was the first celebration of spring. Kids wanted to be outdoors, and they were starved for a major rock festival.

We went in there about a month before the show to start putting in the infrastructure. There were a lot of firsts. We had a mile to cover with the sound, so we needed a massive system. We hired Tycobrahe Sound, owned by our partner, Robert Bogdanovich. They set up and engineered the entire 54,000-watt system with four delay towers, each a quarter of a mile out and fifteen stories tall. They kept the sound level and pressure even all the way to the back of the speedway. It was the biggest sound system ever assembled. It was a sophisticated system with studio-quality EQ and clean amplification. Tycobrahe had the system's core units. Then they went out and rented more gear from some of their competitors. No single sound company had enough equipment to do a system on that scale.

To change bands quickly and efficiently, ABC developed a rail-and-rolling-platform system under sections of the stage. It worked flawlessly. When the performing act finished and came off the stage, the next band's gear would already be set up on the other end. The hundred-foot-long stage slid over into place and the next band was good to go. On the empty side, the next band's gear would get set up. The whole process took about a minute for set changes. Nothing like this had ever been done before at a festival.

The biggest special effect of the day was the "flying spinning piano" used by Keith Emerson of Emerson, Lake & Palmer. During a classical prog-rock piece, Emerson and the hollow grand piano he was pretending to play were raised about thirty feet in the air and then began spinning forward. There was a T-bar built onto the piano that Keith wrapped his legs around tightly as the piano started doing 360s.

There were no giant screens. They didn't have them yet. That's why the sound system had to be great all the way to the back. As far as California Jam's impact on the concert business, the Goodyear Blimp flew around overhead capturing the size and scope of the concert, functioning as a drone does today. The concert went so smoothly that it was almost boring. It ran like a military operation. We finally proved that large outdoor concerts could make money and be safe.

On a humorous note, we had all the acts stay across the freeway at a big truck stop motel. It was right on the side of the freeway across from the speedway. To make sure kids didn't find out they were there, we had the motel put up lettering on their marquee sign that said: WELCOME WESTERN PEACE OFFICERS ASSOCIATION. Nobody went near the place, and the parking lot remained empty. We had a helicopter shuttle the acts over the freeway from the motel to a landing pad behind the stage.

Chapter 15

Rise of Exurbia

In the late 1970s, divorce rates in suburbia and exurbia climbed, particularly in the Midwest's Rust Belt. The postwar American vision of prosperity was shifting. Women won reproductive rights and more of them entered the workforce to make up earnings lost by husbands who had been laid off. Many women stopped marrying for financial security, and men without meaningful work felt they had lost their purpose and status. Children in high-stress households tended to become insecure, anxious, and aimless. Life was even more challenging for children living in single-parent households. Hard rock bands with songs about the emotional hardships of suburban and exurban life connected with teens. These bands became even more significant with the introduction of the Sony Walkman in 1979, which for the first time made music portable, solitary, and more personal. Artists such as Alice Cooper, Steve Miller, and Bruce Springsteen understood the darkness that had fallen over working-class homes, especially in the country's heartland.

Alice Cooper
(lead singer and songwriter in the band Alice Cooper)

In 1968, I was living with my band in Los Angeles and running out of money. We needed a manager. Someone told us about Shep Gordon. We went over to his house. He sized up the five of us and saw a band open to try just about anything to get on the map. At that point, he was right. Shep became our manager with a handshake. Soon after, we signed with Straight Records, Frank Zappa's label. But our first two albums in 1969 and '70 bombed. That's when we started to worry. Nothing was happening for us.

Despite all of this, we never talked about quitting. The five of us had dropped out of college and put all our eggs in one basket. We knew we had something no other band had: theatricality. Most California bands then were made up of hippies. We were edgier, darker, and predisposed to be dramatic. We were all art students who had grown up sitting in front of TV sets watching sci-fi and horror movies. In the spring of 1970, we went out on the road to promote our second album. Shep joined us about a month into the tour. He saw that audience response in the Midwest was very different than in L.A.

Shep Gordon
(Alice Cooper band manager)

I suggested that the band relocate to the Midwest, where they were catching on with audiences just as the economy was starting to slide into recession. The Midwest is a huge market, and the Rust Belt had been hit hard. Alice's music was so rebellious for its time. Rebellion is what feeds pop stars. If parents think something is disgusting or inappropriate, kids cling to it. What makes something big is the cultural ride.

Alice Cooper

The dark stuff we were doing onstage fit right in. A lot of bands in the Midwest had a hard, driving sound. Regional bands like Iggy and the Stooges and the MC5. For a lot of kids at our Midwest concerts, they had taken factory jobs but hated them, despite the money being decent. Or they were out of work. The future didn't seem bright for many of them. Hard rocking bands felt their frustration and fed their outrage. So rather than have us zigzag all over the place to play any gig that popped up, Shep wanted us to break in at Midwest venues where we had developed a strong following.

Word of mouth spread in early '70, and fans were ready. Soon, we needed a place to live and to rehearse 24/7. We couldn't live out of our van, as we had been doing. Our road manager, Leo Fenn, found us a ranch just outside Pontiac, Michigan, about forty-five minutes north of Detroit. Shep wanted us to develop the lurid and despicable Alice character I played in our act. Canadian radio stations played us, and their signals were strong enough to reach much of the Midwest.

Shep Gordon

With Alice Cooper, there was no real traction until the band moved to Pontiac, Michigan, and toured the Midwest heavily. That's when we had our peeing-on-a-gas-station-wall moment. All managers focus on what has to be done to break out. The question was *how* do you do it. For Alice, it was the chicken. We couldn't sell ten tickets to his gigs until the chicken. It was our defining moment when we became the face of a wave. Becoming the face of a wave is always a bit of luck, but it's always educated luck. The chicken was an accident.

At our hotels on tour in 1969, there were feather pillows and CO_2 tanks for fire extinguishers. We took them to shows. At the end, Alice would rip open a pillow and shoot the CO_2 on it. The stage and the first twenty rows were covered in feathers, which picked up the lights. It was visually exciting and a great ending.

When we drove into Varsity Stadium for the Toronto Rock and Roll Revival festival, I saw feral chickens walking around outside. While Alice was onstage, I went out with one of the pillow cases and two security guys and caught a chicken. I thought we'd throw it out onstage to see what would happen. They had already started their show, so I never had a chance to tell Alice.

When the band got to the part with the feathers, the security guy threw the live chicken onstage in the pillow case. I thought chickens could fly. What did I know? Out comes the chicken and it just plops down in the audience. The audience behaved like an audience, and everyone grabbed for the chicken and pulled it apart. They killed the chicken. The next day, the review said Alice had ripped the head off and drunk its blood. That was our break. For years and years, we never denied it. We figured, let's just go with the story. After that one night, we never used a chicken again.

In every city we played after that, city councils had meetings about how to stop this disgusting Alice. Which is what we had prayed for. Everyone was busy trying to create Peter Pan. We created Captain Hook. To up our game, instead of doing just songs, we had a theatrical play worked out. And the story always involved a townsperson who did horrible acts. Finally, the town rises up and executes him. He does all these things dressed in black but comes back, resurrected, in white, redeemed.

Steve Miller
(Steve Miller Band founder, singer-songwriter, and lead guitarist)

Once audiences started coming to Steve Miller Band concerts in the Midwest, our fan base expanded rapidly. I already had urban fans because I had been hanging out in New York and I was living in San Francisco. So I knew those audiences. But I also grew up in Texas and went to college in Wisconsin. I knew all about what was going on in the country's heartland in the 1970s—the oil crisis, the factory closings, rise of malls and main street decay, and economic hardship. I wrote a lot of songs for those people.

The real center and heart of what we did came from the Midwest. I loved playing Kansas City, St. Louis, Minneapolis, Wisconsin, and Nebraska. The music of the South is where the essence of American music comes from. Down there, you have blues, country, and rock. That's all Southern stuff. The thing that differentiated me from artists like the Grateful Dead or Bob Dylan were my roots. I was living in Texas seeing great artists locally and listening to Southern radio in the '50s, so I heard artists like Howlin' Wolf, Bo Diddley, Little Walter, and Jimmy Reed on the radio. The real rock 'n' rollers passed through Dallas all the time.

Later, on tours in more rural areas, it felt like we were bringing the audience the culture from the coasts. Those light shows, the music, what we were doing all wrapped up in Americana—it felt like we were culture ambassadors. And the middle of the country responded to it. We played football stadiums all over the country. It was 80,000 people a night, which was amazing at the time. And they thought so, too. Performing was fun because I knew what life was like when it was 102 degrees and there was nothing to do on the weekends in Texas. It was confining and repressive. As a result, life could be boring and hard with little access to culture. Kids were overjoyed to be out experiencing the stuff they'd heard about on the radio or seen on album jackets. They got to see the people they liked. Bands were the closest thing they had to seeing the new culture in action. When those audiences heard their forgotten lives in the lyrics of your songs backed by an electric guitar, they showed their love at shows and bought your albums.

Max Weinberg
(Bruce Springsteen's E Street Band drummer)

In the early days, we played two two-and-a-half-hour shows a night. We were young then, so you could get by on your energy. Along the way, you began to realize that performing rock was serious stuff and you had to take care of yourself. We all felt this way. For me, drumming is very physical. What Bruce did was outrageously physical. In the beginning, the old theaters and clubs we played had columns and balconies and ladders. Wherever we played, Bruce incorporated those elements into the show. He'd climb a ladder or shimmy up a column or run to the back of a theater and suddenly end up singing in the balcony. He would incorporate these things and none of it was planned. We'd be playing and off he'd go. You couldn't find him until the audience spotted him. It was labor and audiences could relate.

That really endeared him to audiences in the Midwest and elsewhere. They loved when he came out there among them. They went crazy. In previous years, rock had become distant and separated from the people in the seats. A lot of performers stopped seeing themselves in the audience. The whole idea of the glam rocker and rock star as cooler than the audience had come to dominate concerts. What Bruce did was bring the music back down to earth and connect with people emotionally in the seats. His ethos has always been: "If I'm true to myself, the audience will be true to me and will accept what I'm doing." They might not like everything he's doing, but they will accept that this is his way of expressing himself.

With the E Street Band, you had a group of guys who were fully present when they hit the stage. We were like a "flying wedge." The easiest thing in the world is to get psyched up to play with Bruce and the E Street Band. Even when you're sick or if you're tired, you hit that stage ready to go. It's a sacred place. In the early days, Bruce wasn't about coaching. You got up there, rolled up your sleeves, and did the job. We shot for greatness every night. We watched him opening the valves all the way. You had to match his intensity. It wasn't necessarily a conscious effort. It was more that doing so was the job. That's what was expected. Offstage, he was just as disciplined and focused.

One of the things he did that was really smart was leaving for the next city after a concert. He liked driving at night. What that did was keep us safe and out of so-called entangling alliances. He didn't want us to be around the partying culture. Our approach, in Bruce's words, was to blow into a town, blow the roof off the place, blow right out, and get to the next town. Sometimes when we were done at midnight, we'd have to wait until 4:00 a.m. to leave while he was wrapping up media interviews. This was during the '75 to '78 period. Every night he'd do three or four hours with the media. Then we'd drive up to six or seven hours. You'd grab a couple of hours sleep and then go play again.

By 1977, we had a stripped-down Silver Eagle bus that was basically a commuter bus. We put army cots in it. What was nice about it was how streamlined and light it was. When you started riding in those big, lux rock star tour buses, they were certainly comfortable. But they were very slow because they were so heavy. Ours was so spare it was super fast. We had a great driver during that period who drove eighty to ninety miles per hour at night. If you can make it in three and a half hours, you'd rather do that than be in there for six.

In the late '70s, we were increasingly popular in areas outside of cities, particularly in the Midwest. We were from the suburbs and proud of it. Other bands sang about the bleak teenage wastelands in exurbia. Great things happen in regions outside of the city. Regional, rural audiences heard that in our music and identified with Bruce and the band. We were of them. In Bruce's case, where he grew up in Freehold, New Jersey, it was rural down there. It's more suburban now, but back in the '60s it wasn't at all developed. When Bruce was growing up, his mom was a legal secretary and became the family breadwinner. Instead of doing what many rockers did then, which was to reinvent themselves with a tough urban image, we were proud to be from South Jersey—across the Raritan River.

By 1978, the band's live performances grew in length. Bruce didn't want to leave anything on the stage, so in the process, he worked until he was exhausted and had exhausted the audience. We played hard and we played long. People talked about the band's energy. That was true. We were very energetic, particularly compared to what was on FM radio then. Even when some of the soft rock groups were on, it didn't sound or look all-out. Our approach was different. We were like a freight train. I remember Bruce saying that one of the reasons there's less saxophone on "Darkness" was because the saxophone is so intimate and cool. He limited Clarence [Clemons] to iconic solos. I remember him saying, "We're not cool. We're hot. We're in your face."

Around this time, Bruce wanted to write songs about the dignity of work. Whether you're on an assembly line or in the financial world, the dignity of work was central. For me, I was playing the drums, so there were some references. As a boss, Bruce wasn't a micromanager. He's inspirational. He said to me: "Picture yourself, picture the drums." He's a big fan of Westerns and director John Ford. He said that as the drummer, I was Monument Valley, I created the landscape across which the characters ride and the action takes place. When he described that to me, I got my role. It was reflected in my drumming.

I started to simplify everything on tour. It wasn't about playing drums; it was about being this presence, the backdrop. I'm the mountain ranges, the rock formations, the scenery. They don't ever move and the action takes place in front of what I'm doing. One of the things that changed when we started to play arenas was my drumming. As we played bigger gigs, my drumming got more and more simple. Too many fills and flash can take away from the tension in the music.

By 1984, when our *Born in the U.S.A.* album was released, my drumming had become bigger as stadium concerts for us became the norm. I remember seeing the Rolling Stones in the '70s and realizing how simply Charlie Watts was playing. I could hear everything he was doing, mostly on the snare and hi-hat and occasionally on the small tom. He hardly ever played the big tom. But in '84, on tour in support of the album, I played "Born in the U.SA." hard. The song featured me on a solo, and that was rare. Re-creating that studio moment in stadiums is what I shot for every time we played it.

The Born in the U.S.A. stadium tour was incredible. We called it Bossmania, with sort of a nod to Beatlemania. It was like that. Particularly the first six or eight months were just wild. We had to sneak in and out of hotels. In contrast to where we were before that, this finally felt like the big time. Based on the looks on people's faces, they were awestruck. For us, it was awe-inspiring. Bruce had avoided stadiums for ten years. By the time he finally decided to do stadiums, we were ready.

To get physically in shape for our tours, Bruce started weightlifting in around '82 and got into condition so we could work harder. On the road and at home, he worked out every day. He said it was perfect. You take a heavy object and you move it three feet to another place and you move it back. I guess that's true, and it develops muscles and discipline.

When we were onstage, we worked. Offstage, the key was to avoid doing something stupid to screw this thing up or reflect badly on Bruce. A band's work ethic and how it behaves starts from the top down. Bruce was extraordinarily serious about his work and his life and avoided at all costs the excesses that rock had become. Pete Townshend once said, "You go backstage at a Bruce Springsteen show, it's like being in a hospital." It's clinical and orderly. There's no scene, no hangers-on. Naps were cool. Sweating was cool.

The concert that stands out for me was in 1981. New Jersey's Brendan Byrne Arena opened on July 2, and that night we played the first of six concerts. Everybody called it the Meadowlands. I can remember standing in the tunnel leading to the stage. They had this giant metal door that you pulled up with a chain. When closed, it was one solid metal shutter, but it really was composed of many slats. As you pulled it up, the slats opened.

The door wasn't mechanical. It needed two guys pulling on a metal chain. We're standing there waiting to take the stage. As they pulled the door halfway up, the slats opened and you could see that the arena lights were still on. It was preshow, with people milling around. Suddenly, the lights went off. The two guys pulled the gate higher, to a point where we could duck under it. There was this huge roar. It was our first show back from our European tour for *The River*. Our American leg was coming up. The whole thing at that moment felt like being in the Roman Colosseum, but we were the lions. You heard the clanking of this chain and the grated door going up to release us.

When the lights went out, an ungodly roar went up and continued after we took the stage and through the first song. We couldn't even hear ourselves, even with our monitor speakers. I remember saying to myself, this must be what performing was like for the Beatles, where it's so loud you can't hear yourself. It was a hometown crowd, so there must have been quite a bit of tailgating. I think they were screaming because they felt they had a say. Through their support, they had helped small-town guys from Jersey become big. At that moment, we were them and they were us.

PART 4
The 1980s

The 1980s began with the most spectacular and costly rock concert tour to date—Pink Floyd's The Wall. Though the tour ran from February 7, 1980, to June 17, 1981, only thirty-one shows were performed. The entire production had to be broken down and reassembled at venues in Los Angeles, New York, and London—a mammoth undertaking. Despite its abbreviated schedule, the tour became a highly ambitious model for what was possible at rock concerts in terms of size, social statement, and special effects.

Six weeks after the tour ended, MTV began broadcasting on cable TV, requiring rock bands and their record labels to invest more heavily in their visual appeal on videos and in concert. But perhaps the most significant change in the rock concert business in the early 1980s was the proliferation of bank credit cards and the rise of computerized ticketing and new pricing models for seats. Both would dramatically boost box office revenue in the years ahead and completely transform the rock concert business. They also would anger rock fans who could no longer afford to attend as many concerts as they had in the past and fans who never seemed to wind up with great seats.

Arguably, the last major all-star concert with relatively low ticket prices put on by old-school promoters was Live Aid in 1985. Performed simultaneously at Wembley Stadium in London and JFK

Stadium in Philadelphia and covered by ABC and MTV, the charity event featured top rock acts appearing without special effects. Most U.S. fans paid just $35 a ticket for the all-day event ($86 in 2021 dollars), though there were a small number of $50 seats ($122 in 2021 dollars). In the years that followed, the rock concert would grow increasingly expensive and corporate, with arenas and stadiums named for companies, sponsorships by corporations, and in-venue advertising promoting products. The very conformity and corporate control that earlier generations had rebelled against would wind up controlling the space.

Chapter 16

NOT JUST ANOTHER BRICK

If you were a successful rock musician in 1980, you thought long and hard when planning your next concert tour. The more cinematic your show felt and sounded, the bigger the buzz and the more seats you'd fill. The good news was that whatever you could imagine was increasingly doable, provided you had the money and hired the right people. The industry had grown to a point where no matter what you imagined, there were niche companies that could pull it off. A giant wall that goes up onstage and tumbles down at the end? Surreal large-scale inflatables hovering over the audience? A surround-sound speaker system? A plane slamming into a wall? No problem. Pink Floyd's The Wall had all of that and more. It was the first live show to prove that the surreal fantasies of an active imagination were not only possible but also could be executed flawlessly at a high level.

Roger Waters
   (Pink Floyd cofounder, bassist, and singer-songwriter)

I remember writing *The Wall* in 1977 at Bourne Hill House in Horsham, West Sussex, England, where I was living. The theatrical concept of a wall came from our In the Flesh tour in 1977, when I spit on noisy fans in Montreal and felt bad about it. I had the idea of doing a rock show by building a wall between the audience and the band. The wall would metaphorically express the feelings I had about the divide between the people in the seats and any potential that musicians might have for creating something that loosely may be called art.

Back in the late 1970s, the Beatles already had their revolution in England. There was a great felt connection with the music of the Black struggle in America and the political struggles central to Woody Guthrie and all the later stuff in American folk music. It all tied back to a European tradition of protest, starting with the troubadour and moving up through to British folk singer Ewan MacColl and the political folk movement in the '30s and '40s. There was a perceived and felt connection with protest in all of this.

Don't forget about all the early acoustic folk that happened prior to Bob Dylan. He's so enigmatic and opaque about whether he was political in any way or not. But we know in our heart of hearts that he couldn't have written "Blowin' in the Wind" without having understood the politics behind the song and being deeply committed to the politics. A lot of the power from the music and song comes from his attachment to Woody Guthrie and Ramblin' Jack Elliott and others who came before him and showed him the way.

"The Wall" was and remains a political statement about our times, a protest against barriers and isolation. The theatrical rock show we created attempted to show how individuals and institutions box us in and try to mandate how we feel and behave and why the walls that try to silence us must come down.

Gerald Scarfe
(*The Wall* album cartoonist whose work inspired the tour's inflatable characters)

In 1971, the BBC sent me to Los Angeles to create a short film using a new animation technique. But the technique didn't work the way it was supposed to. Since I was already there, I kept an illustrated diary and drew everything American that I could think of, from the Empire State Building to Mickey Mouse and Black Power symbols. In Los Angeles, I made an eighteen-minute stream-of-consciousness short of my diary images dissolving into each other. The BBC aired my film, *Long Drawn-Out*

Trip, only once, in 1973. We couldn't get the rights to the music I used in the soundtrack, so it hasn't aired since.

Soon after the short's broadcast, Pink Floyd's Roger Waters and Nick Mason reached out to me. They had watched my animated film and loved it. The first project I worked on for them was illustrating a concert program for their 1974–75 tour in the U.K. and the U.S. They wanted a comic in the center with caricatures of band members. Then, in '77, I created surreal animated short clips that they used as backdrop films on their Wish You Were Here and In the Flesh tours.

Sometime in 1978, Roger called and said he wanted me to work with him on his next project. He came over to my house in London with a tape and played it for me. The one-and-a-half-hour recording featured Roger screaming into a tape recorder. It was a very rough outline of a project he called The Wall. I listened in silence. He sang rough versions of songs and screamed a narrative.

Roger told me the backstory about his life, his family, and that more recently he'd spat on a member of the audience behaving badly at one of Pink Floyd's gigs. He was disgusted with himself and realized there was a wall growing between him and his audience, between him and those who he wanted to reach. Then he went on to philosophize about all walls, the walls we build in ourselves to protect our vulnerability from those who can hurt us, those who know how to hurt us, and those who know how to put the knife in the right spots—people like girlfriends, boyfriends, husbands, wives, fathers who weren't there, and cruel schoolteachers. The narrative followed the life of a character called Pink, who was a stand-in for Roger and everyone else who had endured such pain.

My initial silence was really from fascination. Over the years, I've come to realize what a huge symbol a wall really is. Roger was using it as a metaphor for all walls everywhere. He universalized the whole thing. I came to realize that Roger's story was my story. The whole thing with *The Wall* started with me designing the album cover, because that's where you've got to begin. Roger never came in and micromanaged what I was doing. He showed me great respect all the way through. The album came out in 1979.

The concert included inflatable characters based on my illustrations. It was like a Roman circus. I can't think of anything quite like it. Of course, there had been gigantic rock concerts with lots of lasers and lights and God knows what else, but this had other dimensions. It was like *Ben-Hur*. The story was being told visually as well as through music and sound effects. One night, Roger took me into the hall. We stood at the back. I remember him saying to me: "You're a rock star." I said I wasn't. I was just a political cartoonist. He said, "No, no, listen, listen." They were showing my animation of sexual flowers projected on the wall that went up. A roar went up from the crowd when they saw my drawing. It felt fantastic.

Ken Schaffer
(Schaffer-Vega diversity system inventor)

In 1979, Pink Floyd built the biggest stage ever for their planned tour for *The Wall*. It was set up in a blimp hangar north of London. By then, I had enough confidence in my Schaffer-Vega wireless guitar and bass units to just ship the twelve they'd ordered rather than bring them over personally to troubleshoot. They had ordered backups for the backups because their entire stage was designed around the concept of movement. My device allowed them to play anywhere onstage, high or low, left or right.

The morning they received the units, I got a frantic call in New York from their production manager in London. He was cursing me up and down. He said the units weren't working properly during rehearsals. I was incredulous. All the units were bad? Once he calmed down, he said the problem was the delay. I was still puzzled. The wireless units had no delay. They worked at the speed of light. I asked how big the stage was. That's when I realized Pink Floyd's wedge monitors—the small speakers onstage that let them hear what they were playing—were two hundred feet away. Sound travels a foot per millisecond, but two hundred feet is a fifth of a second. So from that distance, they were a fifth of a second out of sync—enough to spoil a performance.

The solution was simple. In New York, I went out and bought these crystal-controlled single-frequency FM transmitters. I also picked up a bunch of pocket-size receivers and $1 earbuds, the flesh-colored kind sold with transistor radios then that could be plugged into the receivers. Then I flew over with a dozen of these things. At their rehearsal space, we connected transmitters to the monitor board, one for each player. That's how we eliminated the delay between the guitars and the monitor.

Rocky Paulson
(The Wall concert rigger)

In the early 1970s, I was working as a rigger for NBC. As riggers, we hoisted and secured lighting, video, sound, props, special effects, and scenery into place above a stage for Disney on Parade. They were among the biggest, most technologically advanced touring productions at the time. We'd climb those steel structures, squeeze into weird places, and pull up wire rope for hoists to suspend or "fly" things. We also created flying tracks for stage versions of *Peter Pan* and *Mary Poppins*.

When the NBC-Disney shows ended in mid-1976, I returned home to San Francisco. Rock concerts were becoming more elaborate and required skilled labor to deal with all the gear. In the years before I worked for NBC, rigging was done mostly with block and tackle—wire rope, pulleys, and hemp ropes. We never hung things that were heavier than you could lift with that primitive system. Then in the mid-'70s, we started using chain hoists so we could lift heavier elements. Rock concerts were exploding.

Part of the reason for the rise in rock concert attendance in the late 1970s is that seats considered unsatisfactory became freed up. Up until then, bands had most of their sound and lighting systems on the stage. Impressive, but the problem with ground-supported sound and lighting was that large blocks of seating in arenas remained empty because the view was obstructed and the sound was poor. Venues simply didn't sell tickets in these areas. But the need to maximize revenue forced venues to free up all seats. A new rigging approach emerged that was driven by profits and physics.

To free up seating and provide a straight line of sight to performers onstage, the solution was to "fly" sound and lighting up above the stage.

255

Once we figured out how to get the tons of gear up there, a significant percentage of seating that was dormant became active. Riggers then developed the use of trusses—metal bars to which speakers and lighting could be attached and were hoisted up and hung from the ceiling.

The Disney riggers—those of us who had worked on the Disney on Parade shows—were among the few who knew what could be done in each arena and how to get systems up there securely. We also knew how long it would take to rig a show at different venues. In San Francisco, I stayed local, rigging arenas for various shows. Best of all, I was home more, my wife was happy, and I wasn't touring. Soon I started to get calls about short tours and went out with Jethro Tull in early '77. When I got home, I promised my wife no more tours. But a couple days later, I got a call from London from Pink Floyd's production team.

They wanted me to do the rigging for their In the Flesh U.S. tour. I asked the guy on the phone how many lights they wanted to hang. He said none. I asked him how much sound. He said none. Both their lighting and sound systems were on the ground and supported from the stage. He said they needed to hang these inflatables. As he's telling me this, I'm thinking about balloons, the easiest job in the world. When I arrived in Miami, the "balloons" turned out to be thirty- to forty-foot-long inflatables, including a pig that they wanted flown out over the audience and back.

They had inflatables of a typical American family—a mother, a father, and two and a half children. The half child was sliced in half. There also was a car and a refrigerator. All had to be suspended. Each inflatable was massive. I was taking thousands of spools of half-inch wire rope and running them from one end of the venue to the other. The inflatables had to be attached to wire rope suspended horizontally, high above the stage. The ends were attached hundreds of feet apart and pulled up tight. It was the hardest thing I ever had to do. That's where a lot of The Wall's rigging technology and strategies were developed, during the In the Flesh tour.

So when Roger, architect-designer Mark Fisher, and engineer Jonathan Park wanted to do this again for The Wall, I decided to build a monorail system to fly the pig. The system I created resolved a few problems. The old pig for the In the Flesh tour looked like a balloon. We had a big fan fill it up. Then we tied a knot in the leg and sent it out. But air would leak out and the pig would soften up. For The Wall, I ran an electric line along a monorail and down to the pig so we could put a fan in the pig and keep it fully inflated all the time. We also used aircraft landing lights for the pig's eyes.

Most important was how the pig moved. Instead of yanking on ropes to pull the pig across wire suspended above the audience, I designed a trolley system that could be driven remotely back and forth along a monorail I-beam. The pig was suspended from the monorail from its back, which was attached to a rotate frame that would allow the pig to turn around at the end of the line and travel back in the other direction rather than move backward. All of this plus the power lines were hoisted and secured above the audience.

Roger also wanted a World War II plane to crash into the wall. So they built a model plane with a twelve- to fifteen-foot wingspan. We suspended a wire rope from the ceiling, starting in the back and running on a downward angle and passing just over the well. The plane was mounted on top of the wire rope on trolley wheels and secured to a wire rope above. On cue, a rigger would release the plane, which would zip down the wire and crash through the top of the wall on one side of the stage, knocking several cardboard bricks backward. The plane wasn't damaged. It came to a controlled stop backstage. The bricks were replaced during the performance.

The biggest innovation was the main wall assembled during the show on center stage that Mark designed and built and Jonathan engineered. The bricks were essentially empty cardboard boxes. They folded flat to travel and became square or rectangular, depending on the brick, before the show. The bricks didn't have tops or bottoms and were hollow inside. A special white paint was applied that allowed for film and images to be projected on them.

The goal was for the wall to be assembled during the show without the audience seeing workers behind building it. At the end, the bricks needed to tumble down but not fall into the audience. They hired Genie Industries from Seattle to build five special tower platforms. Genie made what they called man lifts that telescoped up and down behind the wall with workers on them to elevate or lower the platform. Several of the man lifts were placed side by side. When they were all the way down, they were flush to the stage floor.

As the crew on a platform needed to place bricks higher and higher throughout the show, the platforms were raised. The crew members were called the Wallies. They wore black and were always hidden by the wall. The other challenge that needed an engineering solution was gravity. As bricks are stacked, the more unstable they become. You didn't want these bricks wobbling and falling accidentally during the show. So, every twenty feet along the wall, there were pneumatic telescoping poles that went up inside the bricks but never exceeded the height of the highest one to avoid exposure. When the cardboard bricks were added to the wall, these poles would go up inside to hold them securely in place. It was an internal spine of sorts.

On the very tops of these interior poles were little rockers that could be operated to move the top part forward or backward. When it was time at the end for the bricks to come tumbling down, the poles would be lowered and you'd operate the rockers to push the bricks forward or backward, depending on how they wanted the collapse to take place. In other words, as the pole was lowered, the rockers on top could shove bricks forward or backward.

To keep bricks from falling into the seats, the operators made most of them fall backward, away from the audience. Even though some fell forward, the seats began twenty feet away from the wall. Remember, the bricks weren't giant bouncing Styrofoam bricks. They were made of cardboard. When they fell, they were light enough that they landed stationary. Even if they fell off the stage, they wouldn't reach the seats.

To set up The Wall, we needed to arrive at a venue a week before the concert to get the job done. A day before we finished setting up, the band would come in to do a little sound check. A full rehearsal was done the afternoon of opening night. The breakdown and truck loading always took at least a day. We used about twenty large semitrailer trucks. They carried the stage, the inflatables folded up, the lighting, the sound, the sound mixing equipment, the rigging equipment, all the band equipment, the rear screens, the bricks, and four 35mm projectors similar to what movie theaters used. One was a rear-screen projector. It was mounted in the stands behind the screen. So it projected on the rear of the screen, before the wall went up. For the wall projection, there were three projectors mounted out in the house on scaffolding.

Roger has never been given proper credit for The Wall or the development of rock concert stage production. It's one thing to have ideas. It's another to know how to get them done. He hired the right people and let them solve problems creatively and sometimes expensively. Money was no object if it solved a problem innovatively and safely. From a staging standpoint, The Wall set the tone for rock concerts in the '80s and changed the concert business in many ways—the scale, the technology, the sound, the choreography of theatrical and pyrotechnic elements, and the multimedia. The bar was raised. I've never seen anything as crazy as what Pink Floyd did on that tour.

Stan Miller
(The Wall sound-system designer)

In June 1978, some of Pink Floyd's sound people, including their production manager, Robbie Williams, came to hear Bob Dylan perform at Earl's Court in London. I was providing Bob with sound, and the system was attached to trusses and hoisted up. Patrick Stansfield, our production manager, nicknamed it the flying junkyard, because that's what all those different speakers looked like. Robbie liked Bob's setup and said it was the first time he'd heard a system that gave an artist's vocals clear intelligibility. That was because I was using devices that functioned like a nozzle on the end of a hose to direct the sound.

Robbie next flew to San Francisco in February 1979 to hear Neil Diamond at the Cow Palace. It was the same system I had designed for Bob's concert a year earlier. Robbie liked it and told me about the upcoming tour Pink Floyd was planning for *The Wall*. He hired me to design a wraparound quadrophonic sound system. It was the most expensive system I'd ever built up to that point.

I delivered it to the Los Angeles Memorial Sports Arena in January 1980, where Pink Floyd was rehearsing a month in advance of the

259

tour's February 7 start date. They had me and my team accompany the U.S. tour to troubleshoot. During the rehearsals, my team took notes and measured the volume in different locations to be sure there were no dead zones.

They needed a month for rigging, fixing things, working out kinks, building the wall, testing the wall's collapse, testing the hydraulic lifts, and so many other technical things. In their infancy, rock concerts of this scale were a matter of trial and error. Nothing was an exact science. While I had done large arena concerts before, The Wall was the most complex and intricate show I'd been involved in. Everything was experimental.

On the sound side, we tested it to see how loud the band could play before the system distorted. We watched amplifiers to see that they were sustaining their power. One of the things we learned early on is that you needed way more amplifier power than we had initially. If you don't have enough, that's what winds up blowing components. We also found that solid-state amps had way more power than tube units.

The rehearsals sounded great. Then on the night of the first show, the band put the pedal to the metal and blew our forty fifteen-inch speakers, which meant they stopped working. That was approximately half of them. After that show, we had to lower the entire system to the floor, and the speaker boxes had to be taken apart and fixed. They all had to be finished by the next night. The amps and speakers were all Altecs. Fortunately, Altec's manufacturing facilities were in Anaheim, so it wasn't too far away. We were doing multichannel stuff with speakers around the rear and under the seats that was cutting-edge and ahead of its time. The sound enveloped the audience and made them feel more engaged.

The final show in L.A. was on February 13. Then everything was loaded into trucks that drove across the country to New York's Nassau Coliseum. The first night's performance there was February 24. After five nights in New York, Pink Floyd took the sound system to Europe on tour. Britannia Row, their sound production company run by Robbie, had purchased the system. We trained their sound people on installing and repairing it. I'm a classical music buff, and the things they were doing musically were very symphonic and exciting. The Wall was like staging an opera. The sound had to be just as spectacular.

Dave DiMartino
(Rock journalist who reviewed The Wall concert in *Creem*)

When you think about it, Pink Floyd's The Wall tour in 1980 and '81 was dark stuff. At its core, the concert was a rock opera about emotional torture and repression laced with surreal imagery, quad sound, and cinematic effects. I saw The Wall in New York at the Nassau Coliseum. I had seen Pink Floyd in concert several times before when they used quadrophonic sound and was impressed. You knew you were experiencing something unique then. But The Wall was something else and became a turning point in live music.

The Wall was a whole different level of rock concert—a big theatrical thing. From the seats, Pink Floyd's stage set for The Wall looked like it required hundreds of people to create, set up, and manage during the show as the wall went up. I'd never seen a rock performance so elaborate. You could tell that boatloads of money were being spent and that the result was pretty cool. Given punk's rise and popularity using stripped-down, minimalist production, you'd think The Wall's elaborate message show would be a souring, ponderous experience. But it wasn't. It was a shock to the system. The Wall was theater. It was opera. Of course, what set it apart was the centerpiece—the construction of a large wall, which made the stage seem like a movie set.

The whole notion of constructing a wall, brick by brick, while Pink Floyd performed was ambitious and satisfying. I liked the album very much and thought the show was a magnificent visual adaptation of the audio. It was an incredible thing to see unwind for the first time. There was anxiety and tremendous anticipation.

During the concert, you knew that if they were building a wall that big, it certainly was going to come down somehow. I thought, "What's the wall going to look like when done? When it comes down, will it be loud? Is there going to be a disruption to the scheduling of the show?

Are the huge white bricks going to hit people in the seats? How can they possibly make it a smooth performance?" All feelings you'd experience at the circus during daredevil acts.

What made The Wall special wasn't just the visual effects. There was intellect behind much of what was going on, from the imagery of marching fascist hammers to the airplanes to the death of Roger Waters's father. Thematically, the format was geared to put the fear of God into the audience. And yet Pink Floyd didn't bite off more than they could chew. Had effects failed or the sound gone dead or the plane missed its mark, you might have felt they had screwed up. Instead, the show was successfully executed. There was a wow feeling.

As far as The Wall raising the bar, the impact of musical theater and production values along with its impact on the live rock scene was relevant then. The larger the scale, the more significant the music sounded and felt. The size of the wall and the enormity of the sound probably led to the viability of giant video screens at rock concerts. In some ways, the giant LED display screens that arrived in the late 1980s would replace much of the theatrical stuff. Seeing the artists up close from a great distance eliminated the need for a large-scale theatrical presentation to keep the eyes busy. Replicating The Wall was too costly for most bands back then. But rock artists and bands such as Bruce Springsteen, Prince, AC/DC, Queen, and others did work harder to put on mind-blowing, high-energy shows. To hold on to your stadium-size audiences, you no longer could just stand there and play.

The Wall was a turning point but a short-lived one. The following year, everything Pink Floyd was shooting for onstage suddenly became prehistoric with the launch of MTV in '81. All of the gear Pink Floyd was hauling around and setting up for visual excitement could now be taped in a studio or on a set for a music video. But the live visual experience of The Wall had value and was unforgettable. Aside from leaving you in awe, The Wall let you feel what you were seeing. It hit all of your senses. You also could experience the concert by looking directly at the stage or left and right. You weren't locked into one particular perspective on a screen, the way you were with a music video.

So The Wall was a game changer in terms of vision and production. Roger Waters had the desire and the drive, and Pink Floyd created a market for taking the rock concert to a much higher level. Equally impressive was that Pink Floyd—not their record company—paid for The Wall themselves.

Chapter 17

KILLING THE RADIO STAR

When MTV went live just after midnight on August 1, 1981, only a relatively small percentage of viewers saw the debut of the music video channel. Most people in major cities either weren't yet wired for cable TV or didn't have the new channel as part of their cable package. Many lower-income areas also didn't have MTV because cable wasn't initially available in areas where residents weren't likely to be able to afford a monthly subscription. But as buzz and demand grew and cable became ubiquitous, MTV was a must, especially in households with kids. For the first time, you could see artists on TV playing current rock hits in three-minute clips. Once viewers saw artists perform hits that they heard on the radio, they wanted to buy the albums and to see the bands live in concert.

Sue Steinberg
(MTV executive producer)

Almost immediately after the launch of MTV, rock became glossier and more visual. Thanks to MTV, songs became popular faster among friends, short-form videos became culturally acceptable, and our VJs' banter format became a forerunner to reality TV. We had scripts for the VJs, but they weren't stiff or sitcom in tone. They were natural, as if they were hanging out in your parents' basement or in a college dorm. VJs were expected to know the music and be able to ad-lib things about the artists leading into videos. We supplemented the scripts by giving them research on the music and bands. A couple of VJs could do it off the top of their heads because they had been radio DJs, like Mark Goodman and J. J. Jackson.

I recruited the VJs who would cover our demographics. Nina Blackwood was our sexy, Debbie Harry–type VJ. Mark Goodman was appealing to girls and knew his music. J. J. Jackson had TV experience and knew rock 'n' roll. Alan Hunter was a nice, sweet all-American boy. And Martha Quinn was the quirky, upbeat girl next door. She came along forty-eight hours before launch, after another female VJ didn't work out.

On the evening of Friday, July 31, 1981, we were in countdown mode for our launch at midnight. We were scrambling and scurrying. And then, with seconds until midnight, MTV went to its on-screen countdown. Footage rolled of the first space shuttle, *Columbia*, lifting off; John Lack, MTV's COO, announced, "Ladies and gentlemen, rock 'n' roll"; Jonathan Elias and John Petersen played MTV's now-famous recorded rock guitar theme; and footage appeared of Neil Armstrong planting the color MTV logo flag on the moon. Everything was perfect. Except as each VJ introduced the next, the wrong person came up on the screen. They were out of sequence and everyone's jaw dropped.

Once we were around-the-clock live, the goal was to get MTV to look and feel like something. We needed to have something more than an endless rotation of music videos. In the beginning, we actually didn't have that many music videos. If MTV was truly going to be music television, we had to offer viewers more. I thought we should take a cue from *Rolling Stone* magazine and offer kids what we could in the way of music news until we could expand. I thought MTV, ultimately, would become a lifestyle channel the way that *Rolling Stone* became a music lifestyle magazine. We had no competition, so we had the luxury of becoming anything we wanted, so long as we became something.

One of our regular features was MTV tour news. Upcoming rock concert dates were easy to get from venues and managers. Each hour, we'd have a VJ give updated tour information while an image was on the screen. Viewers loved it, since we often had the information before it appeared in newspaper ads. Record companies were happy for the promotion. They loved being part of the food chain: concert dates were announced, viewers bought tickets, and then they went out and bought the band's latest album so they'd be up to speed.

I went to more concerts after we launched because I worked at MTV and had easy access to tickets. MTV was a force from the start. Nothing else covered rock in the video format all day, every day. My sense was that because of MTV's steady growth and rapid entry into the culture, seeing bands live that you saw on TV became a bigger deal. After MTV's launch, everything about rock became a visual experience. For anyone under thirty, MTV was like the British invasion all over again. In New York, where MTV wasn't available yet on cable TV, people went to friends' houses in the suburbs to watch for hours. Even the MTV team had to go to a bar across the Hudson in New Jersey just to watch the launch live.

Live music changed after MTV. The slickness of videos became part of the performing culture. The appeal and success of videos pushed acts to give audiences a show, and there had to be a styled look. Guys who could play a synthesizer suddenly were drowning in work. And concerts tried to emulate the coolness of videos on TV. Even David Bowie got this early with "Let's Dance" in 1983. New wave bands, in particular, became more popular after the launch of MTV. Visually astute artists such as Elvis Costello, Culture Club, Blondie, the Cars, Cyndi Lauper, Talking Heads, Duran Duran, and the Police all had hit videos, which created an appetite to see them live.

Mark Goodman
(Original MTV VJ from 1981 to 1987)

In the '60s, the Beatles changed music, fashion, film, and television. They influenced virtually everything. The same was true for MTV in the 1980s. The channel provided bands with a new platform to reach audiences and gave them and the music a visual personality. As with the Beatles, MTV caused a shift in many different parts of the culture.

In 1980, I was a DJ at WMMR-FM in Philadelphia. That year, I moved to WPLJ-FM in New York, which at the time was the #1 rock station in the #1 market. I was thrilled to get the job. I started in July but by March 1981, I hated it. WPLJ was all hits, and we weren't touching on anything that I truly loved—punk and new wave music that had gained fans and was influencing music in a big way. There had to be more to radio than Meat Loaf and Bad Company. One day, a radio colleague I had worked with in Philadelphia called to see how I was doing. I told him about my disappointment. He told me about a friend of ours who had become a TV producer at Warner-Amex. They were casting for a new 24/7 channel that showed music videos.

In its infancy, cable TV didn't have the greatest reputation as it tried to gain its balance, so I was skeptical about the venture's viability. What held my interest in the project was that it was being seriously funded by a corporate entity—Warner Communications and American Express. On top of that, Bob Pittman was running it, and I had known him as a successful radio programmer at WNBC for several years. He was in his twenties and known in the industry as a wunderkind. I thought that music television produced by the joint venture and Bob had a real shot to be something. At the very least, I hoped, it would be a place where I could play some newer music.

The concept behind MTV—aside from the ingenious idea of airing music videos—was to bond with the rock-loving public. The channel was designed to be a rock station initially. When we launched MTV in '81, we had had two newsbreaks per hour. One of those breaks was devoted to concert dates for specific rock bands. It was a big thing for us to present concert dates to viewers. All music fans wanted to keep up with the touring schedule of their favorite bands, and MTV made it quick and easy.

Music videos offered fans a new way to see their favorite artists, and they provided new artists with a new avenue to invade a fan's consciousness. Some were high-concept videos that told stories, others were straight-up performances. Either way, fans were all in to watch, over and over again. In our first year after MTV's launch, we were just happy to have any videos at all from the record companies. British artists had been using video in the U.K. to promote themselves for years. That's why they were camera ready for MTV's format. Labels were happy to give us videos of their artists. Each time a video aired, it was like a 3'30" commercial for the band featured. Once the labels realized that MTV sold

267

records and concert tickets, labels started producing more videos, and artists started to insist on a video budget in their contracts.

For our news segments, MTV sent the VJs out to emcee concerts or report on music news stories. Eventually, we had a news department that packaged music information every hour. So covering concerts and doing interviews was part of the territory as a VJ. But from the artist's perspective, getting your video on MTV was really what it was all about, especially after the first year. Videos could break a band on a national level, especially obscure ones. As the months rolled on, record labels hired more exciting, avant-garde directors, designers, and stylists to give bands in the videos an image and an edge.

By broadcasting British artists' videos, MTV introduced many new acts to American listeners they may never have known or bothered with. In turn, seeing these bands compelled viewers to give them a chance. The new romantics, British metal, new wave, and other genres became popular and influenced other bands, concert performances, and viewers' tastes. Tours were a big part of a band becoming known and having hits. If MTV was playing your video and the video was selling your records, it would open new markets for an expansion of your tour dates, which led to merchandise and record sales.

Though we were on MTV playing music videos all day, VJs were virtually unknown in many places. But when we showed up at concerts in New Jersey, Westchester, or Long Island, where MTV was thriving, we'd be mobbed. Among my favorite concerts then were the Clash, who played a series of seventeen concerts at Bond's in New York in May and June 1981, before MTV launched. I went to a bunch of those. I'd never seen anything like them before.

The other side of that coin was seeing Bruce Springsteen at the Brendan Byrne Arena in the summer of 1984, during the E Street Band's Born in the U.S.A. tour. Bruce did ten nights there, and I was at every one of them. I did his first full television interview for MTV at the arena. At the time of the tour, Bruce was already a star. But that album blasted him into superstardom. There was nothing like a Bruce show. Back then, the band was like James Brown's Famous Flames. They were so tight. I would watch drummer Max Weinberg and the other guys. They'd be watching Bruce because he was liable to call an audible change at any moment. You never knew where he was going to go next.

MTV played a major role in sending Bruce's career to a new level. The videos for his *Born in the U.S.A.* album featured Bruce performing in concert, like "Dancing in the Dark" and "Glory Days." Before these, he hadn't appeared in his videos. I asked him about his change of heart during my interview backstage. He said his nieces and nephews were asking why he wasn't on MTV in his videos. His shift was mostly to make them happy. The "Dancing in the Dark" video was particularly powerful. It featured a squeaky-clean Bruce in a white cutoff T-shirt and Courtney Cox, planted in the audience and coming up out of the seats to dance with him. After that aired repeatedly on MTV, every girl wanted to sit down front at a Bruce concert hoping to be chosen as the next Courtney Cox.

Bono and U2 in the early '80s had the same level of genuine passion. The concerts during the massive Joshua Tree U.S. tour vaulted the band from cool alt-Irish band to massive superstars. Bono's efforts to bond with the audience were spectacular. I still believe that the twenty-four-hour format of MTV created a universe and urgency for live music unlike anything *American Bandstand* or *The Midnight Special* could ever do. We allowed music to grow in ways no one imagined.

When MTV launched in 1981, there were 23.2 million cable subscribers in the United States, or 28.3 percent of all households that owned a TV. In '83, those numbers jumped to 34.1 million subscribers, or 40.5 percent of households with a TV. By then, MTV was a must. That summer, a new wave band popular on MTV, Talking Heads, was touring in support of their "Speaking in Tongues" hit album. On August 19 and 21, the band was at New York's Forest Hills Stadium performing what would become one of the most praised concerts of their career.

Tina Weymouth
(Talking Heads and Tom Tom Club bassist and singer-songwriter)

From the stage at our Forest Hills concert in August 1983, the temperature and humidity were perfect for playing and hearing. Bodies were packed shoulder to shoulder in the tennis stadium seats. We got this communal energy coming from the crowd. The bass's sound tends to push all the air forward to move the sound of all the other instruments. We had the right warmth in the air for my bass's sound to roll up into the stands from the stage and carry everything else with it. It was beautiful.

Chris Frantz
(Talking Heads and Tom Tom Club drummer)

From where I was sitting behind my drums, I could see Madonna dancing barefoot in the wings, and Mick Jagger was standing there with Jerry Hall. There were a number of superstars there that night. We knew the concert was going to be special. New York was our home base. That's where we started and grew up with the band, so it was a big deal for us to be there. We knew from our experience playing in Central Park that anything outdoors in New York in the summer would be great.

Tina Weymouth

The sound system was terrific. We leased it from Pink Floyd's Britannia Row sound rental company. We had a brilliant engineer at the mixing board—Jeff Hooper. He was making music out of music. If the sound person isn't good, the band is screwed no matter how well you play. Late in our second set, we switched gears and the band that Chris and I had formed, Tom Tom Club, played our hit "Genius of Love," which had been released as an import a year earlier. The reason we did that song was so David could change into his big suit.

Gail Blacker
(David Byrne's "big suit" designer)

In 1981, I met Talking Heads' guitarist Jerry Harrison and his girlfriend, Linda, at a tent hotel in Yucatán, Mexico. We developed a friendship. Back in New York, Jerry told David Byrne to see me about a project they had in mind. Of course, I was familiar with David and Talking Heads. When we met at my studio, I found him to be gentle and soft-spoken. He explained his idea for an oversized suit for a performance.

He had recently been to Japan, where he saw classical Japanese theater that inspired his vision: large and square from the front, sliver-thin from the side. This was my first costume-design request, although in my Soho storefront, my one-of-a-kind clothing was quite theatrical. This was the start of the video era, which from the performer's standpoint combined rock and theater.

I chose a soft gray Italian breathable linen. Then I thought about how to create the illusion of the suit's look that David was trying to pull off. The real challenge was creating the underframe David would wear to support the suit. I used a stiff nylon netting used in clothing construction to create the volume by folding and pleating it. The netting was attached to a band that David wore around his waist. This is what enabled the suit to have the form David was looking for. Then more netting and interfacing was used to build out the shoulder area, and various pads were used to preserve the shape.

Cotton fusible interfacing was pressed on in certain places to maintain the form but not everywhere in order to keep the suit as breathable as possible. The trousers could clip on to the netting waistband and take their shape from there. Constructing the suit's underframe was like designing a building. We also had to take into consideration movability and flexibility, since David's movement couldn't be obstructed in any way. The soft linen chosen was just the right weight that allowed for movement and airiness.

I saw David wear the suit in concert at the Forest Hills concert in 1983. I was proud and overjoyed that it worked perfectly. After the tour, I got calls from other artists. I got a call from Bruce Springsteen's people. They wanted me to do a pair of black jeans for Bruce for his upcoming concert tour. His people said they'd send a limo for me, take me to Bruce's home in New Jersey to take the measurements, and then have me come back to do the fittings.

I had to turn down Bruce. I had to get my next collection out and didn't have a minute to spare. I said to Bruce's people that if he came to my studio in Manhattan, at least for the measurements and the first fitting, I'd do it. But he wouldn't come. Looking back now, of course,

I'm sorry I didn't go out to Jersey. I was a very big fan. But I had a commitment.

The rock concert business grew increasingly profitable and competitive in the early 1980s, giving rise to a greater number of venues in regions. In some cases, these venues were a result of cutthroat competition. One of them was Shoreline Amphitheatre in Mountain View, California.

Danny Scher
(Bill Graham Presents vice president and promoter)

From 1975 to '80, the Bay Area experienced sizable venue growth. You had multiday stadium concerts, outdoor concerts like Day on the Green, and big shows dominated at arenas. In San Francisco, rock went from small places in the early '70s like the Fillmore Auditorium and Berkeley Community Theater to midsize places like Winterland Ballroom. Then in the late '70s, more of our shows were being held at the Oakland Coliseum and the Cow Palace, a 14,500-seat venue. Anyone could call and rent those places. There were no exclusives for individual promoters. Remaining the main promoter in San Francisco was critical for Bill Graham Presents. But at the tail end of the 1970s, a brutal battle began for major venues.

One day in the early 1980s, I got a call from Steve Jensen at International Creative Management. He said he was sorry about what happened at the Concord Pavilion. When I asked what he was talking about, he said we had been thrown out. The Concord Pavilion had made an exclusive deal with Nederlander Concerts. The Concord Pavilion had opened in Concord, California, in 1975 and was owned by the city. It was an amphitheater designed by Frank Gehry and had 12,500 seats. The Nederlander Organization was expanding beyond Broadway.

I called up our guy at the Pavilion who we had been dealing with for years. I also called Concord's parks director, who oversaw the Pavilion. Both confirmed the change. Nederlander's move ignited aggressive competition in the Bay Area. It was the first time a major promoter had come into the market to compete against us. We never called what we had a monopoly, but we certainly controlled the market. Being boxed out of the Pavilion meant trouble. One day it's the Pavilion and the next it could be the Oakland Coliseum.

Almost immediately, our ticket prices started to go up to keep pace with escalating prices that bands demanded to perform. What's more, band managers knew venues were competing to land them. The way we combatted Nederlander was by booking major acts into our theaters around the Concord to give fans concert options other than the Pavilion. Every day I went to work as if I was going to war. I finally told Bill that the only way we were going to beat these guys was to do business differently. I said we could either go broke working out a deal with a venue or we could build our own place and control all of the variables. And that's what we did. We built our own amphitheater in 1985. That's how I developed the Shoreline Amphitheatre in Mountain View, Ca., with 22,500 seats. But the ticket-pricing genie was already out of the bottle. Computers were making it easier to calculate value and maximize prices.

Chapter 18

COMPUTERIZED TICKETING

In the late 1960s, Ticketron became the country's first regional computerized ticket seller—in New York and New Jersey. But you still had to stand in line and sometimes sleep at Ticketron outlets overnight in places like department stores to buy tickets with cash. In 1974, BASS (Bay Area Seating Service), based in San Francisco, was the next regional computerized ticket seller, just as Ticketron expanded nationally in '72. Both sellers faced technology and business limitations that prevented them from becoming fail-safe national ticket vendors. Then came Ticketmaster in 1976, which plodded along until 1982, when Fredric D. Rosen became the company's president and CEO and revolutionized the ticket business. By 1985, Ticketmaster would become the global leader in ticketing and pricing.

Hal Silen
(cofounder of BASS in San Francisco)

In 1973, I was an attorney in Oakland. One of my clients was Roller Derby, headed by Jerry Seltzer, whose father had started the craze in the 1930s. Our firm's office building had a Ticketron outlet in our lobby. The system was always breaking down and screwing up. After Jerry's Roller Derby business went under in '73, he and I started talking. There had to be a better way to sell electronic tickets. The concept was smart, but the computers and software needed to be more stable.

With time on his hands, Jerry found a computer system at the Omni Coliseum in Atlanta that wasn't being used. They had been leasing two Hewlett-Packard systems, and we could pick up the lease from HP. The computers were massive and better taken care of than my children. And I took great care of my kids. To remain operational, the computers needed heating and cooling and humidifiers.

Obviously, we needed funding, but banks wouldn't give us a loan. They didn't want any part of a computer system or electronic ticketing. So I went to everyone I knew—my wife's old ob-gyn, our accountant, our insurance agent, and our family and friends. Jerry did the same. We needed the money for lease payments on the computers and for the software system we were going to develop. We formed Bay Area Seating Services—BASS—in '74, and HP shipped the computers we were leasing across the country to us.

Jerry Seltzer
(cofounder of BASS)

The full name of the new company wasn't really hip for the times. Instead, we went with the acronym BASS. We had an artist draw a fish in a top hat that appeared on every ticket, giving us a human, San Francisco–hippie image. People in the Bay Area would trust a fish in a top hat before a corporation.

Electronic event ticketing clearly was the future. It was fast and convenient, and venues stood to benefit. At the time, computers were the size of refrigerators. They'd crash, and not many people knew how to bring them back online quickly.

Hal Silen

To avoid Ticketron's computer problems, we needed solid, stable software. Jerry and I went down to Stanford University to talk to two guys in the Artificial Intelligence Lab. They said they could create the software we wanted. We rented some space, and the two guys worked twenty-four hours a day. Within four weeks, they had a rudimentary system in place at a much lower cost. We were ready to go. I had done some legal work for promoter Bill Graham, so I went to see him. I told him we'd sell his tickets. Jerry talked to him as well.

Jerry Seltzer

When I went to see Bill and proposed that we become his exclusive ticket seller in Northern California, he asked what would be in it for him. We said we'd raise the service charge to 75 cents and give him the extra quarter on each ticket. He said, "I'm in." Graham had been unhappy with Ticketron, which handled electronic ticketing for him. Then he heard that Ticketron was going to help another promoter produce a festival in New York. He was livid. Ticketron was merely a concert listing service. BASS was becoming a marketing and promotion service. I constantly researched where our ticket sales were coming from. We started with twenty-four outlets in record stores and Sears stores in the Bay Area. Then in the early 1980s, we created a service for phone-in credit card sales. I was determined to replace Ticketron in the marketplace. I never forgave them for failing to tell us about their computer problems and for contributing to the demise of my family's Roller Derby business.

By the early 1980s, BASS was doing well and we wanted to expand into Southern California and beyond. But we didn't have the capital. Ticketmaster had been founded in Phoenix in 1976 as a licensor of computer programs and seller of ticket-system hardware. Then in 1982, the company went into the computerized ticket business when Fred Rosen was named president and CEO. He was taking on Ticketron for dominance in the national ticketing business.

It was time to find allies, so BASS entered into an agreement with Fred and Ticketmaster in 1982 to expand into Southern California. Hal and I sent one of our people to operate the L.A. office. But soon after our person arrived, Fred felt the person wasn't strong enough. Fred said he'd make me a deal. He'd move to L.A. from New York for six months if I'd do the same to see if we could crack the market. I moved down in March 1983. I set up a marketing department and applied the unorthodox marketing strategies I had developed during my Roller Derby days. The turning point for us came in July 1983, when Ticketmaster won the exclusive ticketing contract at the Los Angeles Forum, the center of entertainment and sports in Southern California. Fred let BASS license the Ticketmaster system.

David Mendelsohn
(BASS general manager)

On the concert side, our clients were theaters, coliseums, and stadiums. Through Ticketmaster, we had computerized box offices all over the city. The terminals tapped into our computer system, which held the full inventory of seats. The system had to let all sellers know in real time which seats were available and which weren't. At one point, we had the third-largest telephone system in Northern California that wasn't government controlled. Everything worked by telephone link to the computer. We spent a lot of money leasing phone lines.

By the early 1980s, through Ticketmaster, we had over a hundred ticket centers. They stood in record stores and groceries all over California. We had one hundred phone operators who answered calls from people who wanted to buy tickets. You had to have a credit card to make the purchase. The phone bank was essential by the 1980s. People in the far suburbs of cities didn't have the time to drive in to pick up tickets and then return home.

Fredric D. Rosen
(Ticketmaster president and CEO from 1982 to 1998)

At Ticketmaster, I changed the dynamic of the arena and stadium ticket business in the 1980s and '90s and took the heat for the whole industry. There were a lot of people who didn't like what I was doing and weren't fond of me. Not my clients—the arenas and promoters who made money—but my competitors and some of the managers of the acts and their agents. I was pretty tough. But it was complicated.

The issue was over service fees—the charges we added to the price of tickets for the convenience of buying them without traveling to the venue's box office. All the charges were set by contract, and my goal was to charge what the market would bear. And in the 1980s, consumers always had three options: They could buy tickets by phone and pay a fee for the convenience. They could drive hours to the venue, wait in line, and buy their tickets there. Or they could skip going to the concert altogether.

In the 1980s, ticketing was unlike any other aspect of the rock concert business. Everybody wanted to improve ticketing but, in truth, there was no way to make it better. Concertgoers were always going to hate a third of what was sold—the back third of a venue. Everyone wants to sit as close to the stage as possible. Unless you're sitting in the first ten rows, you're always wishing you were closer. To make matters worse, from your seats, you're staring at seats you wish you had. But you can't make the front rows ten miles long.

My reality was that nobody pays more for a ticket than they want to pay, and that hasn't changed since 1982, when I became Ticketmaster's CEO. Think about it. Nobody is forcing anyone to buy a ticket. If you feel the concert is worth what you're being charged, you make the purchase.

I was an attorney when the Ticketmaster opportunity came along in 1982. I couldn't let it pass. I had a passion for the business. Ticketmaster was started in 1976 by three guys who had just graduated from college and thought electronic ticketing was the future. But they didn't have enough money for a computer.

After a year, they found Charles Hamby, a direct mail marketer, who agreed to fund them. But Hamby misjudged how much was needed to compete with Ticketron. So Hamby convinced Hyatt Hotels Management Corporation to invest. Hyatt was run by the Pritzker family, which also managed the Superdome in New Orleans. They bought out Hamby, but they didn't have much of a sustainable business plan other than using Ticketmaster to sell Superdome tickets. So they sold the company to Burt Kanter, their attorney and tax adviser.

I first met Burt around this time. He had put $3 to $5 million into a bunch of enterprises with hopes that one or more would take off. Burt said to me: "Look, your attention span is better than mine. So here's the deal: I'll make you special counsel to all of these companies because you've got a pretty good business head. You meet me once a month and let me know what's going on in all of them."

And so I got a retainer from all of those companies, including Ticket-master. Ticketmaster was a partner in an operating business in Houston that was comprised of five partners. I'd go to these Ticketmaster meetings in Houston where all decisions required unanimous consent. Needless to say, nothing got done and every meeting was contentious. They'd be complaining about the business and how hard it was to make money. No wonder it was hard. They had borrowed all the money to run the business when the prime lending rate was 22 percent and the company was cash flow even. I thought they were missing the point and the opportunity.

I finally asked, "Why is there a dollar service charge on a forty-dollar ticket?" They said, "Because we sell a five-dollar ticket." At the time, service charges were uniform based on the lowest-priced ticket in the house. I said, "So what? Why can't you have a two-dollar service charge on a forty-dollar ticket and a one-dollar charge on a five-dollar ticket?" They said, "You can't do that." Being a New York wiseass, I said, "Why not? Was that one of the tablets Moses dropped?" Which immediately got them all infuriated.

They didn't want to have multiple service charges on the same event. I was an outsider and looked at business from a commonsense viewpoint. I said, "Look, if you've got a forty-dollar ticket, that has nothing to do with a five-dollar ticket. So we can have multiple service charges." Then I did a little digging and found the real reason why they were clinging to that one-dollar myth. The way their software system was written made it difficult for computers to add varying service charges to different tickets for a single event. They were programmed to add one service charge across the board, regardless of the ticket's price.

I learned a few other things from my research. First, a board meeting in the ticket business can't be a democracy. To run a ticket company, you need total control. One voice. You need to cut through assumptions that don't make good business sense. I was convinced that ticketing could be a very successful business if we were freed from the assumptions about service charges and revenue sharing.

Second, I discovered that about 75 percent to 80 percent of the tickets for rock concerts were sold at a venue's box office in 1982. This meant that we had a huge market waiting for us if we could get consumers to trust our electronic system. Those numbers told me that people were going to the box office to line up and camp out. Neither of these options was very appealing to those looking to buy tickets. And third, the only option, nationally, was Ticketron, which had expanded and was given an allocation of the ticket total by nearly every arena. Ticketron had two computer systems, one for season tickets and one for single tickets. Those two systems weren't integrated, nor did they talk to each other. All of this meant that if you used Ticketron, you could only draw from the tickets they were given, not the entire house.

In the spring of 1982, I went to see Burt about buying his interest in Ticketmaster, which was running out of money. He was going to close it. I said, "Give me a chance to see if I can get it funded." I went to see Jay Pritzker, who agreed to put up $4 million. We formed a great partnership. He was totally supportive, and we became very close. He was a mentor and a second dad to me. We entered into an oral contract that lasted twelve years. Part of the reason he agreed to do a deal was that I had gotten the Chicago White Sox and Jam Productions, Chicago's regional concert promoter, to come onto the system.

When I took over, Ticketmaster wasn't a business. It was an operating system, with everyone saying you can't make money in tickets. Which was a dumb way to think. I found that most people in the business considered ticketing a pain in the ass. Also, if you're not sitting in the first third of the house, you think it's somebody's fault. Ultimately, the ticket company was blamed. And, when the ticket company is making only $1 on every ticket sold, you can't cover your expenses and make a profit. So yes, at the time there was no money in the business.

Ticketron viewed itself as a utility. I viewed Ticketmaster as a business and a marketing company. I saw that there should be tiered service charges on tickets to the same event. I also realized we needed a big phone room to handle calls from ticket buyers and the phone room had to be open the same hours as the music and department stores that hosted your ticket machines. Not select hours, not different days. The same hours. We needed to establish consistency to build trust in convenience.

When I went into arenas and asked if they had a phone room, they'd say yes. Then they'd take me to a room in the box office that had a phone line with two phones. They'd say, "We don't care what you charge on the phone service because nobody buys tickets by phone." I knew immediately that once we had fifty or sixty operators when a rock show went on sale, we'd sell 20 percent to 40 percent of the business by phones. This was right around the time that banks figured out they could market credit cards to anyone who could sign their name on an application.

Unlike Ticketron, I had an integrated computer system that could do season tickets and single tickets. When I went in to talk to arenas about giving me their business, they'd say, "That's nice but we're not paying extra for it. You can have a one-dollar service charge, just like Ticketron." I said, "OK, guys, you don't need me then." And they'd say, "What does that mean?" I'd say, "You've got Ticketron, and yet you complain the equipment's old and their system doesn't work. You're getting more from me, but you want to pay me the same one dollar. What would possess you to think I would do that?"

All of this started with the Los Angeles Forum, the first arena that came on board with us in July 1983. I raised the service charges and gave them a piece. It was the first time an arena was getting a piece of the service charge business from day one. When I landed the Forum, it was for their entire business—sports and entertainment. You couldn't just come in for an arena's rock concert business. You had to pitch everything, which is why an integrated computer system was so important. Venues that owned teams relied on season tickets and group sales for a significant portion of their revenue. I also set up a phone room for orders.

The next thing that came along in terms of the ticketing business was speed. Our system depended on tickets being generated quickly. Nothing good happens from people standing on line. So over a period of time, we were able to generate 2,000 tickets a minute. By selling out fast, the Forum and other arenas were able to add a second and third show. We could tell from the metrics and the computers how fast tickets were selling, which gave us a sense of what the line counts were. Then we'd alert our clients to add shows. Service charges gave us an incentive to build speed into our process.

Ticketmaster also cleaned up the concert business. Venues got accurate accounting. There were no rows that didn't exist on manifests. In the past, this had allowed venues to generate cash "incentives" for artists and managers. Instead, Ticketmaster created honest accounting.

Things started to change industry-wide in the 1980s because other venues heard about us. Owners and arena managers started calling us from all over the country. We delivered a more accurate inventory control system, a faster system, and faster service that made money instead of costing money.

We installed Ticketmaster machines in music stores and department stores. We also had our own proprietary software that we developed. We wrote our own software and designed our own equipment. Everything we did was proprietary. My entire computing staff was two people, but they were really smart. In those days, everyone thought bigger was better when it came to computers. My view was that small is better. This allowed us to buy equipment from a range of companies.

In 1985, there were four shows at the Los Angeles Coliseum for Bruce Springsteen's Born in the U.S.A. tour. Even though we didn't have the Coliseum contract, the Springsteen promoter called and said they didn't trust Ticketron to sell all the tickets and they were worried about selling four stadium shows. They wanted the shows split between the two ticket companies. Ticketmaster got two shows and Ticketron got two.

We sold out our two concerts in less than six hours. Ticketron still had half their inventory left. We were turning people away. I called up the Coliseum and the promoters. I said we shouldn't turn anybody away who wants a ticket. To protect the act, I told him to give me $2 per ticket for everything I sold on the phones and that I'd give the rest to Ticketron and he'd pay the outlet's commission. I also said I'd do it for free, which I did.

That went viral through the business and created the perception that if Ticketron sold your tickets, you were going to leave money on the table. We picked up Ticketron's slack and helped them sell out their inventory. In my mind, this was really the beginning of the end for them, so we helped ensure their demise.

In the process, Ticketmaster transformed the rock concert business. In addition to providing accurate accounting, we began to make people realize the value of what they had. People used to say, "Service charges on tickets should be the same for the first row and the last one." I convinced them that this was a dumb model, because the secondary market was cleaning up by buying good seats cheap and reselling them to scalpers who, in turn, sold them to the public for a fortune.

We also were instrumental in creating the "golden circle." These were the best seats selling for top dollar. The trick was to figure out where those "golden" seats ended in the arena. Someone asked me how we figure that out. I said, "When you run out of tickets." The guy looked at me and said, "What does that mean?" I said, "It's a computer algorithm." We know row A is $100 and row Z is $50. If ticket demand sells seats to row Y, then that's where the golden circle ends and the entire orchestra is the golden circle. But if the computer stops selling $100 seats at row M, you move the $50 price up gradually to row N. The premise underneath all of this is the same—no one pays more for a ticket than it's worth.

We didn't revolutionize the rock concert business. We helped monetize it. We had all the data, so we knew what people would pay to hear certain artists and bands. If Broadway charged $100 to see a show from seats in the orchestra, why was that more valuable than Elton John or David Bowie singing? If a sports team charged $100 to sit in the front row, why couldn't you take the first twenty rows and make them special?

Pricing was an evolutionary change over a period of five to ten years in the 1980s. Part of this change may have had to do with MTV's launch in 1981. Suddenly you could see bands playing hits, which created a greater demand for concerts. But wanting to go and actually paying to go are two different things. To encourage the latter, you needed to build a level of trust with your electronic ticketing system. People had to believe your computer system worked, that the accounting was accurate, and that they were getting the next best available tickets in the house when they purchased tickets.

Yes, there were busy signals when you called in to buy tickets with your credit card. But that's because when a show went on sale, there were hundreds of thousands of attempts to get through. A phone system is a queue. If you're in the queue, you win. If you're not in the queue, you lose. In the 1980s, everything required a wait. But the phone meant the wait happened in your living room or kitchen, not two or three hours away in some store. You hit your phone and if the line was busy, you hit the redial button. Eventually you got through or you didn't, but you never had to put on a coat or spend money on gas.

Ticketmaster took on all the charge-backs and fraudulent transactions, which was approximately 1.5 to 2 percent of our gross ticket sales. We also implemented something called scaling the house. As demand climbed and ticket inventory declined, prices went up. It was like the airlines. Plane tickets are cheaper months in advance, when few seats have been sold. Seats are much more expensive closer to the flight's departure because there are fewer left. The price scales based on demand, inventory, and how fast they're moving.

In the 1970s and early '80s, the rock concert business didn't fully realize what live music was worth. In those days, they worried more about the fans' feelings and keeping prices low. That approach did little more than make a lot of scalpers rich. From our perspective, we were providing the consumer with a tremendous service related to convenience. When we started, everybody thought it was great what we did. They said, "It's really incredible. It's the best available seat. All of this is terrific." Then all of a sudden, they said, "Oh, but I have to pay for it?"

People thought rock should be free of business interests. I didn't come from the music industry. My thinking was that rock and everything around it is a business. Today, every artist is a brand. Service charges should be flexible, arranged through a contract. You should be able to raise the charges or drop them as the market dictates. People didn't understand that. I was just willing to do something most people didn't want to understand.

Chapter 19

AND IN THE END, LIVE AID

Many viewers who watched MTV on July 13, 1985 never left the house. For sixteen hours during the day and into the night, the cable TV music channel broadcast the Live Aid concert from London's Wembley Stadium and Philadelphia's JFK Stadium to a global audience of more than 1.5 billion. ABC covered the last three hours of the U.S. concert. The charity concert featured seventy artists and reportedly raised an estimated $245 million in famine relief for Ethiopia. Only one artist performed at both events—drummer and singer-songwriter Phil Collins, who caught the Concorde SST to the United States after playing in London. But the Philadelphia concert might have ended quite differently if the wrong decision had been made about the stage earlier in the day.

Harvey Goldsmith
   (Live Aid in London copromoter)

Bob Geldof came up with the idea for Live Aid in 1985. Months earlier in 1984, he and James "Midge" Ure had written "Do They Know It's Christmas?" for Band Aid, a supergroup of British and Irish artists. The single raised awareness and a significant sum to help ease the famine in Ethiopia. Bob was persuaded to go to Ethiopia to see what was happening and realized a number of different issues were taking place. One was the level of starvation, which was enormous. And two, the fact that there was a cartel controlling the docks. Relief materials were being purchased and sent, but they weren't going anywhere. They were just sitting at the docks until the right people were paid off. When he returned, he decided more had to be done. That's when Bob started to chase after me about doing a concert.

We didn't really know what we were doing. We had no idea where we were going or what we wanted to do. All we knew is we wanted to do an event to raise money to help. It was about eleven weeks before the concert that we decided we were going to do it. We just knuckled down and got on with it. During that period, Bob and I hoped to raise around £1 million, or about $1.5 million, from the London concert. However, Bob said it wouldn't be enough to make a difference.

Bob decided we also needed to add New York to give the project a global presence. After protracted discussions with the BBC, we all agreed to make the concerts on the same day following each other. But that presented a time zone challenge. I had good relationships with all of the U.S. promoters. So I called Bill Graham and asked if he wanted to promote the American side of things. He was against playing in New York. He kept pushing Stanford Stadium in California. I insisted we had to play the East Coast because of the time difference.

We were convinced we had to have a cohesive concert with many acts and that it had to be on the East Coast. But we couldn't find a stadium in New York, Boston, or Washington, D.C., that was available. The only promoter who came to the table was Larry Magid in Philadelphia.

Larry Magid
(Live Aid in Philadelphia coproducer)

When Harvey called, I told him it was easier for me to work in Philadelphia, my hometown, where everything was within my grasp. By then, I had put on all-day concerts at JFK Stadium for nine years, shows that routinely did 75,000 to 90,000 people. I told Bill we had twice the capacity at Philadelphia's JFK Stadium than anything else on the East Coast. Bill said he was fine with that but I had to sell Bob and Harvey in London.

I called them and said, "Look, this is Philadelphia, the birthplace of America, the country's first capital, home of the Liberty Bell and the cradle of liberty." I gave them the whole nine yards. I also said, "We don't have a lot of time, just weeks to put on the show." They didn't even have a lot of acts booked yet. Geldof had tried to get Paul McCartney and other high-profile rock acts but had failed. He finally got Elton John, who pulled in McCartney and others. Things started to roll. As a result, we were booking acts up until a week before the concert.

But two important things happened: First, there was an outcry from the London press that there were no Black acts on the bill. Bill turned to me. I reached out and got a half dozen Black performers. Everyone was thrilled. Of course, those performers should have been on the bills from the beginning. But we were working with such a short turnaround. I was working eighteen hours a day or more. This is a time before cell phones, the internet, PDFs, or anything remotely convenient. It was all being done on the phone and in person. On our end, it was just Bill and me.

The second hurdle was that I needed to get permission from the city to hold the concert. Even with a lease, a down payment, and all of the other paperwork in place, we still needed the city's official approval. So I reached out to the mayor through the city's representative. By then I was already committed to doing the show in Philadelphia. I was responsible for co-booking it and laying the groundwork. But I wanted to hold the concert without going through the city's red tape or paying city costs. It was a charity concert, but the mayor had turned us down.

I went ahead anyway. I felt we didn't have a choice. Folding up would have embarrassed everyone and shredded many people's reputations. My belief was that things would iron out. I also came to realize that I had to find another way to explain the concert to the mayor. Which I did. I went back to the city's managing director, James White, and explained the charitable cause and how Philadelphia could play a starring role. He went off to see the mayor and told him the city had to do this.

A day before the concert, we held a press event in a compound in the backstage area. The mayor arrived, leading six or seven people into the compound. We showed the mayor and his team what we were doing. They were proud and so were we. We had an international show that was completely sold out and had been advertising that the last three hours would be shown nationally on ABC with Dick Clark emceeing that portion of the TV show.

There were two dilemmas. The first happened days before the concert. Bill Graham wouldn't recognize that there were other people involved in producing the event. He thought he and I were putting on a live concert when, in fact, it was going to be aired live on TV. So it was a TV event, which it had to be since there was a charity telethon taking place.

But Bill and the TV producers didn't get along in terms of who had control of the concert and when acts went on. Control was vital. Otherwise, the stage would become chaotic. Bob Geldof and Harvey Goldsmith wanted to get rid of Bill. I wouldn't have it. The idea of staging such a sizable event and suddenly throwing a monkey wrench into the gears by saying Graham, who had a verbal agreement, had to go, was just nuts. You just didn't throw a guy like Bill out.

Things came to a head a day before the concert. The TV producers called the police to arrest Bill. He was being difficult and getting in the way of what the TV producers had to do. The producers said he was trespassing. I said to the producers: "No one's getting arrested. We have a show to do. I'll deal with Bill, you deal with TV, and let's get the police out of here. No one's throwing anyone out. And I'm not working without Bill."

The police left and everything calmed down. Bill and I worked it out. Essentially, Bill had wanted control of the show. That was just Bill and his long history. It had gotten down to the silly things. Bill said we were going to have blue VIP passes that let performers and key people on the stage. The TV producers said they were going to have red VIP passes. Bill argued that he didn't want the TV producers' people on the stage; they didn't want our people up there.

But there was a bigger issue before the concert, one that could have ended in disaster if the wrong decision had been made. With a concert of this size, you needed a fluid, efficient way to get an act on and off the stage, set up the next act's gear, and get that act on and then off. It looks easy from the audience's seats, but you have to work out a careful choreography. Fortunately, we had the luxury of time.

TV was switching back and forth between continents. While ABC would air an act performing at London's Wembley Stadium, we would have hosts and show videos on screens for the 90,000 people in the audience in Philadelphia. We'd still have to move fast and be ready on time. We would be on TV time, not casual time. There would be about twenty to twenty-five minutes between acts to work with.

But this wasn't 1969. It was 1985. There had been a lot of technical advancements. Each act had their own way of doing things in terms of the gear they wanted to use. We had to meld that. But we still had the problem of getting acts and all their stuff on and off fast. We discussed the idea of having an electric motorized turntable that rotated sets.

While one act was on, we'd set up the next act's gear backstage, with a white screen acting like a curtain in between. When the performing act left the stage, the stage would automatically turn. Their gear onstage would wind up backstage while the next act's gear would be out front and ready for them. The other option was to rotate the turntable stage by hand. You'd have metal spokes that seventeen people would use to push and turn the stage 180 degrees.

But we worried that the manual stage would take us too much time. We went back and forth during our conversations in a trailer near the field. Everyone had their opinion. On the day of the show, I arrived at 5:00 a.m. The stagehand union steward was already there. I went up to him.

We were sitting on the step of the trailer and I said to him: "What do you think? Is that motorized thing going to work?" He said, "Boy, I'd hate to see what might happen if it broke." I instantly visualized the nightmare scenarios. I said, "You just made the decision for me. We're going to go with the seventeen guys turning it manually." The steward said that would be the only way to be sure it always worked. So that's how we did it, without the vibrating motor.

Rob Hyman
(The Hooters cofounder, singer-songwriter, and keyboardist)

When Larry called our management in early '85, he said he wanted to put a local band on Live Aid to represent the city. We were like, "What?"

We had been playing regularly for five years, so we were prepared. Our album *Nervous Night* had just come out, and we had local buzz in Philadelphia. But we didn't have any hits or much of a national presence.

When Larry first told Live Aid's coproducer Bill Graham about what he wanted to do, Bill told Bob Geldof. Bob apparently said, "Who the fuck are the Hooters?" Our band was a local story. We couldn't get arrested in New York, where we struggled to get gigs. Meanwhile, in Philadelphia, we packed clubs. So fair enough to Bob. But Bill and Larry must have done a terrific job convincing him.

At Live Aid, we were scheduled to go on early, at around 9:00 a.m., and perform two of our songs. We followed Joan Baez and were the first band to play. We were a nervous wreck before we went out, but excited. The stakes were huge. We were a relatively new band and the only new band on the Philadelphia bill. After us, everyone was an artist of some note with hits and then some.

When we went out and saw 90,000 people, I said to myself, "Holy shit." I mean, what else can you think? It wasn't our usual gig. Once we launched into our first song, "And We Danced," the sound coming through my monitor speakers was horrible. There was no time to look for someone to adjust them. I didn't even know where that person was. As a musician, what you hear onstage is important and very different from what you hear out in the seats.

All I heard from those speakers was the kick drum ripping my head off. Normally I would hear keyboard, vocals, and everything else in a mix that sounds like music. But our monitor speakers were too loud and the drummer's mix was way up. We just had to play and get through it.

After our second song, "All You Zombies," I came offstage thinking, "That really was pretty bad." The crowd was great, but I had to assume that if it sounded bad to me, it sounded bad to everyone.

The weird thing was when we saw the broadcast later, we sounded great. Bob Clearmountain did the live mix. When I watch us at Live Aid now, there certainly was some extra nervous energy in that performance. We were terrified of falling on our faces.

When we finished, we stayed backstage the entire day. Everyone back there was a big deal. I remember Madonna walked in with her entourage, which was cool. Later, there was Mick Jagger and Bob Dylan and Crosby, Stills & Nash. Everywhere you looked, you saw stars.

The other big thing about Live Aid was the idea that two sister concerts for the same cause were happening simultaneously in two different cities on two different continents. And then Phil Collins arrived after playing in London. In Philadelphia, he performed a three-song set on drums behind Eric Clapton, then performed his own "Against All Odds" and "In the Air Tonight" on piano, finishing on drums behind Jimmy Page and Robert Plant of Led Zeppelin. Everyone was stunned. It was like a magic trick flying over on the Concorde. So cool.

After Live Aid, rock began transforming little by little into a megabusiness. Live Aid certainly was proof that live music had the potential to be a massive moneymaker, if you could get rid of your competition. That certainly didn't go unnoticed among those who would enter the business and did just that. Of course, Live Aid wasn't the last giant charitable rock concert. Farm Aid was in September. And almost as gratifying for us was Amnesty International's Conspiracy of Hope tour the following year. We played for half an hour on that tour and killed it.

But Live Aid definitely gave us a big jolt. After the concert, we hit the road and toured for years. We did videos, we got airplay, we were good live, we opened a bunch of tours, and we just kept playing. Appearing on that Live Aid stage was a valuable ten minutes. It changed our lives. And those ten minutes sort of answered the question: "Who the fuck are the Hooters?" A mantra we still live with today.

Shep Gordon
(talent manager and Hollywood film agent)

I was managing Teddy Pendergrass in 1985 and had him perform at Live Aid in Philadelphia. Live Aid was the end of innocence. Businesses finally saw how concerts could be scaled up. MTV already was a major force and growing. There have been other great concerts after Live Aid, but the innocence was gone.

Business executives were calculating how to monetize the charitable side of musicians. I think Live Aid was the last time that monetizing wasn't even thought about. It was about getting the awareness out about the crisis in Ethiopia. The pure passion and sense of giving by musicians to show that they cared about heartbreaking events and were willing to donate their time and money was infectious. Virtually everyone showed up for Live Aid.

The concert was Teddy Pendergrass's first performance since his paralyzing car accident. Teddy had been off the scene for three years. Philadelphia was his hometown. Nobody really knew anything about his condition. We never let any pictures out. We had never said anything, and all of a sudden he was up onstage with Ashford and Simpson. Days earlier, I had asked the promoters if he could do one song with them. They said yes.

But when I wheeled Teddy up the ramp toward the stage on the day of the concert, he said he couldn't do it, that he was terrified. I told him I loved him but I was wheeling him out there, and he could sing or not. After he was announced by Nick Ashford and the massive audience screamed, he wheeled himself out in his electric wheelchair. There wasn't a dry eye there. What a comeback. Teddy sang "Reach Out and Touch (Somebody's Hand)." He nailed it.

John Oates
(Hall and Oates cofounder, guitarist, and singer-songwriter)

Mick Jagger needed a band at Live Aid in Philly. He was on hiatus from the Rolling Stones in '85 and had just put out a solo album. One of the Live Aid promoters told us Mick wanted to perform but he needed a backing band. We said we'd be happy to back him. Mick liked us. He gave us a list of songs in advance and then came to Studio Instrument Rentals in New York where we were rehearsing.

He took the mic and said, "Let's go." He jumped on the stage and kicked it off doing the Mick Jagger chicken-wing thing, as if performing for 100,000 people. That really surprised me. "Wow," I thought. "He's really doing this?" Mick could have walked through the rehearsal. Instead, he went through the songs as if it was all happening live. It was fun. Playing backup was fun. All we had to do was play and watch Mick rather than being at the mic. During Live Aid, I had the best seat in the house.

I went to the stadium early to see who was there. But I had nowhere to go. Duran Duran had our trailer until they went on. I was thirty-five then. I wasn't a kid. I was fifteen years into a professional career, so I wasn't in awe. I felt I was doing what I should have been doing at that point in my life. I felt we belonged and it was where we should have been, that I was born to do this.

Daryl Hall
(Hall and Oates cofounder, guitarist, keyboardist, and singer-songwriter)

We went on sometime after 9:00 p.m. First we performed two of our songs before Eddie Kendricks and David Ruffin came out for a Temptations revue. You sensed something big was going on. I felt that what I was involved in was going to be remembered. Then Mick came on around 10:00 p.m. He sang three songs before bringing out Tina Turner. Everyone was really into it.

John Oates

Headlining what was the biggest rock show ever put together was exciting. It was being simulcast worldwide; we were in Philadelphia, our hometown; and it was a time in our career when we were on top of the world. It was the hyped-up, jacked-up '80s and a really important moment. Rock went global and the music was taken to a new level on TV. Rock, that day, was on par with the World Series or the Super Bowl. It had arrived on a massive scale as a universal cultural event around the world. Everyone understood how big it was. Mick tearing off Tina's miniskirt while they sang "It's Only Rock 'n' Roll" was a complete surprise.

Daryl Hall

Live Aid felt like a turning point in rock. Ticket prices hadn't exploded yet. The concert was an extravaganza and yet it wasn't. It was pretty loose and didn't have that corporate sheen yet. Everything was still pretty innocent. And yet we were accomplishing something by coming together to help Ethiopia in a massive stadium that was packed. It was a music summit of sorts, with artists who mattered in two different cities, some of whom had been performing since the late 1950s when they were kids. What I felt more than anything was the communality of music. Everyone recognized we were a big family.

Larry Magid

The concert that day was great. Turning the stage manually took a little longer but it worked. As soon as the show ended, hundreds of performers and crew swarmed the stage to sing "We Are the World." Lionel Richie, Kenny Loggins, Smokey Robinson, and other artists who weren't in the show had come just to sing the song at the end. We even had a chorus back there. It was a great way to end the concert. After the song, we cleared everyone off. We had to break down the turntable and the stage. Everyone left the stage. And that's when it happened.

The turntable with the unused motorized apparatus underneath crashed through the stage to the ground. All of the weight had been too much for the stage. Had we used the motorized mechanism, the crash might have happened sooner, during a performance earlier in the day. People certainly could have been injured or killed. Thankfully no one was hurt when the turntable fell through the stage.

Overall, the concert was smooth. There were a few glitches. A couple of acts played a little longer than they were supposed to and were cut off at the end. For example, at the end, Bob Dylan was playing with Ronnie Wood and Keith Richards when TV coverage cut off in the middle of their last song. We had to be off the air. That was the deal with ABC.

The question for us as producers was: How would we ever top this? It was such a huge, ambitious event. Bigger, more elaborate, and technologically sophisticated concerts would come later, in the 1990s. But that's because affordable digital technology finally caught up to the dreams and imaginations of people who put on concerts.

In many ways, Live Aid was the last pure rock concert. There was none of the elaborate staging, explosions, and dazzle that you saw in later years. Many acts played in broad daylight, without dramatic lighting or special effects. They played with emotion and without pretention and for a good cause. The concert unified everyone who was there and on two continents. For a day, the world felt like a smaller, better place. We had pulled it off.

EPILOGUE

The rock concert didn't disappear the day after Live Aid ended. It continued on, entering a new phase when strategies developed by industry pioneers of the 1960s, '70s, and '80s were leveraged by a smaller number of powerful live-entertainment companies. As the years rolled on and these companies acquired niche- and concert-related businesses, the high-end performance landscape widened to include more lucrative music categories such as country, pop, rap, and Latin. Though rock remains a sizable box-office draw, the rock concert has become less of an agent for social change and more of a nostalgia business for legacy artists.

In the late 1980s and '90s, grunge and alternative rock bands thrived initially by performing new forms of rock at clubs, amphitheaters, and arenas named for corporate sponsors, and at an expanding number of boutique music festivals nationwide. But by the 2000s, the rock concert had fizzled as a rite of passage and was more of an event parents took children to for the experience. By then, the youth culture was spending more time with new affordable technology and sharing their life changes and anxieties in real time. The arrival of the high-speed modem, at-home internet access, email, the MP3, music downloading, iTunes, and cell phones all gave teens digital access to recorded music and instant communication with friends.

In the 2010s, new and improved technology such as smartphones, texting, social media, apps, music streaming, and YouTube let young people carry on live communication with multiple peers at once, share music, and legally listen to free music through streaming services. Concert ticket prices continued to climb, and prime seating became virtually impossible to access at box offices or through online ticket sites. As with professional sports, sitting close to the action now required connections or a willingness to pay hefty prices at ticket brokers.

In the decades following Live Aid, rock played a less revolutionary role as well. This trend continued even though political and social issues such as climate change, plastic pollution, racism, police brutality, mass shootings, workplace sexual harassment, voting suppression, and hate crimes all have emerged or increased. Rock struggled as an influential force while other forms of popular music became more meaningful to the youth culture. Even the electric guitar—rock's workhorse and onetime symbol of teenage pushback and independence—has been marginalized by the evolving digital landscape. Rock heroes wailing away onstage on an electric guitar have slowly disappeared, replaced at megastar pop music concerts by choreography and sophisticated electronic instruments in the stage's shadows.

To some extent, rock's decline as a cheerleader for change is a result of higher financial stakes that followed increased box office revenue and concert dependency. With album sales now negligible thanks to years of free downloading, file-sharing, and free streaming, artists need all the fans they can seat at the largest possible venues. For many rock musicians, tours have become their major source of income, a vital financial pipeline that was turned off during the COVID-19 pandemic of 2020. Scandal and bad press also have been perilous. Artists are more at risk now of losing vast segments of their lucrative concert-going audience over a social-media backlash in response to politically incorrect statements, past or present #MeToo events, racial slurs, and even false claims.

But by forfeiting the moral high ground, rock and the rock concert's purpose in the post-1985 era has been diminished. In an age when the youth culture communicates throughout the day with friends, a concert experience hardly offers the same rite of passage or meeting-of-the-tribes moment it once did. Many teens at odds with parents or struggling socially in school can escape simply by going online. As for music, access to an infinite number of global choices is now available for free online through YouTube and streaming music services. Of course, many parents who are rock fans are overjoyed by the playlists of children who have "discovered" classic rock artists through friends and social networks.

Between 1950 and 1985, rock empowered several young generations to demand an end to injustice and motivated them to invent a better world. Whether that was truly accomplished is a matter of debate. But for rock to survive in its original form as an artistic expression of outrage and pushback, the music and its public performance will have to connect meaningfully with the youth culture's current concerns and agenda. Otherwise, rock and the rock concert risk fading away with the generation that was most inspired by its rise.

FIFTY BEST LIVE ALBUMS, CONCERT FILMS, AND ROCK DOCS

There are thousands of live rock albums and videos, but not all of them altered the history of the rock concert. The following lists aren't meant to be definitive. They simply are choices that feature powerful performances and were milestones in the thirty-five-year period covered in this book. Many of the albums can be heard on music streaming services and most of the videos can be viewed on YouTube and other video streaming platforms or on DVD or Blu-ray. I've also included a list of fifty of my favorite rock documentaries, which remain educational deep dives into moments in time that changed rock and the culture at large.

Fifty Best Live Albums

1950s

1951—Hunter Hancock Presents Blues and Rhythm Midnight Matinee (Route 66)
1954–56—Elvis Presley: Complete Louisiana Hayride Archives (MRS)
1955—Bill Haley and His Comets: Rock 'n' Roll Show (Hydra)
1956–58—Alan Freed's Rock n' Roll Dance Party, Vols. 1–5 (WINS)
1957–58—Buddy Holly: Off the Record, On the Air (Rollercoaster)
1958—Blues in the Night: Newport Jazz Festival 1958 (Phontastic)

1960s

1963—Bo Diddley's Beach Party (Checker)
1964—Jerry Lee Lewis: Live at the Star-Club (Philips)
1964—Ike and Tina Turner: Revue Live (Kent)
1964—Beach Boys Concert (Capitol)
1964—Five Live Yardbirds (Columbia)
1964–65—The Beatles: Live at the Hollywood Bowl (Universal/Apple)
1966—The Rolling Stones: Got Live If You Want It! (London)
1966—Bob Dylan: The 1966 Live Recordings (Legacy)
1966—Otis Redding: Live at the Whisky a Go Go (Stax)
1967—Monterey International Pop Festival (Rhino)
1968—Cream: Goodbye Tour Live 1968 (UMC)
1968—Janis Joplin: Live at the Carousel Ballroom (Columbia/Legacy)
1968—Jefferson Airplane: Bless Its Pointed Little Head (RCA)
1968—Sly and the Family Stone: Live at the Fillmore East (Epic/Legacy)
1969—Get Yer Ya-Ya's Out! The Rolling Stones in Concert (London)
1969—Grateful Dead: Live/Dead (Warner Bros.)
1969—Woodstock: Back to the Garden (Rhino)

1970s

1970—The Who: Live at Leeds (Decca)
1970—Jimi Hendrix: Band of Gypsies (Capitol)
1970—The Doors: Absolutely Live (Elektra)
1971—The Concert for Bangladesh (Apple)
1971—Emerson, Lake & Palmer: Pictures at an Exhibition (Rhino)
1971—The Allman Brothers Band: At Fillmore East (Capricorn)
1972—Deep Purple: Made in Japan (Rhino/Warner)
1973—Led Zeppelin: The Song Remains the Same (Swan Song)
1973—Lou Reed: Rock 'n' Roll Animal (RCA)
1974—CSNY 1974: Crosby, Stills, Nash & Young (Rhino)
1974—Joni Mitchell: Miles of Aisles (Asylum)
1975—Bruce Springsteen: Live at the Roxy (Springsteen.net)
1976—David Bowie: David Live (RCA)
1977—The Ramones: It's Alive (Sire)
1977—Steve Miller Band: Live! Breaking Ground (Sailor/Capitol/UMe)

1978—The Clash: From Here to Eternity: Live (Epic)

1978—AC/DC: If You Want Blood You've Got it (Atlantic)

1978—Neil Young and Crazy Horse: Live Rust (Reprise)

1978—The Band: The Last Waltz (Warner Bros.)

1979—No Nukes Concert (Asylum)

1979—Queen: Live Killers (Elektra)

1980s

1980—Is There Anybody Out There: The Wall Live 1980–81 (EMI)

1983—The Police: Live! (A&M)

1983—U2: Under a Blood Red Sky (Island)

1983—Talking Heads: Stop Making Sense (Sire/Warner)

1984—Bruce Springsteen: Brendan Byrne Arena (live.brucespringsteen.net)

1985—Live Aid (Band Aid Trust)

Fifty Best Rock Concert Films

1950s

1956—Rock Around the Clock

1956—The Girl Can't Help It

1956—Rock, Rock, Rock!

1956—Don't Knock the Rock

1957—Mister Rock and Roll

1958—Jazz on a Summer's Day (with Chuck Berry)

1960s

1963—Peter, Paul and Mary at Newport 1963–65

1964—T.A.M.I. Show

1965—The Other Side of the Mirror: Bob Dylan Live at Newport

1965—The Beatles at Shea Stadium

1965—Roy Orbison: The Monument Concert

1965—The Beatles: Eight Days A Week, the Touring Years

1966—The Big T.N.T. Show

1967—Monterey Pop

1968—The Doors: Live at the Bowl

1968—Aretha Franklin: Legendary Concertgebouw Concert

1968—James Brown: Man to Man

1968—Elvis: The Comeback Special

1969—Woodstock

1969—Celebration at Big Sur

1969—The Beatles: Let It Be

1970s

1970—Jimi Hendrix: Blue Wild Angel: Live at the Isle of Wight

1970—The Who: Live at the Isle of Wight Festival

1970—Joni Mitchell: Both Sides Now, Live at the Isle of Wight Festival

1971—Pink Floyd: Live at Pompeii

1971—Ike & Tina: On the Road: 1971–72

1971—Joe Cocker: Mad Dogs & Englishmen

1972—Deep Purple: Made in Japan

1972—Wattstax

1972—The London Rock 'n' Roll Show

1972—T. Rex: Born to Boogie

1972—Elvis on Tour

1973—Led Zeppelin: The Song Remains the Same

1973—David Bowie: Ziggy Stardust and the Spiders From Mars

1974—Soul Power

1974—Deep Purple: California Jam

1974—The Who: Live at Charlton, London

1976—Paul McCartney and Wings: Rockshow

1977—Frank Zappa: Baby Snakes

1977—Ramones: It's Alive

1978—Blondie: Live 1978

1978—Grateful Dead: The Closing of Winterland

1978—Fela Kuti: Berliner Jazztage '78

1978—Jethro Tull: Live at Madison Square Garden

1979—The Cars: Recorded Live on Musikladen

1979—Neil Young: Rust Never Sleeps

1980s

1982—Queen on Fire: Live at the Bowl
1984—Talking Heads: Stop Making Sense
1984—Yes: 9012 Live
1985—Live Aid

Fifty Best Rock Documentaries

Chicago Blues (1972)

B. B. King: The Life of Riley (2014)

Devil at the Crossroads (2019)

BBC: Dancing in the Street: Whole Lotta Shakin' (1996)

BBC: Story of American Folk Music (2014)

The Weavers: Wasn't That a Time! (1982)

PBS: The March on Washington (2013)

BBC: Beach Boys: Wouldn't It Be Nice (2005)

The Wrecking Crew (2008)

What's Happening! The Beatles in the U.S.A. (1964)

BBC: Blues Britannia (2009)

Rolling Stones: Charlie Is My Darling—Ireland 1965 (2012)

Bob Dylan: Dont Look Back (1967)

BBC: The Motown Invasion (2011)

Rolling Stones: Sympathy for the Devil (1968)

BBC: Summer of Love: How Hippies Changed the World (2017)

Gimme Shelter (1970)

Rumble: The Indians Who Rocked the World (2017)

Cocksucker Blues (1972)

John Lennon & the Plastic Ono Band: Sweet Toronto (1971)

John and Yoko: Above Us Only Sky (2018)

Gimme Some Truth: The Making of John Lennon's "Imagine" Album (2000)

Echo in the Canyon (2018)

BBC: Prog Rock Britannia (2009)

BBC: Hotel California: LA from the Byrds to the Eagles (2007)

The Allman Brothers Band: After the Crash (2016)

BBC: Sweet Home Alabama: The Southern Rock Saga (2012)

Ain't in It for My Health: A Film About Levon Helm (2010)

BBC: Kings of Glam (2006)

Super Duper Alice Cooper (2014)

New York Dolls: All Dolled Up (2005)

End of the Century: The Story of the Ramones (2004)

Fillmore: The Last Days (1972)

Gimme Danger: The Stooges (2016)

George Clinton: The Mothership Connection (1998)

Fleetwood Mac: Rumours (1997)

The Who: The Kids Are Alright (1979)

The Clash: New Year's Day '77 (2015)

The Decline of Western Civilization (1981)

U2: Rattle and Hum (1988)

Neil Young: Year of the Horse (1997)

Ginger Baker: Beware of Mr. Baker (2012)

AC/DC: Dirty Deeds (2012)

Grateful Dead: Long, Strange Trip (2017)

No Direction Home: Bob Dylan (2005)

Hip-Hop Evolution (2016)

Joan Jett: Bad Reputation (2018)

David Crosby: Remember My Name (2019)

Zappa (2020)

Summer of Soul (2021)

SOURCE LIST

Ian Anderson—Jethro Tull founder, lead singer, songwriter, acoustic guitarist, and flutist.

Ernie Andrews—Los Angeles jazz, blues, and pop vocalist.

Joan Baez—Folk singer, guitarist, and social and political activist.

Amir Bar-Lev—Director of the documentaries *My Kid Could Paint That*, *The Tillman Story*, *Happy Valley*, and *Long Strange Trip*, a six-part miniseries on the Grateful Dead.

Tony Barrow—English publicist for the Beatles between 1962 and 1968 who coined the phrase "Fab Four."

Al Bell—Stax Records co-owner, songwriter, and coexecutive producer of the daylong Wattstax festival in Los Angeles.

Gail Blacker—Fashion designer and creator of David Byrne's "big suit" that he wore during the Talking Heads 1983 tour.

Joe Boyd—Record producer and production manager of the 1965 Newport Folk Festival.

Craig Braun—Graphic designer who helped transform the album sleeve into an interactive experience, including the banana-peel cover for *The Velvet Underground & Nico* and the zipper cover for the Rolling Stones' *Sticky Fingers*. He also finalized the Stones' official lips-and-tongue logo.

Robert "Toe-Cutter" Burton—Rock band roadie.

Marshall Chess—Record producer, founding president of Rolling Stones Records, film producer, and son of Leonard Chess, cofounder of Chess Records.

Alice Cooper—Singer-songwriter and founder of the band Alice Cooper, whose development of shock rock helped influence the sound and look of punk and heavy metal.

Cameron Crowe—*Rolling Stone* journalist at age fifteen and the author of *Fast Times at Ridgemont High*. He wrote and directed *Jerry Maguire*, *Almost Famous*, and *Vanilla Sky*, and produced the documentary *David Crosby: Remember My Name*.

Henry Diltz—Rock photographer whose images appear on the covers of more than 250 albums, including the Doors' *Morrison Hotel*, James Taylor's *Sweet Baby James*, and Crosby, Stills & Nash's debut album.

Dave DiMartino—Rock journalist and author whose work has appeared in *Creem*, *Billboard*, *Entertainment Weekly*, *Rolling Stone*, *Mojo*, *Spin*, and the *Village Voice*.

Sepp Donahower—Cofounder of Pacific Presentations and coproducer of California Jam 1974, which set the record for paid attendance at a rock concert up until that point.

Bob Eubanks—Disc jockey, game show host, and producer of the Beatles at the Hollywood Bowl in 1964 and '65 and at Dodger Stadium in '66.

Nick Fasciano—Graphic artist and album cover designer whose work includes the band Chicago's first nine studio albums.

Mike Fisher—Cofounder and band manager of Heart.

Roger Fisher—Cofounder and lead guitarist of Heart.

Pete Foxx—Singer-guitarist and original member of the Flairs, a Los Angeles R&B vocal group.

Chris Frantz—Cofounder, singer-songwriter, and drummer of Talking Heads and Tom Tom Club.

Lance Freed—President of Rondor Music International, a music publishing company, and son of radio disc jockey Alan Freed, an early champion of rock 'n' roll.

Harvey Goldsmith—English promoter of rock concerts and charity concerts and copromoter of Live Aid in London.

Mark Goodman—Radio disc jockey and one of the original five MTV VJs from 1981 to 1987.

Shep Gordon—Hollywood agent, producer, and manager of recording artists including Alice Cooper, the Gipsy Kings, Pink Floyd, Teddy Pendergrass, and Luther Vandross.

Scott Gorham—Songwriter and lead guitarist of Irish-rock band Thin Lizzy.

Daryl Hall—Singer-songwriter, multi-instrumentalist, and cofounder of Hall and Oates.

Bill Hanley—Considered the "father of festival sound." Founder of Hanley Sound and designer of systems for the 1965 Newport Folk

Festival, the Beatles' North American tour in 1966, Woodstock in 1969, and many other rock concerts.

Rob Hyman—Singer-songwriter, keyboardist, and cofounder of the Hooters and cowriter with Cyndi Lauper of "Time After Time."

Wanda Jackson—Singer-songwriter, guitarist, and rockabilly pioneer who was the first female artist to tour with Elvis Presley in 1955.

Jimmy Johnson—Chicago R&B and electric blues guitarist and singer.

Norma Kamali—Fashion designer best known for creating the sleeping-bag coat in 1973 and the red bathing suit Farrah Fawcett wore in her 1976 poster as well as outfitting rock bands, including the New York Dolls and Todd Rundgren in the early 1970s.

Jim Koplik—Rock concert promoter best known for coproducing Summer Jam at Watkins Glen, New York, in 1973, attended by an estimated 600,000 fans.

Artie Kornfeld—Musician, composer of more than seventy-five hit songs, and cocreator of the first Woodstock Music and Art Festival.

Michael Lang—Cocreator of the first Woodstock Music and Art Festival, organizer of the Altamont Free Concert, and coproducer of the first Miami Pop Festival.

Don Law—Rock concert promoter and producer and president of Live Nation/New England.

Chuck Leavell—Pianist for the Allman Brothers Band from 1972 to 1976 and for the Rolling Stones since 1982.

Bill Legend—English musician and drummer for T. Rex.

Tommy LiPuma—Pop and jazz record producer and cofounder of Blue Thumb Records.

Larry Magid—Concert promoter and Broadway producer who cofounded the Electric Factory in Philadelphia and coproduced Live Aid at the city's JFK Stadium.

Jerry Martini—Sly and the Family Stone cofounder and saxophonist.

Elizabeth Marvel—Film and TV actress and self-described Deadhead.

Albert Maysles—Documentary filmmaker and codirector of *What's Happening! The Beatles in the U.S.A.*, *Gimme Shelter*, and other films.

Michael McClure—San Francisco Beat poet, playwright, novelist, and documentary filmmaker.

Country Joe McDonald—Cofounder of Country Joe and the Fish, lead singer, guitarist, and songwriter.

Big Jay McNeely—Flamboyant tenor saxophonist whose hit record "The Deacon's Hop" in 1949 helped establish jump blues, the basis of R&B and rock 'n' roll.

David Mendelsohn—General manager of San Francisco's Bay Area Seating Service (BASS), an early electronic ticketing company.

Jimmy Merchant—singer-songwriter and original member of the Teenagers, a New York vocal group that at one point featured lead singer Frankie Lymon.

Helen Meyer—Cofounder of Meyer Sound Laboratories in Berkeley, California, an early designer and creator of concert speaker systems.

John Meyer—Cofounder and CEO of Meyer Sound Laboratories in Berkeley, California, an early designer and creator of concert speaker systems.

Jerry Mickelson—Cofounder of Chicago's Jam Productions, a producer of live entertainment since 1972.

Stan Miller—Founder of Stanal Sound, an early designer of loudspeaker systems for rock tours, including for Pink Floyd's The Wall in 1980 and '81.

Steve Miller—Singer-songwriter, guitarist, keyboardist, and founder of the Steve Miller Band.

Chip Monck—Early pioneer of rock concert and festival staging and lighting who worked on the Newport Jazz and Folk Festivals, Monterey Pop, Miami Pop, Woodstock and Altamont, the Concert for Bangladesh, and Rolling Stones tours from 1969 to 1972.

Tony Newman—Drummer for Sounds Incorporated, a British studio and backup band that opened for the Beatles' U.S. tour in 1965.

John Oates—Singer-songwriter, guitarist, and cofounder of Hall and Oates.

Ric O'Barry—Founder and director of the Dolphin Project who trained the five dolphins that appeared in TV's *Flipper* in the 1960s and coproduced the first Miami Pop Festival.

Rocky Paulson—Founder of Stage Rigging Inc. and concert rigger for the U.S. leg of Pink Floyd's The Wall tour.

D. A. Pennebaker—Documentary filmmaker and director of the 1965 Bob Dylan documentary *Dont Look Back* as well as *Alice Cooper, Ziggy Stardust and the Spiders from Mars,* and *Monterey Pop.*

Jerry Pompili—House manager of Bill Graham's Fillmore East.

Cynthia Robinson—Singer, trumpeter, and cofounder of Sly and the Family Stone.

Fredric D. Rosen—Attorney, philanthropist, and Ticketmaster president and CEO from 1982 to 1998.

Joel Rosenman—Cocreator and cofinancier of the first Woodstock Music and Art Festival.

Amalie R. Rothschild—Filmmaker and photographer best known for her images taken at the Fillmore East, Woodstock, and other rock events from 1968 to 1974.

Todd Rundgren—Utopia founder, singer-songwriter, multi-instrumentalist, and producer.

Art Rupe—Founder of Specialty Records and producer of Fats Domino, Little Richard, and other R&B and rock 'n' roll artists.

Ethan Russell—Studio and concert photographer of the Beatles, the Rolling Stones, Janis Joplin, the Who, and many other rock artists and bands.

Gerald Scarfe—English cartoonist and animator whose surrealist illustrations appeared in film clips and a music video for Pink Floyd's In the Flesh tour and on the band's *The Wall* album, inspiring the tour's inflatable characters.

Ken Schaffer—Inventor of the Schaffer-Vega diversity system that allowed electric guitarists and bassists to play wirelessly onstage.

Danny Scher—Rock concert promoter, vice president of Bill Graham Presents, developer of Shoreline Amphitheatre in Mountain View, California, and cofounder of DanSun Productions.

Jerry Seltzer—Cofounder of San Francisco's Bay Area Seating Service (BASS), an early electronic ticketing company.

Hal Silen—Cofounder of BASS electronic ticketing.

Barbara Hearn Smith—Elvis Presley's girlfriend from 1956 to '57.

Byther Smith—Chicago singer and electric blues guitarist.

Ronnie Spector—Cofounder and lead singer of the Ronettes.

Chris Stein—Songwriter, guitarist, and cofounder of Blondie.

Seymour Stein—Cofounder of Sire Records who is credited with coining the term "new wave" and signing and promoting the postpunk genre.

Sue Steinberg—Cofounder of MTV who served as the music channel's original executive producer.

Mike Stoller—R&B and rock 'n' roll songwriter and producer who teamed with Jerry Leiber to cowrite more than seventy hits, including "Hound Dog," "Kansas City," "Jailhouse Rock," and "There Goes My Baby."

Noel Paul Stookey—Singer-songwriter, guitarist, and member of the folk trio Peter, Paul and Mary.

Lesley Trattner—Daughter of Leo Mintz, owner of Cleveland's Rendezvous Records who is often credited with offhandedly coining the term "rock 'n' roll."

Fred Vail—Radio disc jockey, producer, and first concert promoter of the Beach Boys.

Bill Walton—Sportscaster and former NBA center for the Portland Trailblazers, San Diego Clippers, and Boston Celtics, a two-time championship winner, NBA Hall of Fame inductee, and self-described Deadhead.

Roger Waters—Bassist, singer-songwriter, and cofounder of Pink Floyd.

George Wein—Founder of the Newport Jazz Festival in 1954, cofounder of the Newport Folk Festival in 1959, and founder of the New Orleans Jazz and Heritage Festival in 1970.

Max Weinberg—Drummer in Bruce Springsteen and the E Street Band since 1974.

Bob Weir—Lead singer, songwriter, guitarist, and cofounder of the Grateful Dead.

Tina Weymouth—Singer-songwriter and founding bassist of Talking Heads and Tom Tom Club.

Kay Wheeler—President of Elvis Presley's first national fan club and promoter of his first stadium concert at the Cotton Bowl in Dallas, Texas, in October 1956.

Joshua White—Creator and producer of the Joshua Light Show, best known for projecting a liquid light show on a screen behind performing artists at the Fillmore East.

Bob Willoughby—Photographer who specialized in Hollywood, jazz, film, and dance stars as well as early R&B artists such as Big Jay McNeely.

Peter Yarrow—Singer-songwriter, guitarist, and member of the folk trio Peter, Paul and Mary.

Angus Young—Lead guitarist, songwriter, and cofounder of AC/DC.

ACKNOWLEDGMENTS

Loving thanks to my wife, Alyse, for her wisdom and support and for always treating me like a rock star. I'm so fortunate to know what it's like to have an adoring fan.

This book wouldn't have been possible without Glen Hartley, my literary agent, and Lynn Chu, my literary attorney, whose praise for my writing is especially appreciated.

I've also been lucky to have a literary powerhouse in my corner. Throughout the project, I've treasured the guidance and wisdom of my editor, Grove Atlantic CEO and publisher Morgan Entrekin, who shares my enthusiasm for pop culture, rock concerts, and music history. I'm also grateful to assistant editor Sara Vitale for her editorial input, eye for detail, and organizational skills.

Also thanks to the Grove Atlantic team: Judy Hottensen, associate publisher; Deb Seager, publicity director; Julia Berner-Tobin, managing editor; Sal Destro, production director; Gretchen Mergenthaler, art director; Norman E. Tuttle, book designer; Paula Cooper Hughes, sharp-eyed copy editor; and Alicia Burns, proofreader.

A special thanks to the book's sources, who generously made time for me and were open and revealing about their role and contribution to the rock concert's development. As for my sources who have since passed away, my deepest condolences to their families. And thanks to the assistants, publicists, managers, spouses, and rock stars who reached out to key sources on my behalf. The names of those who were there for me is too long to list here, but you know who you are.